New Waves in Philosophy

Series Editors: **Vincent F. Hendricks** and **Duncan Pritchard**

Titles include:

Boudewijn DeBruin and Christopher Zurn (*editors*)
NEW WAVES IN POLITICAL PHILOSOPHY

Vincent F. Hendricks and Duncan Pritchard (*editors*)
NEW WAVES IN EPISTEMOLOGY

Yujin Nagasawa and Erik J. Wielenberg (*editors*)
NEW WAVES IN PHILOSOPHY OF RELIGION

Jan Kyrre Berg Olsen, Evan Selinger and Søren Riis (*editors*)
NEW WAVES IN PHILOSOPHY OF TECHNOLOGY

Thomas S. Petersen, Jesper Ryberg and Clark Wolf (*editors*)
NEW WAVES IN APPLIED ETHICS

Kathleen Stock and Katherine Thomson-Jones (*editors*)
NEW WAVES IN AESTHETICS

Forthcoming:

P. D. Magnus and Jacob Busch
NEW WAVES IN PHILOSOPHY OF SCIENCE

Otavio Bueno and Oystein Linnebo
NEW WAVES IN PHILOSOPHY OF MATHEMATICS

Allan Hazlett
NEW WAVES IN METAPHYSICS

Future Volumes:

New Waves in Philosophy of Language
New Waves in Philosophy of Mind
New Waves in Meta-Ethics
New Waves in Ethics
New Waves in Formal Philosophy
New Waves in Philosophy of Law

New Waves in Philosophy
Series Standing Order ISBN 978–0–230–53797–2 (hardcover)
Series Standing Order ISBN 978–0–230–53798–9 (paperback)
(*outside North America only*)

You can receive future titles in this series as they are published by placing a standing order. Please contact your bookseller or, in case of difficulty, write to us at the address below with your name and address, the title of the series and the ISBN quoted above.

Customer Services Department, Macmillan Distribution Ltd, Houndmills, Basingstoke, Hampshire RG21 6XS, England

---

New Waves in Philosophy of Religion

Edited by

Yujin Nagasawa
University of Birmingham, UK

Erik J. Wielenberg
DePauw University, USA

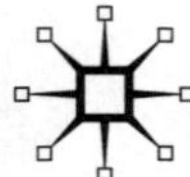

First published 2009 by
PALGRAVE MACMILLAN

Palgrave Macmillan in the UK is an imprint of Macmillan Publishers Limited,
registered in England, company number 785998, of Houndmills, Basingstoke,
Hampshire RG21 6XS.

Palgrave Macmillan in the US is a division of St Martin's Press LLC,
175 Fifth Avenue, New York, NY 10010.

Palgrave Macmillan is the global academic imprint of the above companies
and has companies and representatives throughout the world.

Palgrave® and Macmillan® are registered trademarks in the United States,
the United Kingdom, Europe and other countries.

ISBN-13: 978–0–230–22384–4 hardback
ISBN-10: 0–230–22384–2 hardback
ISBN-13: 978–0–230–22385–1 paperback
ISBN-10: 0–230–22385–0 paperback

This book is printed on paper suitable for recycling and made from fully
managed and sustained forest sources. Logging, pulping and manufacturing
processes are expected to conform to the environmental regulations of the
country of origin.

A catalogue record for this book is available from the British Library.

Library of Congress Cataloging-in-Publication Data
New waves in philosophy of religion / edited by Yujin Nagasawa, Erik
   J. Wielenberg.
        p.   cm.
     Includes index.
     ISBN-13: 978–0–230–22384–4 (hardback : alk. paper)
     ISBN-10: 0–230–22384–2 (Hardback : alk. paper)
     ISBN-13: 978–0–230–22385–1 (pbk. : alk. paper)
     ISBN-10: 0–230–22385–0 (pbk. : alk. paper)
     1. Religion—Philosophy.   I. Nagasawa, Yujin.   II. Wielenberg, Erik
   J. (Erik Joseph), 1972–
     BL51.N46 2009
     210—dc22   2008029969

10   9   8   7   6   5   4   3   2   1
18   17   16   15   14   13   12   11   10   09

Printed and bound in Great Britain by
CPI Antony Rowe, Chippenham and Eastbourne

Contents

List of Contributors

Tim Bayne is University Lecturer in Philosophy of Mind at the University of Oxford and Fellow of St Catherine's College, UK.

Christopher J. Eberle is Associate Professor of Philosophy at the United States Naval Academy, USA.

David Efird is Senior Lecturer in Philosophy at the University of York, UK.

Daniel J. Hill is Lecturer in Philosophy at the University of Liverpool, UK.

Daniel Howard-Snyder is Professor of Philosophy at the University of Western Washington, USA.

Klaas J. Kraay is Associate Professor of Philosophy at Ryerson University, Canada.

Neil A. Manson is Assistant Professor of Philosophy at the University of Mississippi, USA.

T. J. Mawson is Fellow and Tutor in Philosophy at St Peters College, Oxford, UK.

Thaddeus Metz is Professor of Philosophy and Director of the Wits Centre for Ethics, University of the Witwatersrand, South Africa.

Christian B. Miller is Assistant Professor of Philosophy at Wake Forest University, USA.

Yujin Nagasawa is Lecturer in Philosophy at the University of Birmingham, UK.

Alexander R. Pruss is Associate Professor of Philosophy at Baylor University, USA.

Greg Restall is Associate Professor of Philosophy at the University of Melbourne, Australia.

Erik J. Wielenberg is Associate Professor of Philosophy at DePauw University, USA.

Introduction

As part of the *New Waves in Philosophy* series, this volume aims to gather together papers written by some of the best philosophers of religion of the new generation. The quantifier 'some' is important here because we do not claim to have collected papers by *all* the best philosophers of religion of the new generation. The impossibility of such a task is a consequence of the healthy state of contemporary philosophy of religion.

In the early phase of contemporary analytic philosophy, topics in the philosophy of religion were not taken very seriously. Many philosophers, especially those attracted to logical positivism, dismissed religious statements as unverifiable or meaningless. In the last few decades, however, the philosophy of religion has been revived and is flourishing as one of central areas of philosophy. Philosophers of religion, including theists, atheists and agnostics, have developed many of their most important ideas and arguments by adapting significant advancements in metaphysics, epistemology, logic and ethics as well as natural science. This volume provides an opportunity for young and up-and-coming philosophers of religion to review these developments and introduce their own cutting-edge research.

A fundamental topic in the philosophy of religion is that of the divine attributes. Without sufficient understanding of the attributes that theists ascribe to God we cannot meaningfully discuss the existence and non-existence of God. Among the various divine attributes, omnipotence in particular has attracted much attention. Understanding omnipotence is important because it is closely related to the problem of evil, the cosmological argument and a number of other arguments concerning the existence of God. Philosophers have attempted to define omnipotence in terms of states of affairs, propositions and actions. However, most, if not all, of these definitions face persistent counter-examples and entail problematic consequences. In Chapter 1 Daniel J. Hill introduces a new definition of omnipotence in terms of sets. Hill claims that his definition is more sustainable than other existing definitions because it does not involve quantifications over such disputed entities as states of affairs, propositions and actions.

Once we acquire sufficient understanding of God's attributes we can consider the plausibility of His existence. Many theists believe that while there are many possible worlds that God can instantiate, He chose to instantiate only one of them, namely, this world. What if, however, there are infinitely many possible worlds that are unsurpassable, or there is a hierarchy of increasingly better worlds? In these scenarios God does not seem to have a sufficient reason to create this specific world. This is a serious challenge for theists because it could lead to the conclusion that God is not the creator of this world after all. In Chapter 2 Klaas J. Kraay discusses critically a response to this problem, a response according to which God has chosen to create a world *at random*. Kraay argues that such a response succeeds at solving the problem only on the implausible assumption that there is exactly one randomizer available to God, which picks randomly one world from either the infinite set of unsurpassable worlds, or the infinite set of increasingly better worlds.

In Chapter 3 T. J. Mawson addresses a related issue from a different perspective. He considers whether or not we can provide a sufficient explanation for the very existence of anything at all. He discusses three prominent explanations: the theistic explanation (i.e. God is a necessary being so it is metaphysically impossible that there is nothing), Peter van Inwagen's explanation (it is metaphysically possible but infinitely unlikely that there is nothing) and the Axiarchic explanation (it would be overall good were there something rather than nothing and that which would be overall good has to obtain). He argues that none of these explanations is decisively correct. Mawson claims as well that this problem is relevant to the cogency of theism because which explanation we find most plausible depends on the reasons we have for believing in or disbelieving in the existence of God.

The argument for the existence of God that has attracted most attention recently among philosophers, scientists and the general public is the design argument. A modern version of the design argument, which is sometimes called the 'analogy argument', was introduced by the eighteenth-century theologian William Paley. Paley says that the relationship between a watch and a watchmaker is analogous to the relationship between nature and God. If, as the cover art of this book illustrates, we find a watch on the beach and pay close attention to its elaborate design, it is reasonable to infer that there is a watchmaker who designed it. Analogously, Paley says, if we pay close attention to the elaborate design of nature it is reasonable to infer the existence of God. In Chapter 4 Alexander R. Pruss discusses a contemporary version of the analogy argument. The notion of a genetic defect is often analogized to the notion of a bug in a computer program. Pruss cautions that such an analogy does not, however, constitute a sound argument for the existence of a designer because some computer programs are generated by other programs, not necessarily designed independently by programmers. Pruss argues, however, that we can amend such an argument by advancing an analogy, not between a computer program and DNA but between a computer program *designed by a programmer* and DNA. Pruss concludes that the essential question for further debate will be whether in fact DNA shares relevant characteristics with designed computer programs.

In Chapter 5 Neil A. Manson discusses an important, but neglected, issue about the design argument. Analysts of the argument, including both proponents and opponents, focus on such issues as whether apparent evidence of design leads to the existence of a designer and whether such evidence can be explained away naturalistically. Manson points out that, in disputing these issues, the analysts overlook a crucial question, which he calls the 'why design' question: If a designer did exist, why would we expect to find evidence of the design? It is not very obvious, as Manson says, why the designer would design anything in the first place. Manson provides a new framework for addressing this question and explains where the debate on the design argument goes wrong.

Beyond these enduring controversies over the attributes and existence of God, there are many other subjects of dispute in the philosophy of religion. The next four chapters discuss various doctrines that are often endorsed by theists and some related puzzles that arise from them.

In Chapter 6 David Efird tries to construct an axiomatization of the divine command theory on the assumption that the theory is a metaphysical analysis of the properties of moral rightness and moral wrongness. He tries to develop the axiomatization by taking into account such theoretical constraints as Hume's Razor (do not multiply necessities beyond necessity) and Moore's Razor (do not contradict common sense beyond necessity). Efird maintains that his axiomatization requires a Priorian semantics for quantified modal logic.

The best-known alternative to the divine command theory is the divine intention theory, according to which deontological properties are metaphysically grounded in God's relevant intentions rather than in His commands. In Chapter 7 Christian B. Miller tries to develop a third alternative, which he calls the 'divine desire theory'. The theory says that deontological properties are metaphysically grounded in God's relevant desires. Miller explains why the theory is worthy of serious consideration, if not superior to others.

In Chapter 8 Daniel Howard-Snyder focuses on what he calls the 'puzzle of prayers of thanksgiving and praise'. Most traditional theists believe that God is worthy of thanks and praise for His good acts. Yet if God is *essentially* unsurpassably good, then it does not seem even to be an option for God to perform something worse than what he actually does. If so, it is unclear why we should be thankful to God in the first place. Howard-Snyder claims that there are three ways to solve this puzzle: (1) give up the practice of thanks and praising God; (2) give up incompatibilism about free will and determinism; or (3) give up the idea that God is essentially unsurpassably good. Since (2) is not an option for Howard-Snyder, he concludes that theists' endorsement of the offering of prayers of thanksgiving and praise is rational only if God is not essentially unsurpassably good.

In Chapter 9 Tim Bayne and Greg Restall discuss the atonement, a central doctrine in Christian theism. They argue that existing models of the atonement are not compelling because they rely on a naively deontic conception of sin and also because they fail to show an internal connection between the atonement, on the one hand, and Christ's incarnation, death and resurrection, on the other hand. Bayne and Restall then try to develop, by reference to recent work in Pauline scholarship, a participatory model of the atonement, according to which the atonement involves participation in Christ's death and resurrection. They maintain that the new model is exegetically and philosophically plausible and more robust than existing models.

Theism, if it is true, has a number of implications for the existence of human beings. In Chapter 10 Christopher J. Eberle discusses what he calls 'basic human worth'. Western liberal democracies are based on the idea that each human being has a worth, dignity or sacredness that equals that of any other human being. This idea, however, demands justification. Eberle claims tentatively that theism can provide a more adequate account of the thesis than secularism. Eberle admits that there are powerful objections remaining for his theistic account but if they can be met, he says, theism shapes the moral life in at least one more-than-trivial respect.

A common cliché about God is that life is meaningless if He does not exist. Many theists have tried to defend it not as a cliché but as truth. In Chapter 11 Thaddeus Metz observes that life appears meaningless to some because human beings and their surroundings are significantly limited. Many philosophers, even including some atheists, claim, therefore, that in order for life to be meaningful there must be God, who is associated, or identified, with a maximally great being, ideal justice and eternal bliss. In response to such a suggestion critics have introduced various naturalistic accounts that are based on the idea that some imperfect value is sufficient for one's life to be meaningful. Metz assesses these accounts through the following question: What degree of less-than-perfect value is sufficient to grant meaning to life? He tries to articulate and defend a new naturalistic account that deserves serious consideration.

It should be clear by now that this volume covers a wide range of topics from many different perspectives. We believe that each one of the following chapters makes a signification contribution to an ongoing debate in the philosophy of religion.

Acknowledgements

We would like to thank Michael Almeida, Trent Dougherty, Vincent F. Hendricks, Joseph Jedwab, Dan Kaufman, Stephen Maitzen, Graham Oppy, Alvin Plantinga, Duncan Pritchard and Michael Rea for helpful comments on this work and Melanie Blair, Daniel Bunyard and Priyanka Pathak at Palgrave and Suwathiga Velayutham at Integra Software Services for their invaluable editorial support. We would also like to thank Emma Bullock for preparing the index for this volume. We are also grateful, of course, to all the contributors for their excellent work.

1
A New Definition of 'Omnipotence' in Terms of Sets

Daniel J. Hill

1 Background

Almost all the recent attempted definitions of 'omnipotence' in the litera-ture are couched in terms of states of affairs or propositions.[1] The definitions from the scholastics are almost all in terms of actions.[2] There is, however, considerable philosophical debate over whether states of affairs, proposi-tions, and actions really exist.[3] In this essay I wish to investigate whether it is possible to define 'omnipotence' in a new way without quantifying over such disputed entities.

2 A schematic definition?

So, is it possible to give a correct definition of 'omnipotence' without mak-ing reference to states of affairs or the like? A first try might make use of a definition schema and substitution rather than quantification:

1. For every possible being, x, x is omnipotent if and only if x has the power to cause it to be the case that p.

The reason why Definition-Schema 1 is a definition schema rather than a definition proper is that 'p', unlike 'x', is not a variable, but a schematic letter. The assertion would be that, if x is omnipotent, whatever English sen-tence we substitute for the letter 'p' in Definition-Schema 1 yields a truth. The problem is that to be a valid definition schema the converse assertion also needs to be true, that is, it needs to be true that if whatever English sentence we substitute for 'p' in Definition-Schema 1 yields a truth then x is omnipotent. Sadly, this converse assertion is not true, however. Definition-Schema 1 is too weak: it allows to qualify as omnipotent a being whose powers reach as far as does our language, but no farther. In other words, we think, intuitively, that an omnipotent being should have the power to do things far beyond the descriptive powers of English or any other natural language, yet Definition-Schema 1 does not insist on this. The moral of this failed attempt is that any satisfactory definition of 'omnipotence' is going to have to involve quantification over *something*; a mere schema will not suffice.

3   Defining 'omnipotence' in terms of sentences?

So, over what undisputed entities (i.e. entities other than states of affairs, propositions, and actions) can we quantify? *Sentences* certainly exist, and this might tempt us to define 'omnipotence' thus:

2. For every possible being, x, x is omnipotent if and only if for every possible sentence, S, if it is metaphysically possible that S be made true then x has the power to make S true.

Definition 2 is stronger than Definition-Schema 1, as it quantifies over *possible* sentences rather than just allowing substitution of *actual* sentences. Despite this, however, it is still not clear that this definition is sufficiently strong – it still runs the risk of counting as omnipotent a being that we intuitively think not omnipotent. Even if we consider all the sentences that could exist, there are, intuitively, ways the world could be that aren't described by such sentences: it is usual to insist that every sentence must be finitely long, and yet we surely want the definition of 'omnipotence' to imply that every omnipotent being has the power to accomplish tasks that need infinite specification. Also, if every sentence has to be of a physical form (e.g. marks on a paper, or sound waves) then it would seem, since physical forms can be differentiated only by difference in position of atoms and molecules, that there cannot be enough physical forms to express every truth concerning the mental world that we think should be in the power of an omnipotent being.[4] It may be responded that God represents all these truths to himself in mental sentences, and so the definition goes through unchallenged. This response may be correct, but I think that the definition of 'omnipotence' should not presume either that God exists or that he represents truths to himself in the form of sentences.[5]

4   The new definition of 'omnipotence', in terms of sets

At this point it may seem that we have exhausted our options, if we are not going to pursue a definition in terms of sentences, and if we also reject states of affairs, facts, actions, and propositions. We have not, however, rejected all abstract objects; we have not considered such putative mathematical objects as sets and numbers.

The existence of sets is less controversial than the existence of propositions, actions, and states of affairs. This is for two reasons: first, an adequate interpretation of modern-day mathematics requires the idea of a set, and secondly, it is relatively clear as to what sets are supposed to be – collections of a certain kind. And it is relatively clear what collections are supposed to be, and we regularly assume the existence of groups, teams, countries, organizations, companies, and so on, as well as the individuals that compose them. It should also be noted that not all sets are necessary existents; a set exists if and only if its members do, and while mathematicians tend to study pure sets that are frequently considered necessary existents, our discussion will be confined here to impure sets.[6] (Pure sets have no members that are not sets, and their members have no members that are not sets, and so on, whereas impure sets do have members that are not sets, or have members that have members that are not sets, and so on.)

5   First main clause of the new definition

How, then, should we define 'omnipotence' in terms of sets? The first thing we want is that an omnipotent agent be able to create any creatable object and destroy any destructible object: here we do not need to introduce discussion of sets as we have no objection to discussing individual (concrete) objects anyway. This yields the following first main clause of our definition:

3. For every possible being, x, x is omnipotent only if

   3.1 for every other possible being, y, if it is possible that anything has the power to cause it to be directly the case that y actually exists, then x has the power to cause it to be directly the case that y actually exists;

   3.2 and for every possible being, y, if it is possible that anything has the power to cause it to be directly the case that y does not actually exist, then x has the power to cause it to be directly the case that y does not actually exist.

It is necessary to add the subsidiary clauses beginning 'if it is possible that anything has the power' since there may well be necessarily existent entities (such as God himself) that cannot be caused to exist by anything, and cannot be caused not to exist by anything.[7] It is necessary to add the word 'other' in Subsidiary Clause 3.1 because it would not be appropriate for a definition to rule out of court in advance the epistemic possibility that there might be an omnipotent being that might be powerless to cause his own existence, but whose existence might have been brought about by something else. For example, on some understandings of the Trinity the Father causes it to be the case that the Son exists (though not, of course, that he begins to exist) and yet the Son cannot cause it to be the case that he himself exists (since nothing can cause it to be the case that it itself exists), even though he is omnipotent.

Let me explain what I mean by 'cause it to be directly the case that':

4. For every possible being, x, x causes it to be directly the case that p if and only if x causes it to be the case that p, and it is not true that both

    4.1 x causes it to be the case that q;
    4.2 and it is the case that p (at least partly) in virtue of its being the case that q.

5. For every possible being, x, x causes it to be indirectly the case that p if and only if x causes it to be the case that p and it is true that both

    5.1 x causes it to be the case that q;
    5.2 and it is the case that p (at least partly) in virtue of its being the case that q.

Note that these are, strictly speaking, not definitions, but definition schemata: they become definitions when the dummy letters 'p' and 'q' are replaced with real English sentences. It is important to note that 'p' and 'q' are not variables; if they were then they would have to range over really existent things and we would be back with the commitment to propositions that I eschewed at the start. It does not matter if both 'p' and 'q' are replaced by the same English sentence since no sentence of the form 'it is the case that p in virtue of its being the case that p' is true. Note that 'directly' and 'indirectly' qualify 'it is the case that' rather than 'cause'; this is not the same notion as that of a basic action. One reason for this is that I am trying to come up with a definition of 'omnipotence' that does not involve the notion of action, since, as we saw earlier, actions are disputed entities. Another reason is that it would seem to be possible to cause it to be the case that p & q, but without doing so in virtue of *separately* causing it to be the case that p or *separately* causing it to be the case that q. Nevertheless, on my definition one would be causing it to be indirectly the case that p & q, since one would be, *thereby*, either causing it to be the case that p or causing it to be the case that q, and it is the case that p & q partly in virtue of its being the case that p and partly in virtue of its being the case that q.

Let me give some examples to clarify the intuitive notion. Let us assume that Plato caused it to be the case that he freely wrote a dialogue. Did he cause this to be directly the case or did he cause this to be indirectly the case? Surely he caused it to be indirectly the case that he freely wrote a dialogue, since it is the case that he *freely* wrote a dialogue partly in virtue of its being the case that he wrote a dialogue, and surely he caused that also to be indirectly the case, since it is the case that he wrote a dialogue in virtue of its being the case that he moved his arm in a certain way.

Let us assume that Adam caused it to be the case that Adam sinned without being determined to do so by God. Did he cause this to be directly the case or did he cause it to be indirectly the case? Surely he caused it to be indirectly the case that Adam sinned without being determined to do so by God, since it is the case that Adam sinned without being determined to do so by God partly in virtue of its being the case that Adam sinned, and surely he caused that to be indirectly the case, since it is the case that Adam sinned partly in virtue of its being the case that he ate the forbidden fruit, and surely he caused *that* to be indirectly the case, since it is the case that he ate the forbidden fruit partly in virtue of its being the case that he moved his jaw in a certain way.

Why is it necessary to add the word 'directly' in Definition 3? It is necessary to prevent gerrymandered counter-examples, such as the objection that no omnipotent being has the power to cause it to be the case that there actually exists a being whose actual existence is not brought about by an omnipotent being (assuming that it is indeed possible that there be such a being). The definition escapes this objection because nothing can or could cause it to be *directly* the case that there actually exists a being whose actual existence is not brought about by an omnipotent being. Suppose some being, z, caused it to be the case that such a being actually existed, then it would be the case that a being whose actual existence was not brought about by an omnipotent being actually existed partly in virtue of its being the case that there was a being of some sort or other – and z would have caused this to be the case too. (It would also be the case partly in virtue of its being the case that z brought it about and partly in virtue of its being the case that z was not omnipotent, but this latter fact is not relevant here, since (we may assume) z did not cause it to be the case that z was not omnipotent.) Hence, if some being, z, caused it to be the case that there actually existed a being whose actual existence was not caused by an omnipotent being, z would not cause it to be *directly* the case that there actually existed a being whose actual existence was not caused by an omnipotent being. (This same answer also suffices if the objection is reworked in terms of 'a being whose actual existence is not brought about by an omnipotent being to be directly the case' or 'a being whose actual existence is not brought about by an omnipotent being to be indirectly the case'.)

It may be wondered why we did not have a clause featuring 'causing it to be *in*directly the case that' in Definition 3. The answer is that it was not necessary: if a being, z, has the power, for every being whose actual existence can be caused directly to be the case, to cause it to be directly the case that that being actually exists, z will thereby have the power to cause actually to exist every being whose actual existence we would intuitively expect an omnipotent being to have the power to cause indirectly to be the case.[8] For example, suppose that the aggregate of Mt Everest and George Bush actually exists (as I think it does). Is it possible to cause this aggregate's actual existence *directly* to be the case? No. Suppose some being, z, caused it to be the case that the aggregate of Mt Everest and George Bush actually existed.

It would then be the case that the aggregate of Mt Everest and George Bush actually existed partly in virtue of its being the case that Mt Everest actually existed and partly in virtue of its being the case that George Bush actually existed, and it would be the case that either z caused it to be the case that Mt Everest actually existed or z caused it to be the case that George Bush actually existed, whence it follows that z would have caused it to be *indirectly* the case that the aggregate of Mt Everest and George Bush actually existed. Our definition mandates that every omnipotent being has the power to cause it to be *directly* the case that Mt Everest actually exists and the power to cause it to be *directly* the case that George Bush actually exists, since it is possible (even if not for us) to cause, for each of these, it to be directly the case that it actually exists. Hence it follows, without the need for further specification, that every omnipotent being has, by co-exercising its power to cause it to be the case that Mt Everest actually exists and its power to cause it to be the case that George Bush actually exists, the power to cause it to be indirectly the case that the aggregate of Mt Everest and George Bush actually exists.[9]

Even with all this refinement, however, there may still be an objection to Subsidiary Clause 3.1. The objection is that the clause mandates only that for any *one* other possible being every omnipotent being has the power to cause it to be directly the case that that being actually exists (assuming this is possible); it does not insist that every omnipotent being has the power to cause it to be directly the case that *two or more* other possible beings actually exist.[10] Further, even if the definition were changed to reflect this, the change might well be to no avail since it seems that nothing could possibly have the power to cause it to be *directly* the case that two or more other beings actually exist: if some being, x, causes it to be the case that y and z actually exist, surely x causes it to be *indirectly* the case that y and z actually exist since it is the case that y and z actually exist partly in virtue of its being the case that y actually exists, and partly in virtue of its being the case that z actually exists, and since it must be that either x causes it to be the case that y actually exists or x causes it to be the case that z actually exists. The force of the objection is that Subsidiary Clause 3.1 is deficient because it wrongly fails to prevent from qualifying as omnipotent a being that lacks the power to cause it to be the case that two or more other beings actually exist.

One possible response to this is analogous to the response I defended in Hill (2005, pp. 178–81) to the objection that my definition there was too weak. This response is to argue that if some putatively omnipotent being, x, has, for every possible being, y, the power to cause it to be directly the case that y actually exists (if it is possible for anything to cause it to be directly the case that y actually exists), then x has the power to cause the actual existence of any number, finite or infinite, of possible beings. The argument makes use of the following schematic analysis of the locution '*x* has the power to cause it to be (directly or indirectly) the case that *p*':

6. For every possible being, *x*, *x* has the power to cause it (directly or indirectly) to be the case that *p* if and only if it is the case that, supposing *x* had the opportunity, know-how, and the overriding desire to cause it to be the case that *p*, then *x* would cause it to be the case that *p*.[11]

The terms 'opportunity', 'know-how', and 'overriding desire' are included because, intuitively, *x* might have the power to cause it to be the case that *p*, and yet not desire to exercise that power, or might not know how to exercise it (as I may have the power to ride a bicycle, being physically fit, but may not know how to), or might not have the opportunity to exercise it (as I may have the power to write my name but lack the opportunity if there is no writing implement to hand).

Now, the objection that we are facing goes like this: suppose *x* has the power to cause it to be directly the case that y_1 actually exists and the power to cause it to be directly the case that y_2 actually exists (as is mandated by Definition 3) then, so the objection goes, it may yet be that *x* lacks the power to cause it to be directly or indirectly the case that y_1 and y_2 actually exist. In this case, Subsidiary Clause 3.1 would wrongly allow *x* to qualify as omnipotent.

To apply Analysis 6 to our problem, we note first that if a putatively omnipotent being, *x*, had the opportunity, know-how, and the overriding desire to cause it to be the case that y_1 and y_2 actually exist, then surely, at least if *x* were rational, *x* would also have the opportunity, know-how, and the overriding desire to cause it to be the case that y_1 actually exist, and the opportunity, know-how, and the overriding desire to cause it to be the case that y_2 actually exist, whence it would follow, since *x* is supposed to satisfy Clause 3.1, that y_1 actually exist and that y_2 actually exist (assuming it possible that y_1 and y_2 be caused actually to exist). In other words, if a putatively omnipotent being, *x*, had the opportunity, know-how, and the overriding desire to cause it to be the case that y_1 and y_2 actually exist, then *x* would cause it to be the case that y_1 and y_2 actually exist, whence it follows by Analysis 6 that *x* does indeed have the power to cause it to be the case that y_1 and y_2 actually exist.

Admittedly, this argument does presume that *x* is rational and so if *x* desires to cause it to be the case that y_1 and y_2 actually exist, then *x* desires to cause it to be the case that y_1 actually exist, and *x* desires to cause it to be the case that y_2 actually exist, and so the argument will not work on those rare occasions on which we want to consider a possible irrational omnipotent being. (It seems plausible that if something has the opportunity and know-how to cause it to be the case that some possible beings y_1 and y_2 actually exist, then it also has the opportunity and know-how to cause it to be the case that y_1 actually exist, and the opportunity and know-how to cause it to be the case that y_2 actually exist.) It might be countered that, even for a rational being, desire to cause it to be the case that y_1 and y_2 actually exist might not imply desire to cause it to be the case that y_1 actually exist and desire to cause it to be the case that y_2 actually exist, since it might be that the being wants to create Adam and Eve, but does not want to create Adam on his own or Eve on her own. But the addition of the phrase 'on his own' gives the game away here: it certainly is not the case that if a perfectly rational being, x, has the overriding desire to cause it to be the case that y_1 and y_2 actually exist it necessarily follows that x has the overriding desire to cause it to be the case that y_1 actually exist *on its own*. Indeed, the very fact that x desires to cause it to be the case that both y_1 and y_2 actually exist shows that x does not desire to cause it to be the case that y_1 actually exist on its own.

Another objection to Main Clause 3 would be that while Subsidiary Clause 3.1 mandates that, in order to be omnipotent, a being, x, has to have the power for every other possible being, y, to cause it to be directly the case that y actually exist (assuming such is possible) and for every possible being, y, to cause it to be directly the case that y not actually exist (assuming such is possible), it *not* mandate that in order to be omnipotent x has to have the power for two other beings, y_1 and y_2, to cause it to be the case that y_1 actually exist and y_2 not actually exist (assuming such is possible). The force of the objection is that Main Clause 3 wrongly allows to qualify as omnipotent something that is intuitively not omnipotent for it lacks the power to cause it to be the case that y_1 actually exist and y_2 not actually exist. Once again, however, if we attend to Analysis 6, we can see that this objection misfires. We suppose that x has the overriding desire, opportunity, and know-how to cause it to be the case that y_1 actually exist and y_2 not actually exist. We again assume that x is rational, whence it follows that x has the overriding desire, opportunity, and know-how to cause it to be the case that y_1 actually exist, and the overriding desire, opportunity, and know-how to cause it to be the case that y_2 not actually exist. Since, however, by Subsidiary Clause 3.1, it follows that if x has the overriding desire, opportunity, and know-how to cause it to be the case that y_1 actually exist, x will cause it to be the case that y_1 actually exist, and from Subsidiary Clause 3.2 that if x has the overriding desire, opportunity, and know-how to cause it to be the case that y_2 not actually exist, x will cause it to be the case that y_2 not actually exist; it follows further that if x has the overriding desire, opportunity, and know-how to cause it to be the case that y_1 actually exist and y_2 not actually exist x will cause it to be the case that y_1 actually exist and y_2 not actually exist, that is x has the power to cause it to be the case that y_1 actually exist and y_2 not actually exist.

6 Second main clause of the new definition

For the second main clause of the new definition we need the language of sets, since we wish to say, without quantifying over properties, relations, or any such disputed entities, that an omnipotent being has the power to make anything exist in any particular way.

I shall now briefly argue that the language of sets is up to the job. If an agent causes it to be the case that I am tall that agent thereby causes it to be the case that I am a member of the set of tall things. Conversely, if an agent causes it to be the case that I am a member of the set of tall things it follows that that agent causes it to be the case that I am tall. Further, if an agent causes it to be the case that I am taller than my wife that agent thereby causes it to be the case that the ordered pair of me and my wife is a member of the set of ordered pairs whose first co-ordinate is taller than the second. Conversely, if an agent causes it to be the case that the ordered pair of me and my wife is a member of the set of ordered pairs whose first co-ordinate is taller than the second, it follows that that agent causes it to be the case that I am taller than my wife. In sum, sets can be made to do duty for properties and relations: whenever others say that an agent causes something to have a certain property we can say that the agent causes the thing to be a member of the corresponding set, and whenever others say that an agent causes some things to stand in a relation we can say that the agent causes the ordered pair of those things to be a member of the corresponding set of ordered pairs. (Note that this does not presuppose that there is an existent entity, the relation of membership. Rather, it presupposes that the *predicate* 'is a member of' makes sense, as it does.) We can also say whatever others say about the actualization of states of affairs in terms of the causing it to be the case for certain objects and certain sets that the objects are in the sets. And, of course, there are far more sets than we have physical names for sets, so this avoids the possible problem we noted concerning the proposed definition of 'omnipotence' in terms of sentences.

Here is my suggestion for the second main clause of the new definition:

7. For every possible being, x, x is omnipotent only if for every possible being, y, and every possible set, S, if it is possible that anything have the power to cause it to be the case that y is directly a member of S, then x has that power.

Here, however, I am using 'directly' in a slightly different way from before, so I need slightly to rework my definitions of 'directly' and 'indirectly' to put them in terms of sets:

8. For every possible being, x, and for every possible being, y, and every possible set, S, x causes it to be the case that y is directly a member of S

if and only if x causes it to be the case that y is a member of S and it is not true that both

   8.1   there is a distinct set, T, such that x causes it to be the case that y is a member of T;

   8.2   and y is a member of S (at least partly) in virtue of y's being a member of T.

9. For every possible being, x, and for every possible being, y, and every possible set, S, x causes it to be the case that y is indirectly a member of S if and only if x causes it to be the case that y is a member of S and it is true that both

   9.1   there is a distinct set, T, such that x causes it to be the case that y is a member of T;

   9.2   and y is a member of S (at least partly) in virtue of y's being a member of T.

Note that the definitions do *not* say that

10. For every possible being, x, and for every possible being, y, and every possible set, S, x causes it to be the case that y is directly a member of S if and only x causes it to be the case that y is a member of S, and it is not true that both

   10.1 x causes it to be the case that p;

   10.2   and y is a member of S (partly) in virtue of its being the case that p.

11. For every possible being x and for every possible being y, and every possible set S, x causes it to be the case that y is indirectly a member of S if and only if x causes it to be the case that y is a member of S, and it is true that both

   11.1 x causes it to be the case that p;

   11.2   and y is a member of S (partly) in virtue of its being the case that p.

The reason why Definition-Schema 10 and Definition-Schema 11 are not the definitions (strictly, definition schemata) is that it would seem that, if they were the definitions, it would be impossible to cause it to be the case that anything were directly a member of any set. This is because it would appear that it is only ever possible to cause it to be the case that something is a member of the set of blue things, say, by causing it to be the case that that thing is blue, and that thing would be a member of the set of blue things in virtue of its being the case that it was blue.[12]

We needed to include the word 'directly' to Main Clause 7 to avoid the following objection: it might be objected that I have the power to cause it to be the case that I am in the set of those that freely go walking (I use 'freely' in the libertarian manner, according to which freedom is incompatible with determinism), but that nothing distinct from me has the power to cause it to be the case that I am in the set of those that freely go walking, because if something distinct from me causes it to be the case that I am in the set of those that go walking I shall not be in the set of those that *freely* go walking at all. So it appears that nothing can be omnipotent, for nothing but me has the power to cause it to be the case that I am in the set of those that freely go walking, and I lack the power to cause it to be the case that my wife is in the set of those that freely go walking. The answer to this puzzle is that nothing, not even I, has the power to cause it to be the case that I am *directly* in the set of those that freely go walking; rather, I cause it to be the case that I am *indirectly* in the set of those that freely go walking. We can see this since I also cause it to be the case that I am in the (distinct) set of those that go walking, and I am a member of the set of those that freely go walking partly in virtue of my being a member of the distinct set of those that go walking (and partly in virtue of my being a member of the set of uncompelled people, or something like that). But Main Clause 7 *does* mandate that every omnipotent being has the power to cause it to be the case that I am directly in the set of those that go walking.

It may be objected that we need to add a clause saying 'if it is possible that anything have the power to cause it to be the case that y is directly a *non*-member of S, then x has that power'. In fact, however, such a clause is both incorrect and unnecessary. In the first place, it is incorrect because it is impossible for any being, x, to cause it to be the case that any other thing, y, *directly* be a non-member of any set, S, since x would always cause it to be the case that y were a non-member of S by causing it to be the case that y were a member of some other non-overlapping set, T, and y would be a non-member of S in virtue of being a member of T. For example, consider the set of blue things. One can cause it to be the case that something is a non-member of the set of blue things only by causing it to be the case that it is a member of the set of red things, or the set of pink things, and so on. Secondly, the proposed second clause is unnecessary since if x causes it to be the case that y is directly in the set of red things then x thereby causes it to be the case that y is indirectly a non-member of the set of blue things since nothing can be in both sets.

This last point may, however, prompt a more serious objection: one way of causing it to be the case that something is a non-member of the set of blue things would seem to be by causing it to be the case that it is a member of the set of colourless things. Here we hit a problem, however, since it turns out that, on standard Zermelo–Fraenkel set theory, there is no set of colourless things, since there are too many colourless things to be gathered into a set (every possible set is itself colourless, so all the uncountably many sets would have to be contained in the set of colourless things,[13] but it turns out that there can be no set containing all sets on standard Zermelo–Fraenkel set theory). So it seems as though there is a problem with Main Clause 7: it wrongly fails to rule out from qualifying as omnipotent a being that lacks the power to cause it to be the case that something is colourless.

One possible response to this is to reject Zermelo–Fraenkel set theory in exchange for another set theory, such as Quine's NF or NFU set theory.[14] In fact, I think this is the right thing to do for quite independent reasons, but I can see that this may be too high a price to pay for some.

Another possible response is to argue that if one causes it to be the case that some concrete physical thing is colourless one will also cause it to be the case that it is a concrete colourless physical thing, and, hence, that it is a member of the set of concrete colourless physical things. This is indeed a set, for it contains only concrete physical things as members and even if there are infinitely many of them they can still be gathered into a set, even under Zermelo–Fraenkel set theory. So, since Main Clause 7 does mandate that a being, to be omnipotent, must have the power to cause something to be a member of the set of concrete colourless physical things, it does also mandate that a being, to be omnipotent, must have the power to cause it to be the case that something is colourless.

Quine's NF set theory in fact also allows (unlike Zermelo–Fraenkel set theory) a universal set, that is, a set that contains everything that actually exists. This allows us to dispense with the first clause, Main Clause 3, of our definition. This is dispensable since to cause it to be the case that something, y, actually exist is equivalent to causing it to be the case that y is a member of the set of all possible things that actually exist, and to cause it to be the case that y not actually exist is equivalent to causing it to be the case that y is a member of the set of all possible things that do not actually exist. It may be responded that this last set is surely by definition empty, but I wish to allow simulated quantification over possible, but non-actual beings here. In fact, this is already allowed in the definition anyway, for it begins 'for every *possible* being' – we do not restrict our attention to actual beings. I shall postpone detailed defence of this practice till after I have expounded the third main clause of the definition.

7   Third main clause of the definition

Let us now turn to the third main clause of the definition. Other philosophers would say here that an omnipotent being can make any things stand in any relation. We, however, are eschewing this realistic idiom, and so we need to restate their point in terms of sets. A first go at this would be the following:

12. For every possible being, x, x is omnipotent only if for every possible ordered n-tuple of possible beings, $< y_1, \ldots, y_n >$, and every possible set, S, if it is possible that anything have the power to cause it to be the case that the n-tuple is directly a member of S, then x has that power.

The problem with this clause is that philosophers of a realistic bent would say that an omnipotent being also must have the power to make infinitely many beings possess a property or stand in a relation: for example, to instantiate some possible arrangement of angels. To capture what they are saying in our terms, we need to broaden Main Clause 12 thus:

13. For every possible being, x, x is omnipotent only if for every possible ordered sequence of possible beings, and every possible set, S, if it is possible that anything have the power to cause it to be the case that the sequence is directly a member of S, then x has that power.

Note that we cannot say 'the power to cause it to be the case that the members of the sequence are directly members of S', since it is the sequence that is ordered, not the members, so the proposed change would lose the order that we need to distinguish John's loving Mary from Mary's loving John. It is essential that the order be preserved, else we should wrongly allow to qualify as omnipotent a being that had the power to cause it to be the case that John loved Mary but not the power to cause it to be the case that Mary loved John. Our formulation is slightly less natural, but logically watertight, for if John loves Mary then the ordered pair <John, Mary> is a member of the set of ordered pairs whose first co-ordinate loves the second.

Again, we need to include the word 'directly' to rule out counter-examples concerning freedom, such as the following: I have the power freely to murder Joe Bloggs, so I have the power to cause it to be the case that the ordered pair <Daniel Hill, Joe Bloggs> is a member of the set of all ordered pairs whose first co-ordinate freely murders the second. Since nothing can cause it to be the case that something different freely does anything,[15] no possible being different from me has the power to cause it to be the case that the ordered pair <Daniel Hill, Joe Bloggs> is a member of the set of all ordered pairs whose first co-ordinate freely murders the second. So it looks as though nothing can be omnipotent, since it is possible for me, but nothing else, to cause it to be the case that the ordered pair <Daniel Hill, Joe Bloggs> is a member of the set of all ordered pairs whose first co-ordinate freely murders the second, and possible for Joe Bloggs, but nothing else, to cause it to be the case that the ordered pair <Joe Bloggs, Daniel Hill> is a member of the set of all ordered pairs whose first co-ordinate freely murders the second. The solution to this puzzle is, of course, that it is not possible for *anything*, not even for me, to cause it to be the case that the ordered pair <Daniel Hill, Joe Bloggs> is *directly* a member of the set of all ordered pairs whose first co-ordinate freely murders the second. Suppose I cause it to be the case that the ordered pair <Daniel Hill, Joe Bloggs> is a member of the set of all ordered pairs whose first co-ordinate freely murders the second. I will have done so by causing it to be the case that the ordered pair <Daniel Hill, Joe Bloggs> is a member of the set of all ordered pairs whose first co-ordinate kills the second, and the ordered pair <Daniel Hill, Joe Bloggs> will be a member of the set of all ordered pairs whose first co-ordinate freely murders the second partly in virtue of being a member of the set of all ordered pairs whose first co-ordinate kills the second[16] (and partly in virtue of my being a member of the set of all beings that act illegally, and partly in virtue of my being a member of the set of all beings that act intentionally, and partly in virtue of my being a member of the set of all beings that act freely). So this is not a counter-example to Main Clause 13, as the addition of the word 'directly' there precludes such counter-examples.

It also turns out that we can subsume the second main clause, Main Clause 7, under this, the third main clause, Main Clause 13. This is because causing it to be the case that something, y, is a member of some set, S, is equivalent to causing it to be the case that the ordered sequence $<y>$ is a member of the set, S', of all 1-tuples whose members are members of S.[17] The first main clause, Main Clause 3, can be subsumed under this one since causing it to be the case that something, y, actually exist is equivalent to causing it to be the case that the ordered sequence $<y>$ is a member of the set, S', of all 1-tuples whose members are members of the set of all actually existing objects.[18]

8   The definition in full

If we put together all the clauses we get the final definition:

14. For every possible being, x, x is omnipotent if and only if

    14.1 for every other possible being, y, if it is possible that anything have the power to cause it to be directly the case that y actually exist, then x has the power to cause it to be directly the case that y actually exist;

    14.2 and for every possible being, y, if it is possible that anything have the power to cause it to be directly the case that y not actually exist, then x has the power to cause it to be directly the case that y not actually exist;

    14.3 and for every possible being, y, and every possible set, S, if it is possible that anything have the power to cause it to be the case that y be directly a member of S, then x has that power;

> 14.4 for every possible ordered sequence of possible beings, and every
> possible set, S, if it is possible that anything have the power to
> cause it to be the case that the sequence be directly a member of S,
> then x has that power.

The brief form of this consists of just the final clause, provided that one adopts Quine's NF set theory or some similar remedy to allow existence to be subsumed under some set:

15. For every possible being, x, x is omnipotent if and only if, for every possible ordered sequence of possible beings, and every possible set, S, if it is possible that anything have the power to cause it to be the case that the sequence be directly a member of S, then x has that power.

Now, it might seem at first as though we get into trouble in Definition 14 by splitting up the simple idea that the realist has of actualizing a state of affairs into three or four clauses. For example, it may be objected that my Definition 14 does not insist that an omnipotent being have the power to, as the realist would put it, 'actualize a conjunctive state of affairs', such as that (supposedly) named by 'a snowflake's falling and a ball's existing'. So it might be, to put the objection without reference to states of affairs, that Definition 14 wrongly allows to qualify as omnipotent a being that fulfils each individual clause by itself, and so has the power to cause it to be the case that a snowflake fall (from Clause 14.3) and the power to cause it to be the case that a ball exist (from Clause 14.1), and yet lacks the power to cause it to be the case that a snowflake fall and a ball exist. Once more we can put to use our analysis of 'has the power to' in Analysis 6. We suppose x has the opportunity, know-how, and overriding desire to cause it to be the case that a snowflake falls and a ball exist. We once again assume that x is fully rational, whence it follows that x has the opportunity, know-how, and overriding desire to cause it to be the case that a snowflake fall and the opportunity, know-how, and overriding desire to cause it to be the case that a ball exist. But, by Analysis 6, it then follows that, assuming x meets Clause 14.3, if x has the opportunity, know-how, and overriding desire to cause it to be the case that a snowflake fall then x does cause it to be the case that a snowflake falls, and by Analysis 6 again, assuming x meets Clause 14.1, it follows that if x has the opportunity, know-how, and overriding desire to cause it to be the case that a ball exist then x does cause it to be the case that a ball exist. It follows hence that if x does indeed have the opportunity, know-how, and overriding desire to cause it to be the case that a snowflake fall and a ball exist then it will indeed follow that a snowflake falls and a ball exists, that is, x has the power to cause it to be the case that a snowflake fall and a ball exist.

9 Quantification over merely possible beings

One problem with Definition 14 (and many of the other definitions presented *en route*) is that it seems to quantify over non-existent objects, viz. merely possible beings. These cannot be restricted to actual beings, as we do not want to say that it is sufficient to qualify for omnipotence that one have the power to cause actually to exist only actual beings! Does Definition 14 then imply realism, in the style of David Lewis,[19] concerning possible but non-actual entities?

It should be noted that this is not a problem peculiar to Definition 14 and the other definitions presented *en route*. On the contrary, even homely sentences such as the following seem to involve quantification over non-existent objects:

16. I could have had a younger sister

16 can perhaps be paraphrased away; David Lewis presents the more challenging case of:

17. A red thing could resemble an orange thing more closely than a red thing could resemble a blue thing.[20]

Lewis asserts that this implies sentences such as the following:

18. There exist non-actual red objects, non-actual orange objects, and non-actual blue objects.

The problem is that most of us do not want to accept sentences such as Sentence 18, but do want to accept sentences such as Sentence 17. Suppose that such sentences as Sentence 17 cannot be paraphrased away without cross-modal comparison, with its implications as exhibited in Sentence 18, what then? I want to argue that we should adopt the approach of modal fictionalism, as pioneered by Gideon Rosen.[21] This involves saying that sentences such as Sentence 18, while not really true, are treated as true because they are true according to the fiction of the modal realist's theory, just as we often treat sentences such as the following as true because they are true according to certain well-known fictions:

19. Sherlock Holmes lived at 221B Baker Street.[22]

We might well seem to use quantification too:

20. Sherlock Holmes was cleverer than all the other detectives in London.

It might well be asked, concerning Sentence 20, how we can quantify over non-existent things, fictional detectives. The answer is that we do not quantify over them; we merely report that in the fictional stories by Conan Doyle they seem to be quantified over. But how can Conan Doyle quantify over them if they do not exist? He does not really quantify over them; he just pretends to, in just the same way as he does not really assert that a detective lives in 221B Baker Street, he merely pretends to assert that (which is why Conan Doyle was a storyteller, not a liar). So, Sentence 20 is equivalent to, and to be analysed as, that shown below:

21. According to the stories by Conan Doyle, Sherlock Holmes was cleverer than all the other detectives in London.

To return to our examples concerning omnipotence, we can accept Definition 14 or Definition 15 without taking it literally as regards quantification over merely possible beings. We take literally the following analysis:

22. According to the modal realist's fiction, for every possible being, x, x is omnipotent if and only if, for every possible ordered sequence of possible beings, and every possible set, S, if it is possible that anything have the power to cause it to be the case that the sequence be directly a member of S, then x has that power.

The modal realist does not really quantify over non-actual beings, though he or she thinks that that is what he or she is doing; rather, the modal realist simulates quantification over non-actual beings, just as Conan Doyle simulates quantification over London detectives. It might at first seem odd for me to suggest that the modal realist simulates quantification without realizing it, but this is no odder than what happens when someone reads out Sentence 20 without being sure whether it is fact or fiction: such a person would simulate quantification without realizing that that was what he or she was doing. So, I admit that Definition 15 literally implies:

23. There exist non-actual beings.

We do not accept Sentence 23, because we do not take Definition 15 literally, but we do accept the following, taken literally:

24. According to the modal realist, there exist non-actual beings.

This concludes my defence of Definition 14 and Definition 15 against the charge that they involve illicit quantification over non-existent objects.

At this point, the reader may expostulate that I am not playing fair since I earlier rejected a definition of 'omnipotence' couched in terms of actions or states of affairs on the grounds that it would quantify over entities whose existence is disputed. The reader may well ask why I did not treat this definition as an instance of fictional quantification. There are, however, two important dissimilarities between the two cases. The first dissimilarity is that in the case of modal language such as 'could' we have, I assert, *independent* need to embrace fictionalism to deal with sentences such as Sentence 16 and Sentence 17, so I am merely using existing tools. On the other hand, in the case of language such as 'action', 'state of affairs', 'proposition', and so on, I assert that we do not have *independent* need to embrace fictionalism, although there is not space to defend that assertion here.

The second important difference is that in the case of definitions such as Definition 14 it is clear what the quantification is supposed to be over – objects just like the familiar ones, but non-actual. On the other hand, in the case of language such as 'action', 'state of affairs', and so on, it is by no means clear to me just what these nouns are supposed to *mean*, just what the objects they are supposedly used to pick out are meant to *be*. While I know perfectly well what a sister is, and so can understand 'the sister I never had' even though the phrase does not pick out anything in reality, I do not know at all what a proposition or a state of affairs or an action is supposed to be, and so I do not really understand what the word 'proposition' or 'action' or the phrase 'state of affairs' is supposed to signify (though of course I am aware what realists concerning these supposed things *say* when asked what the objects in which they believe are). And if I cannot understand the story told by the realist concerning actions and states of affairs I cannot avail myself of a fictionalist treatment of it, because I shall fail to understand the fiction and so be unable to use it coherently, just as I could not sensibly discuss whether Holmes was the greatest detective if the stories by Conan Doyle contradicted themselves on this point, or if I could not understand the use of 'detective' or 'greatest' by the author.

10   Conclusion

In this essay I have attempted to produce a definition of 'omnipotence' that did not involve quantification over disputed entities such as states of affairs, propositions, actions, and the like, defending it along the way against objections, and trying to argue for some of the philosophical implications of the definition (the existence of sets, the direct/indirect distinction, etc.). I have not, of course, shown that anything actually is omnipotent, but I hope that this new definition will be of service to theists that want to ascribe omnipotence to their God without subscribing to excess baggage in the shape of actions, propositions, or states of affairs.[23]

Notes

1. See, for example, Flint and Freddoso (1983); Wierenga (1983); Hoffman and Rosenkrantz (1988); Wielenberg (2000); Hill (2005, pp. 125–191).
2. See, for example, Thomas Aquinas, *Summa Theologiae*, Ia.25.3.*resp.*
3. Peter van Inwagen expresses scepticism concerning the existence of events (and, thus, of actions) in Inwagen (2007, p. 210). Peter Geach argues that event-talk can be paraphrased away in Geach (1965), reprinted in Inwagen and Zimmerman (1998, see especially p. 200). Geach also denies the existence of facts (and, presumably, therefore, of states of affairs): see Geach (1963) reprinted in Geach (1972, pp. 13–31; see especially p. 23). Quine (1976, p. 200) denies the existence of propositions.
4. For example, we intuitively think that an omnipotent agent should have the power to create uncountably many angels, and to get each of them to thinking of a particular real number. *This* task can be finitely described ('the task of making true the finite sentence "there exist uncountably many angels, each of them thinking of a particular real number" '), but we might want, for every possible assignment of angels to real numbers, an omnipotent agent to have the power to cause it to be the case that that assignment be instantiated. The specification of some of these assignments could not be achieved even with an infinitely long sentence.
5. William Alston, for example, denies that God has beliefs (and, presumably, that God uses sentences) – see Alston (1986).
6. For a defence of the notion that sets exist if and only if their members do, see Fine (1981).
7. The first part of this is controversial, but it would certainly be inappropriate for a definition of 'omnipotence' to *presume* that everything can be caused to exist and can be caused not to exist.
8. That is, excluding gerrymandered entities. The purpose of introducing the distinction between causing p directly to be the case and causing p indirectly to be the case is to separate off what we intuitively think an omnipotent agent should have the power to do from what we intuitively think of as not real tasks at all, but logical tricks that test definitions in a merely verbal fashion.
9. Of course, not every set of powers can be co-exercised – one cannot co-exercise the power to create George Bush and the power to prevent George Bush's creation. Nevertheless, this fact does not have any implications for the definition of 'omnipotence', as it concerns not the possession of powers (as omnipotence does), but their exercise, which is a separate matter. Many hold that God, for example, has the power to do wrong, but cannot exercise it. For a defence of this view, see Hill (2005, pp. 151–159).
10. There is, of course, an analogous objection concerning Subsidiary Clause 3.2.
11. For a brief discussion and defence of this analysis, see Hill (2005, pp. 127–129).
12. Some may object that there is no difference here between something's being blue and its being a member of the set of blue things. It is risky to assert this, however, since, for example, it is possible to cause it to be the case that something is colourless but not, on standard Zermelo–Fraenkel set theory, to cause it to be the case that the thing is a member of the set of colourless things, for there is no such set – see below.
13. There will still be uncountably many sets even if we restrict ourselves to impure sets.

14. Quine introduced his NF set theory in 1937. For an introduction to NF, see Holmes (1998) and Forster (1995). For a discussion of the current state of research on NF and NFU (New Foundations with *Urelemente*), see http://plato.stanford. edu/entries/quine-nf/ and http://math.boisestate.edu/~holmes/holmes/nf.html.
15. We obviously continue to presuppose libertarianism here. Note that Plantinga's 'weak sense' of 'bring it about that' is compatible with bringing it about that somebody else does something freely. This is why I write 'cause it to be the case that' rather than 'bring it about that'. See Plantinga (1974, pp. 172–173).
16. And the ordered pair is a member of *this* set partly in virtue of being a member of the set of all ordered pairs whose first co-ordinate strikes the second, or partly in virtue of being a member of the set of all ordered pairs whose first co-ordinate shoots the second, or ...
17. If the reader does not like the notion of a 1-tuple, then we may say instead that causing it to be the case that something, y, is a member of some set, S, is equivalent to causing it to be the case that the ordered pair $<y, y>$ is a member of the set, S', of all ordered pairs whose members are identical with each other and also members of S.
18. Or, if the reader prefers, equivalent to causing it to be the case that the ordered pair $<y, y>$ is a member of the set of ordered pairs whose first member is actually identical with its second member.
19. See Lewis (1986).
20. Ibid., p. 13.
21. Rosen (1990).
22. Ibid., p. 331.
23. I would like to thank my commentator from this volume, Klaas Kraay, for extremely helpful comments. I would also like to thank the editors of this volume, Erik Wielenberg and Yujin Nagasawa, for helpful comments and encouragement. My thinking on omnipotence has been immeasurably enriched over the years by conversations with my friend Joseph Jedwab, and it is to him that I am most grateful.

References

Alston, William P. 'Does God Have Beliefs?', *Religious Studies*, 22 (1986) 287–306.
Fine, Kit. 'First-Order Modal Theories I – Sets', *Noûs*, 15 (1981) 177–205.
Flint, Thomas P. and Alfred J. Freddoso. 'Maximal Power', in (Freddoso, 1983, pp. 81–113).
Forster, Thomas. *Set Theory with a Universal Set* (Oxford: Clarendon Press, 1995).
Freddoso, Alfred J., ed. *The Existence and Nature of God* (Notre Dame, IN: University of Notre Dame Press, 1983).
Geach, Peter. 'Aristotle on Conjunctive Propositions', *Ratio*, 5 (1963) 33–45.
Geach, Peter. 'Some Problems about Time', *Proceedings of the British Academy*, 51 (1965) 321–336.
Geach, Peter. *Logic Matters* (Berkeley: University of California, 1972).
Hill, Daniel J. *Divinity and Maximal Greatness* (Abingdon: Routledge, 2005).
Hoffman, Joshua and Gary S. Rosenkrantz. 'Omnipotence Redux', *Philosophy and Phenomenological Research*, 49 (1988) 283–301.
Holmes, M.R. *Elementary Set Theory with a Universal Set* (volume 10 of the Cahiers du Centre de logique, Louvain-la-Neuve: Academia, 1998).

Inwagen, Peter van. 'A Materialist Ontology of the Human Person', in (Inwagen and Zimmerman, 2007, pp. 199–215).

Inwagen, Peter van and Dean W. Zimmerman, eds. *Metaphysics: The Big Questions* (Oxford: Blackwell, 1998).

Inwagen, Peter van and Dean W. Zimmerman, eds. *Persons: Human and Divine* (Oxford: OUP, 2007).

Lewis, David. *On the Plurality of Worlds* (Oxford: Blackwell, 1986).

Plantinga, Alvin. *The Nature of Necessity* (Oxford: Clarendon Press, 1974).

Quine, W. V. 'New Foundations for Mathematical Logic', *American Mathematical Monthly*, 44 (1937) 70–80.

Quine, W. V. *The Ways of Paradox* (Cambridge: Harvard University Press, 1976, revised edition).

Rosen, Gideon. 'Modal Fictionalism', *Mind*, 99 (1990) 327–354.

Wielenberg, Erik. 'Omnipotence Again', *Faith and Philosophy*, 17 (2000) 26–47.

Wierenga, Edward R. 'Omnipotence Defined', *Philosophy and Phenomenological Research*, 43 (1983) 363–375.

2
Can God Choose a World at Random?

Klaas J. Kraay

1 Creation and the axiological status of worlds

Theism holds that there exists a being who is unsurpassable in power, knowledge, and goodness, and who is the creator and sustainer of all that is. In contemporary analytic philosophy of religion, the act of creation is construed like this: God surveys the set of actualizable worlds,[1] and freely selects exactly one for actualization on the basis of its axiological properties. Discussions of creation, then, typically assume that worlds have axiological status, and that they can (at least in principle) be evaluated: some are good, others are bad; some are better, others are worse.[2] I will proceed on these assumptions. Philosophers disagree about what the axiological properties relevant to worlds are, but they can be divided into two kinds: *world-good*-making properties (WGMPs) and *world-bad*-making properties (WBMPs). The overall axiological status of a world, *ceteris paribus*, depends on these properties.[3] To simplify matters, let us assume *necessitarianism*: the actual set of WGMPs and WBMPs could not possibly have had different members than it does.[4] Finally, let us assume, again for simplicity, that all worlds are both *commensurable* and *comparable* with respect to these properties.[5]

2 Three hierarchies of worlds; three arguments for atheism

The axiological considerations from Section 1 suggest that there are three candidate hierarchies of actualizable worlds worth considering:

(1) Famously, Leibniz and others have held that there is exactly one unsurpassable world. (Hereafter, I will call this view EOUW).
(2) Alternatively, one might agree that some actualizable world is unsurpassable, but deny that *just* one is.[6] On this view, it is generally thought that for any world *w* having axiological status *s*, there is a trivially different variant *w'* that also has axiological status *s*. Moreover, it is typically

thought that there are infinitely many such variants.[7] On this view (hereafter IMUW), there are infinitely many unsurpassable worlds.

(3) Some philosophers have claimed that there are no unsurpassable worlds (hereafter NUW).[8] On this view, there is an infinite hierarchy of increasingly better worlds.

Objections to theism have been levelled on each hierarchy:

(1) Famously, on EOUW it has been urged, *a priori*, that a perfect being would actualize the unique best world, and *a posteriori*, that this expectation has not been met. In short, it is claimed that the actual world is surpassable, and that this disconfirms theism.[9]

(2) It has been claimed, *a priori*, that IMUW is inconsistent with theism. If there are infinitely many unsurpassable worlds, God would not have *sufficient* reason to actualize any particular one.[10] But on theism, God is supposed to be the explanation for this world's being actual, and God requires sufficient reasons for action. So, since there is an actual world, it was not actualized by God.[11]

(3) Finally, it has been suggested, *a priori*, that NUW precludes theism. If there are no unsurpassable words, God cannot have *sufficient* reason for actualizing any particular world, since there are infinitely many *better* worlds that could be actualized instead. But again, on theism, God is supposed to be the explanation for this world's being actual, and God requires sufficient reasons for action. So, since there is an actual world, it was not actualized by God.[12]

Since the three hierarchies are mutually exclusive and jointly exhaustive,[13] these three objections constitute an unpalatable trilemma for theism. Recently, however, two ways out have been suggested for the theist: on both IMUW and NUW, philosophers have urged, God can defensibly select a world to actualize *at random*. In Section 3, I set out the motivation for this move, and in the remainder of the chapter, I evaluate it.[14]

3 Sufficient reasons and randomization

The objections to theism on IMUW and NUW both concern God's choice of which world to actualize. They both allege that, in the face of these respective hierarchies, God's choice of a world cannot be rational, since God cannot have sufficient reason to actualize any particular world. On IMUW, it is claimed, God has insufficient reason to select any particular world, since there are infinitely many *equally good* candidates. And on NUW, it is claimed, God has insufficient reason to select any particular world, since for any world there are infinitely many *better* candidates.

It is sometimes thought that the problem for theism here is this: granting that God could have no principled reason for selecting a world in these scenarios, God would be paralyzed, stymied, or hamstrung – unable to actualize *any* world.[15] This is a mistake. No matter which hierarchy of worlds is correct, if theism is true, God cannot fail to actualize some world or other. On theism, which world is actual depends upon God. God may freely decide to create, say, creatures or a universe. If God *creates*, then God is responsible for the resulting world's being actual. If, on the other hand, God creates nothing, the resulting world is *bare* – save for whatever uncreated existents (such as numbers) there are. But here, too, God is responsible for this world's being actual. Accordingly, on theism, it is impossible that God fails to actualize some world or other. The problem for theism on IMUW and NUW, then, is *not* that God – while existing – is somehow frustrated in his desire to actualize a world. The problem is much more serious: if God must have a *sufficient reason* for selecting a world to actualize, then IMUW and NUW are both logically incompatible with theism.

In response, philosophers have denied that God must have a sufficient reason for selecting a world to actualize on IMUW and NUW.[16] They point out that in ordinary human affairs, when rational choice is thwarted by the absence of sufficient reasons, practical considerations make it reasonable for us to choose *at random*. These philosophers urge that God may do the same, while remaining unsurpassable in all relevant respects.[17] If this is defensible, then the objections to theism on IMUW and NUW are defanged. In Section 4, I consider whether God could choose a world at random on IMUW, and in Section 5, I consider the same question on NUW. In both cases, I conclude that this is a defensible strategy for God only on the enormously implausible assumption that there is *exactly one* randomizing device or procedure available.

4 Randomization on IMUW

Suppose that IMUW is correct. Lloyd Strickland (2006) urges that, on this view, God need not have sufficient reason for his choice of world: God can defensibly choose at random. In this section, I evaluate Strickland's claim. Suppose that there is exactly one possible randomizing device or procedure that God could use. If so, then provided that the principle of sufficient reason admits an exception in this context, this seems like a satisfactory solution for the theist.[18] But Strickland says that

> *prima facie* it seems possible that there will be *more than one* such [device or] procedure available to God, and if there are many … then it seems possible, even quite likely, that some, or even all, of them will be *equally good* but not bettered by any other.

> (2006, p. 153)

Strickland offers no defence of either claim. Let us consider each in turn.

Why think that there is more than one randomizing device or procedure on IMUW? Randomizing *devices* are physical objects which output a random number. It is well known that there are numerous indeterministic features or processes in the actual world. Accordingly, theists should not find it difficult to imagine that God could construct a variety of indeterministic devices to generate random numbers.[19] In addition, it seems plausible to suppose that for any randomizing device, there could be another trivially different device – perhaps even infinitely many such devices. Moreover, devices could be combined in various ways to generate new devices. As for non-physical randomization *procedures*, if there are any, there are many. The reason is simple: for any randomization procedure *r*, it is possible to construct a different randomization procedure *s* which uses *r*, and then performs a mathematical operation on the deliverances of *r* to generate a new result. Perhaps, for example, *s* takes the result of *r* and adds one (or indeed any other number). This new result is every bit as random as the deliverances of *r*, although the procedure is different. Finally, *hybrids* are possible: combinations of devices and procedures. Accordingly, it seems extremely plausible to grant that there is more than one randomizer on IMUW.

I now turn to Strickland's second undefended claim that some randomizers are *unsurpassable*. How might one defend such a claim? Randomizers, like other things, are presumably to be evaluated with respect to their axiological properties, like *good-making* properties and *bad-making* properties.[20] Certain plausible good-making properties of randomizers seem to have intrinsic maxima. Perhaps, for example, *simplicity of construction or method* is a good-making property of randomizers. Perhaps *speed of operation* is another. Both these properties seem to have intrinsic maxima, and reflection on them might suggest that there is at least one unsurpassable randomizer. (The alternative, after all, is difficult to imagine: surely there could not be more and more ever-*simpler* or ever-*faster* randomizers, *ad infinitum*!)[21] On the other hand, it is less clear that other good-making properties of randomizers have intrinsic maxima: consider, for example, aesthetic properties. Here it might seem difficult to imagine how some randomizer could be *unsurpassably* beautiful.

The overall axiological status of a randomizer, *ceteris paribus*, depends on the axiological properties it exhibits. But it is difficult to tell exactly what role any given property plays in the overall axiological status of a randomizer, and how the various properties work together to shape this overall axiological status. Accordingly, it is far from clear that Strickland is entitled to assume that some – let alone all! – randomizers are unsurpassable. In what follows, I consider both alternatives: I first consider the issue on the assumption that there are unsurpassable randomizers (Section 4.1) and I then consider the issue on the assumption that there are no such randomizers, but instead an infinite hierarchy of increasingly better randomizers (Section 4.2).

4.1   Unsurpassable randomizers on IMUW

Suppose that, on IMUW, the idea of an unsurpassable randomizer is coherent. This suggests three possibilities: either there is *exactly one* such randomizer, or else there are *multiple but finitely many* such randomizers, or else there are *infinitely* many. I will take each in turn.

Suppose first that there is *exactly one* unsurpassable randomizing device or procedure available to God on IMUW. If so, it is reasonable to expect that God would use it. (After all, it is available for use, and surely God would be surpassable for using a surpassable randomizer when an unsurpassable one is available.) But it is implausible to think that there is exactly one unsurpassable randomizer, since it is plausible to suppose that for any unsurpassable randomizer, there is a trivially different randomizer which has the same axiological status.[22] If there are multiple unsurpassable randomizers, there are either *finitely* many or *infinitely* many. I consider these scenarios next.

Suppose that there are *multiple but finitely many* unsurpassable randomizers available to God. One might expect that God would be entitled to select any *one* of these: they are equivalent, after all. But, as Strickland points out, it is difficult to see how God could rationally select exactly one for use. God's choice of a randomizer will itself either be random or non-random. A non-random choice cannot be rational, since there is no sufficient reason for selecting any one randomizer from such a set. But a *random* choice of randomizers cannot be rational either: this way regress lies.[23] (Since this argument will be appealed to again below, it will be helpful to name it: Argument A.)

In the face of this dilemma, Strickland suggests that God should use *all* of the finitely many unsurpassable randomizers:

> if God is faced with ten different-but-equally good random-selection procedures [or devices] to choose from, there is nothing to prevent Him from selecting them all in the way that there is something preventing Him from selecting all equally best worlds. And the decision to select all available selection procedures can hardly be said to be irrational either, unlike the remainder of God's options, which are to choose none of the procedures, or just one of them (for which He would of course have no reason at all). So if there are ten procedures [or devices] God can simply select and run them all, and then pool the results. If one of the equally best worlds is selected more often than any other, then that is the world He [actualizes], and if the combined results of all the random procedures [or devices] do not favour any one world over the others, then God can simply run all of them again until a clear winner does emerge.
>
> (2006, p. 154)

Strickland's pooling method represents an attempt to do something in the face of a difficult choice between randomizers: choose them *all*. But difficulties beset this method. First, it is not evident what it would take for a 'clear winner' to emerge: how much does a world need to be 'favoured', exactly, before clarity is achieved? Second, even if the necessary and sufficient conditions for clarity could be established, it remains possible that these conditions never be satisfied, even over infinitely many poolings. And even if we waive these difficulties, a third, more serious one, remains. Strickland offers no reason for thinking that this pooling method is a *principled* method of world-selection for God. He offers no grounds for thinking that it is more desirable to use *all* of the finitely many randomizers, rather than just one, nor does he offer any reason for thinking that it is desirable to actualize a world that is 'the clear winner' of such a process. Absent an argument for either claim, it is difficult to see why this method should be thought preferable to any other method.[24] (Since these three objections will be appealed to again below, it will be helpful to give them a collective name: Argument B.)

Nor is there a defensible *via media*, such as pooling the results of more than one but not all of the finitely many unsurpassable randomizers. (Strickland does not consider this alternative.) For this to work, God would require a principled method of selecting this proper subset of randomizers whose outputs are to be pooled. No non-random selection method is rational, since there can be no sufficient reason for selecting any particular proper subset: all randomizers in the set are equivalent, after all. And no random method can be rational either, for this way regress lies.[25] (Since this argument will be appealed to again below, it will be helpful to name it: Argument C.) I conclude, then, that if there are multiple but *finitely* many unsurpassable randomizers on IMUW, God cannot select a world for actualization at random.

Suppose, finally, that there are *infinitely many* unsurpassable randomizers. One might then think that God has three alternatives: he might choose (a) *one* from the infinite set; (b) *every* member of the set; or (c) more than one but not every member of the set. Unfortunately, none of these alternatives is acceptable. God cannot select *one* randomizer from the infinite set of unsurpassable randomizers, for the reasons given above as Argument A. Nor can Strickland's suggestion be redeployed in this context: God cannot hope to arrive at a rational choice by pooling the results of *every* member of the infinite set of equivalent randomizers, for the reasons given above as Argument B. And there is no acceptable *via media* between these extremes: God cannot rationally select more than one but not all of the unsurpassable randomizers from this infinite set, in order to then pool the results. Such a method would involve selecting either a finite or an infinite proper subset from the set of all randomizers, and in either case, Argument C would apply.

4.2   No unsurpassable randomizers on IMUW

One alternative remains: suppose that there are *no* unsurpassable randomizers on IMUW: for every randomizer r, there is an axiologically superior randomizer $r+1$.[26] Again, three choices seem to be available: God could (a) use *one* of the randomizers; (b) use them *all* and pool the results; or (c) use a *proper subset* and pool the results. Unfortunately, none of these is defensible.

First, God cannot select *one* randomizer from this set. God's selection must either be random or non-random. The former leads to regress, as noted in Argument A. The latter is indefensible: no non-random selection of a randomizer can be rational, since, no matter which randomizer is selected, there is always *more reason* to select another, better one. Second, God cannot defensibly use *all* members of an infinite set of randomizers and pool the results, for the reasons given above as Argument B. Third, God cannot use a *proper subset* of randomizers and pool the results. After all, God's selection of a proper subset must either be random or non-random. The former alternative leads to regress, as noted in Argument C. The latter alternative is indefensible: no non-random selection of a proper subset of randomizers can be rational, since, no matter which subset is selected, there is always *more reason* to select another, better subset of randomizers.[27]

I have considered various proposals for God's random selection of a world on IMUW, first on the hypothesis that there are multiple unsurpassable randomizers (Section 4.1), and then on the hypothesis that there are none (Section 4.2). In both cases, I have urged that randomization is not a defensible strategy for God. Accordingly, the only scenario on which God can rationally select a world for actualization on IMUW is the one I have urged as extremely implausible: the view that there is *exactly one* randomizing device of procedure available to God. I now turn to a randomization proposal on NUW.

5 Randomization on NUW

NUW holds that there is an infinite hierarchy of increasingly better actualizable worlds. As noted above, it has been suggested, *a priori*, that NUW precludes theism. Daniel and Frances Howard-Snyder (1994, pp. 260–67) reply with the following thought-experiment:[28]

> Jove is an essentially unsurpassable being who desires to actualize a world, but who is unable to actualize a best actualizable world, there being none. Jove divides the set of all actualizable[29] possible worlds into two subsets based on certain axiologically relevant criteria.[30] Worlds in the better subset are given unique integer ordinals: the worst of the lot is '1', the second-worst '2', and so on.[31] Jove selects from the better subset at random, and world no. 777 is actualized.

The Howard-Snyders claim that in this story, Jove's '...creating a world inferior to one he or some other possible being could have created does nothing to impugn his status as essentially...unsurpassable *in any respect whatsoever'* (1994, p. 261).[32] In other words, the Howard-Snyders think that God can defensibly select a world at random on NUW.

On the Howard-Snyders' model, *world-actualizing-actions* involve two steps: (1) God selects a *partition principle* to bisect the set of all actualizable worlds; and (2) God decides on a logically subsequent *decision method* – randomization – to select a world for actualization from the better subset. The Howard-Snyders claim that it is plausible to suppose (or at least not clearly plausible to deny) that there is a unique *best partition principle*, and they stipulate that God acts on it (1996, p. 423). They further claim that, for all we know, there is a unique best randomizer, and they stipulate that God uses it (1994, p. 266). Elsewhere, I have criticized the Howard-Snyders' claim that it is plausible to suppose that there is a best partition principle (Kraay, 2005). Here, however, I set aside this worry, and consider only what the Howard-Snyders say about randomization.

Suppose that there is *exactly one* possible randomizing device or procedure that God could use on NUW. If so, then this seems like a satisfactory solution for the theist. But it is extremely implausible to think that there is just one possible randomizer available to God on NUW (for the reasons offered in Section 4). Accordingly, it is reasonable to suppose that there are multiple randomizers on IMUW. In the final section, I distinguish four multiple randomizer scenarios, and I suggest that none is defensible.

5.1 Four randomizing scenarios on NUW

Suppose, on NUW, that the idea of an unsurpassable randomizer is coherent (as the Howard-Snyders suppose). If so, it seems that there are three possibilities: either there is *exactly one* unsurpassable randomizer; multiple but *finitely* many such randomizers; or else *infinitely* many such randomizers. I take up each in turn. Afterwards, I consider a fourth scenario: perhaps, *pace* the Howard-Snyders, there are *no unsurpassable randomizers* on NUW.

If there is *exactly one* unsurpassable randomizer on NUW, as the Howard-Snyders' thought-experiment stipulates, it is reasonable to expect that God would use it. (After all, it is available for use, and God would surely be surpassable for using a surpassable randomizer when an unsurpassable one is available.) But as I argued in Section 4.1, there is reason to think that if there is one unsurpassable randomizer, there are multiple such randomizers. Accordingly, the Howard-Snyders are not entitled to stipulate that there is exactly one unsurpassable randomizer, and so we must turn to the remaining possibilities.

Suppose that there are *multiple but finitely many* unsurpassable randomizers. Three alternatives seem to be available: God could (a) use one of the randomizers; (b) use them all and pool the results, in the spirit of Strickland; or (c) use a proper subset and pool the results. Unfortunately, none of these alternatives is defensible. God's selection of *one* randomizer from a finite set of unsurpassable randomizers must either be non-random or random. But, as

Argument A shows, neither is acceptable. Similarly, God cannot use them all and pool the results, for the reasons given as Argument B. And, as Argument C shows, God cannot rationally choose a proper subset of unsurpassable randomizers in order to then pool the results.

Next, suppose that there are *infinitely many* unsurpassable randomizers available on NUW. Again, three alternatives seem to be available: God could (a) use one of the randomizers; (b) use them all and pool the results; or (c) use a proper subset and pool the results. Unfortunately, none of these alternatives are defensible, as shown by Arguments A, B, and C, respectively.

Finally, suppose that there are *no unsurpassable randomizers* on NUW: for every randomizer r, there is an axiologically superior randomizer $r + 1$. This view, in fact, is extremely plausible on NUW. Consider what I urged in Section 4: for any randomization procedure r, it is possible to construct a different randomization procedure s which uses r, and then performs a mathematical operation on the deliverances of r to generate a new result. Perhaps, for example, procedure s takes the result of r and adds one (or indeed any other number). Procedure s is just as random as procedure r, and there is good reason for thinking it *better than* r: in every case, s will deliver a better result than r – a superior world. On the plausible view, then, that there are no unsurpassable randomizers on NUW, three alternatives again seem to be available: God could (a) use one of the randomizers; (b) use them all and pool the results; or (c) use a proper subset and pool the results. Unfortunately, none of these alternatives is defensible, for the reasons given in Section 4.2.

I conclude, then, that on the extremely plausible assumption that there are multiple randomizers on NUW, no defensible randomizing scenarios are available to God.

6   Conclusion

In Section 2, I set out the three hierarchies of possible worlds: either there is exactly one unsurpassable world, or infinitely many, or none. In the remainder, I considered arguments for atheism on the latter two hierarchies. On IMUW, it is claimed that God has insufficient reason to select any particular world, since there are infinitely many *equally good* candidates. On NUW, it is claimed that God has insufficient reason to select any particular world, since for any world there are infinitely many *better* candidates. In response, philosophers have suggested that on both scenarios, God need not have a sufficient reason: God can defensibly select a world at random. In Section 4, I argued that randomization is a defensible strategy for God on IMUW only on the extremely implausible view that there is exactly one randomizer available for use. In Section 5, I made the same case on NUW. I conclude, then, that these randomization proposals fail to show how God could defensibly select a world for actualization on IMUW and NUW, respectively. If the theist wishes to block the arguments for atheism on IMUW and NUW, a different account of God's world-choosing activity is needed.[33]

7 Acknowledgement

Ancestors of this chapter were presented to the *British Society for Philosophy of Religion* Conference (Oxford, UK, 11–13 September 2007) and the *Canadian Society of Christian Philosophers Annual Meeting* (Saskatoon, Canada, 30 May 2007). I am grateful to Daniel Hill, Jonathan Strand, and Brandon Watson for helpful comments on drafts, and to the editors of this volume, Yujin Nagasawa and Erik Weilenberg. Finally, I am grateful for the generous research support I received from the Social Sciences and Humanities Research Council of Canada (2005–2007).

Notes

1. It has been plausibly argued that not every possible world is within God's power to actualize (Alvin Plantinga, 1974, pp. 169–74). Accordingly, I hereafter restrict my focus to the set of *actualizable* worlds.
2. States of affairs can bear axiological properties: properties which, *ceteris paribus*, tend to make these states of affairs good or bad. Since *worlds* can be understood to be (maximally compossible) states of affairs, it is reasonable to suppose that worlds can bear axiological properties too.
3. The *ceteris paribus* clause is important, because it may be that certain good-making properties cease to make worlds better past a certain point, or in certain combinations. The same goes, *mutatis mutandis*, for WBMPs. So, while the goodness of a world depends on its axiological properties, this dependency may not be simple.
4. The rival view, which I call *contingentism*, holds that the actual set of WGMPs and WBMPs might have had different members.
5. One might deny that all worlds can be *evaluated* with respect to a stable set of WGMPs: this is to hold that there are *incommensurable* pairs of worlds. Alternatively, one might deny that all worlds can be *compared*. This can be done in two ways: (1) one might hold that there are pairs of worlds which are both incommensurable and (hence) *incomparable*; and (2) one might hold that there are pairs of *commensurable* worlds that are nevertheless incomparable. For simplicity, I set these niceties aside.
6. For a thorough list of philosophers who hold this view, see Lloyd Strickland (2006, p. 141).
7. For example, suppose that w' differs from w by having one more grain of sand on one beach than w does (and whatever is required for this, and whatever ensues from this). It seems reasonable to suppose that for any world w, there are infinitely many such minor variants. Each is a distinct world, and, since the variations are sufficiently minor, all have the same axiological status.
8. See, for example, Richard Swinburne (1979, p. 114).
9. This is, of course, a version of the problem of evil. In response, some theists (notably, Robert Adams, 1972) have rejected the *a priori* claim, while others – too

many to mention here – have denied the *a posteriori* claim, or at least suggested that it has not been (or cannot be) justified.

A small qualification: while I here suggest that arguments for the surpassability of the actual world are *a posteriori*, Ian Wilks has offered a plausible counter-example: *a priori* introspection of one's own thoughts, desires, intentions, and the like, might well convince one that the actual world could be better. (In slogan form: *male cogito ergo malum est*.) In what follows, I ignore this special case.

10. Blumenfeld (1975, p. 166; 1995, 396) and Strickland (2006, pp. 142–43) attribute this worry to Leibniz.
11. For more on this charge, see Blumenfeld (1995, p. 396) and Donald Turner (2003, p. 147).
12. To put the point differently, no being can be unsurpassable on NUW, since no matter what world a putatively unsurpassable being actualizes, that being could be surpassed by a being who actualizes a better world. For arguments in this vein, see Philip Quinn (1982), Stephen Grover (1988), William Rowe (2003, 2004), and Jordan Howard Sobel (2004).
13. I here assume that there is no principled middle ground between the claim that there is exactly one unsurpassable universe, and the claim that there are infinitely many.
14. In what follows, I set aside EOUW and the argument for atheism that it generates.
15. Blumenfeld expresses this idea (on NUW) as follows: 'The nature of such a continuum apparently would keep God fixed eternally on the brink of decision, stymied by the endless and ever more attractive objects of possible choice' (1975, p. 170). Later, Blumenfeld calls this '...the collapse of the possibility of decision, the metaphysical paralysis of the divine motivational system' (1975, p. 172).
16. Lloyd Strickland (2006) makes this case on IMUW, and Daniel and Frances Howard-Snyder (1994) urge it on NUW. As Grover (2003, p. 148) notes, such a position is untenable if the principle of sufficient reason holds exceptionlessly.
17. Nicholas Rescher (1969, pp. 156–57) maintains that it is absurd for God to use a randomizer, since, given his essential omniscience, God would *foreknow* the deliverances of any device or procedure used. Strickland (2006, p. 151) replies that it is reasonable to suppose that there are *no truths* concerning the deliverances of randomizers. The Howard-Snyders (1994, p. 266) agree. On this view, there is simply nothing for God to foreknow, in which case God's lack of knowledge on this point does not count against his omniscience. This is a reasonable reply. Another reasonable reply is to take Rescher head-on and argue that, even if there are truths about the results of randomizers, God's knowledge of them presents no problem for random selection. Space does not permit an exploration of this, but such a reply could be modeled on some of the theistic responses to the problem of divine foreknowledge and human freedom.
18. *En passant*, I register a small worry: does God have sufficient reason to use the *first* result produced by the randomizer? A critic might object that God has just as much reason to use the result produced by the randomizer on its *second* running, and on its *third*, and so on. This, of course, leads to regress. I'm not convinced that this worry is decisive, but there is no space to argue so here.
19. Any such device, it should be noted, would be part of the world selected for actualization on the basis of that device's use. This will serve to fix certain parameters

of that world: for example, nothing logically inconsistent with the existence of this device could be part of the resulting world.

20. I assume, for simplicity, that all randomizers are commensurable and comparable with respect to a stable set of axiological properties.

21. To argue otherwise, one would have to shoulder the burden of proving that randomizers *asymptotically* approach the relevant limits (of *perfect* simplicity and *instantaneous* operation, respectively).

22. This is an application of the general argument for the existence of multiple randomizers given above in Section 4. Brandon Watson isn't persuaded:

> [Kraay] overlooks the possible response that, if God Himself is considered the randomizing device, then the reply to the claim that there is only one unsurpassable randomizer doesn't work, since that reply assumes that the randomizer is something distinct from God that is selected by Him. And it would be hard to argue that God couldn't Himself be a randomizer with someone who is already claiming that God can choose randomly. (http://branemrys.blogspot.com/2007/04/notes-and-links.html)

I grant that *if* God can plausibly be deemed a randomizer, theists should expect this randomizer to be unsurpassable. But can God really *be* (considered) a randomizer? Traditional monotheists will surely deny that God *is* (to be thought) a physical randomizing device or a non-physical randomizing procedure.

23. Strickland (2006, pp. 153–54). The Howard-Snyders (1994, p. 266) also note this.

24. It is plausible to think that pooling the results of a set of randomizers is, in effect, just another randomization procedure. But if so, then Strickland cannot claim that this procedure surpasses all others, since *ex hypothesi* there are multiple unsurpassable randomizers. I thank Jonathan Strand and Daniel Hill for helping me to see this.

25. Even if there were a principled way for God to select a proper subset, the considerations advanced as Argument B would still apply.

26. The Howard-Snyders deem this to be an epistemic possibility (1994, p. 266). In Section 5.1, I will deem this view plausible on NUW.

27. A better subset might be a set comprised of *wholly* better members, for example, or a set comprised of better members *on average*. Of course, any such subset could in turn be surpassed by another, *ad infinitum*. Even if there were a principled way for God to select a proper subset, the considerations advanced as Argument B would still apply.

28. Their stated targets are Quinn (1982) and Rowe (2003). Random selection on NUW is also endorsed by Swinburne (1979, p. 115) and Leftow (2005, p. 275).

29. The Howard-Snyders appear to assume that every possible world is actualizable: 'Out of his goodness, Jove decides to create. Since he is all-powerful, there is nothing but the bounds of possibility to prevent him from getting what he wants' (1994, p. 260). But see Note 1.

30. The Howard-Snyders say little about what the sorting criteria might be – they merely offer candidates:

> For example, he puts on his left worlds in which some inhabitants live lives that aren't worth living and on his right worlds in which every inhabitant's life is worth living; he puts on his left worlds in which some horror fail to serve

> an outweighing good and on his right worlds in which no horror fails to serve
> an outweighing good. (We encourage the reader to use her own criteria.)
>
> (1994, p. 260)

31. The Howard-Snyders assume for simplicity that there are no ties: each world has
    a unique axiological status. If there are ties (as is plausible to suppose) then I
    presume that the Howard-Snyders would say that God should use the randomizer
    twice: once to select a world ordinal, and then once more to select a world from
    the set of worlds having that axiological status.
32. The Howard-Snyders here speak of 'creating' possible worlds, but, strictly speak-
    ing, possible worlds are states of affairs which can neither be created nor
    destroyed, so 'actualizing' is a better term.
33. Jonathan Strand, commenting on an earlier draft of this chapter, offers such an
    account: he suggests that God could 'just pick' a world for actualization, without
    using either a randomizing device or procedure. On this model, God's selection
    of a world is utterly arbitrary – there is no basis for God's choice whatsoever –
    but it is not random. Space does not permit a detailed examination of this
    model, but I note two worries. First, this model may not be coherent, since it
    may be illegitimate to stipulate that 'just picking' is not a randomizing proce-
    dure. Second, supposing this account is coherent, I suspect that there will be
    grave concerns about the unsurpassability of a being who 'just picks' a world for
    actualization.

References

Adams, R. 'Must God Create the Best?', *Philosophical Review* 81 (1972) 317–32.

Blumenfeld, D. 'Is the Best Possible World Possible?', *Journal of Philosophy* 84 (1975)
163–77.

——. 'Perfection and Happiness in the Best Possible World', in N. Jolley (Ed.),
Cambridge Companion to Leibniz (Cambridge: Cambridge University Press, 1995),
pp. 382–410.

Grover, S. 'Why Only the Best is Good Enough', *Analysis* 48 (1988) 224.

——. 'This World, "Adams Worlds", and the Best of All Possible Worlds', *Religious
Studies* 39 (2003) 145–63.

Howard-Snyder, D. and Howard-Snyder, F. 'How an Unsurpassable Being Can Create a
Surpassable World', *Faith and Philosophy* 11 (1994) 260–68.

——. 'The *Real* Problem of No Best World', *Faith and Philosophy* 13 (1996) 422–25.

Kraay, K. 'William L. Rowe's *A Priori* Argument for Atheism', *Faith and Philosophy* 22
(2005) 211–34.

Leftow, B. 'No Best World, Creaturely Freedom', *Religious Studies* 41 (2005) 269–85.

Plantinga, A. *The Nature of Necessity* (Oxford: Clarendon Press, 1974).

Quinn, P. 'God, Moral Perfection, and Possible Worlds', in F. Sontag and M. D. Bryant
(Eds), *God: The Contemporary Discussion* (New York: The Rose of Sharon Press, Inc.,
1982), pp. 197–213.

Rescher, N. 'Choice without Preference: A Study of the History and of the Logic of
the Problem of "Burdian's Ass"', in N. Rescher (Ed.), *Essays in Philosophical Analysis*
(Pittsburgh, University of Pittsburgh Press, 1969), pp. 111–57.

Rowe, W. 'The Problem of Divine Perfection and Freedom', in E. Stump (Ed.), *Reasoned
Faith* (Ithaca: Cornell University Press, 2003), pp. 223–33.

——. *Can God Be Free?* (Oxford: Oxford University Press, 2004).

Sobel, H. *Logic and Theism: Arguments for and against Beliefs in God* (Cambridge: Cambridge University Press, 2004).
Strickland, L. 'God's Problem of Multiple Choice', *Religious Studies* 42 (2006) 141–57.
Swinburne, R. *The Existence of God* (Oxford: Clarendon Press, 1979).
Turner, D. 'The Many-Universes Solution to the Problem of Evil', in R. Gale and A. Pruss (Eds), *The Existence of God, International Research Library of Philosophy* (Aldershof: Ashgate, 2003), pp. 1–17.

3
Why is There Anything at All?

T. J. Mawson

To be clear at the outset, the things the existence of which our question is asking about are concrete things. The existence of abstract objects, such as pi, in contrast to concrete, such as the bust of Seneca that I have in my College room, is not our problem. This is not to say that there may not be a legitimate question about why there are any abstract objects at all, but just to carve that question, be it legitimate or not, off from our question, which is why there are any concrete objects at all. As I have said elsewhere (Mawson, 2005, p. 128), it is not at all easy to say what the distinction between concrete and abstract objects consists of; it may be that the distinction is a basic one, incapable of explication in terms of anything else. Be that as it may, we have an intuitive grasp of the distinction such that we know that my bust of Seneca is a concrete object and pi is not and we know these things more surely than we do the premises of any argument for any particular characterization of concreteness and abstractness; that being so, we may quite properly use this knowledge to test any putative characterizations of concreteness and abstractness. Any characterization of concreteness that has as a consequence that my bust of Seneca is not concrete or that pi is not abstract is, *ipso facto*, rationally unacceptable to us. In connection with the theistic answer to our question, which we shall discuss in more detail in a moment, it is important to note now that our intuitive grasp on the concrete/abstract distinction places any person – an agent with free will; someone who knows things and exhibits moral properties; and someone who has performed actions and will perform yet others – definitively on the concrete side. Given that the God of classical theism, if He exists, is a person – he is perfectly free; he knows everything and displays perfect moral goodness; and he has performed actions (e.g. creation) and will perform yet others (e.g. the Last Judgement) – so God, if he exists, is definitely a concrete object.[1]

The question 'Why is there anything at all?' is sometimes dismissed out of hand as illegitimately presupposing that nothingness would have been more likely than 'somethingess' and thus that there being something is especially in need of explanation. 'To ask "why is there something rather than nothing?" assumes that nothing(ness) is the natural state that does not need to be explained, while deviations or divergences from nothingness have to be explained... There is, so to speak, a presumption in favor of nothingness' (Nozick, 1981, p. 122). Certainly, this presumption has been behind the question in the minds of some of those who have asked it.[2] But one need not make any such presumption in asking the question.[3] One is free to suggest that had there been nothing, then the question 'Why is there nothing at all?' would have been just as much in need of an answer (although there would, of course, then have been nobody around to feel that need). However, things being (as they are), the question that is of interest is 'Why is there anything at all?' or, equivalently, 'Why is there something rather than nothing?' In other words, one can cheerfully accept the figurative if not literal truth of the claim made by the man who says in reply to one's telling him that one is wondering why there is something rather than nothing, 'If there had been nothing, you'd still be complaining.'[4]

The question is sometimes dismissed as unanswerable in principle. It is maintained that one can only explain the existence of something by making reference to something that one already supposes to exist for the purposes of proffering that explanation; thus one cannot, even in principle, explain why there is anything at all. However, the principle that is being supposed here is not sound. If one can come to an understanding of how it is that something could not have been otherwise than the way that it is, this is the most satisfactory answer one can possibly reach to the question of why that thing is as it is. Thus, for all we know at the start of an investigation, there may be a fully satisfactory answer to the question of why there is anything at all to be obtained by showing how it is that in fact there *could not* have been nothing, a fully satisfactory answer that does not begin then by presupposing the existence of something in the allegedly inescapable and problematic fashion. In what follows, we shall consider three suggestions that take this form.

Explanations of why something obtains which demonstrate the impossibility of alternatives are ones the satisfactoriness of which increases with the strength of the modality one finds oneself able to employ in them. To understand that every putative alternative to what obtains is in fact physically impossible is to have reached an explanation of why what obtains does obtain that is satisfactory for the purposes of everyday life. (Here everyday life is being understood as life in which the laws of nature are not taken to be part of what needs explaining.) 'Why is your lodger lying on the floor?' 'Because, given that I've just knocked him out cold, he physically couldn't have done anything other than fall over and lie there.' A stronger sort of impossibility, metaphysical impossibility, is sufficient to dispel at least some of the whimsies that may be entertained if one ceases to take the laws of nature as a given. 'Why not think the baby caused *itself* to come into existence in your daughter's womb?' 'Because of metaphysical necessity nothing can cause itself to come into existence. Hand me my shotgun; revive the lodger; and get my daughter and a parson in here.' And, finally, the logical impossibility of any alternative is the most satisfactory explanation of all. 'Why will marrying your daughter off to the lodger stop her being a "disgraced spinster"?' 'Because spinsters are by definition simply unmarried women.' This suggests then that a satisfactory answer to the question 'Why is there anything at all?' would be reached were we to be able to show the physical, metaphysical, or logical impossibility of there being nothing. It is obvious that the question of why there is anything at all cannot have an answer in terms of its being physically impossible that there be nothing, as physical impossibilities are generated only once there is something (and something physical as well). So we must turn to consider metaphysical and logical impossibilities. Here there is, in principle, room for an answer and here there is, in practice, much dispute.

To Parfit (1998), it seems metaphysically possible that there could have been nothing. Of course it is not metaphysically possible now, now that there is something, for there nevertheless to have been nothing. But Parfit suggests that just as it is – our intuition tells us – logically and metaphysically possible that, instead of there being what there is, there could have been something else, so it is logically and metaphysically possible that instead of there being anything, there could have been nothing at all. Whilst, on any plausible account, intuition, even reflective intuition, is not an infallible guide to logical let alone metaphysical possibility, it is the only guide we have and thus it is to be trusted in the absence of special considerations. It is conceivable that there have been nothing; there doesn't seem to be anything logically or metaphysically 'repugnant' to the suggestion as we think it through. Thus we should conclude that there could well have been nothing. This is not to presuppose then an anti-realist conception of necessity, just that our perceptions of necessity are the best evidence we could get of the reality of it.

Parfit (1998, p. 7) calls the possibility of there being nothing the 'Null possibility' and suggests that if its possibility is not immediately obvious, the easiest way to see it is to imagine there being just one simple thing and then imagine away even that simple thing.[5] Following Parfit's suggestion then, let us imagine that the only thing that exists is a universe in which there is just one lump of iron. It is possible now to imagine away that 'last' object, leaving nothing at all behind. As one imagines away the lump in this fashion, there is nothing apparently incoherent or repugnant to one's metaphysical imagination, the – admittedly fallible – mark of one's stumbling across a logical or metaphysical impossibility. Having deployed a similar thought experiment to this, Parfit thus concludes that it is a metaphysical as well as a logical possibility that there be nothing concrete – no universe, no minds, nothing at all. And, that being so, Parfit would be inclined to think that there can be no satisfactory answer to our title question in terms of its being metaphysically impossible that there be nothing. *A fortiori*, there can be no satisfactory answer to the question of why there is anything at all in terms of its being logically impossible that there be nothing, for metaphysical possibility is a subset of logical possibility. Parfit's own thought then continues on a line to which we shall return in a moment. But according to some we need not follow Parfit down that line for the argument of this paragraph has already gone wrong. It went wrong in allowing that it is metaphysically possible that there could have been nothing.

Of the subtraction sort of thought experiment that Parfit suggests gives us reason to suppose that it is logically and metaphysically possible that there be nothing, Rundle says this:

> talk of imagining there was nothing . . . run[s] the risk of being treated as if a matter of imagining nothing, and that is refraining from imagining anything. Either that, or, I suggest, it is to imagine things lacking where there might have been something: we suppose we can imagine stars ceasing to exist one by one – like so many lights going out – but we still look to where they were. It makes sense to suppose a reversal of the development described – objects now start reappearing before us in the space which had been vacated. We have not discarded the setting; something we might search in vain, but something – a previously occupied region – none the less.
>
> (Rundle, 2004, p. 111)

So Rundle concludes that 'attempts to think away everything amount to envisaging a region of space which has been evacuated of its every occupant, an exercise which gives no more substance to the possibility of there being nothing than does envisaging an empty cupboard' (Rundle, 2004, p. 116). As the tenor of these passages implicitly suggests and Rundle later explicitly articulates, on his view it is actually physical stuff (in an attenuated sense that allows empty space to count as physical stuff) the non-existence of which is inconceivable. Thus Rundle is inclined to answer the question of why there is anything at all by asserting that it is actually impossible (probably he would say logically as well metaphysically) for there not to be something and equally impossible for whatever there is not to be a universe (where a universe is just any collection of physical stuff in the attenuated sense just mentioned). According to Rundle then, there had to be some physical universe, but there did not have to be the universe that there is. Thus he maintains 'the claim that there has to be something without having to demonstrate that there is something [in particular] that has to be' (Rundle, 2004, p.110) and without needing to maintain – that which would surely be implausible – that this universe in all its particularity could not have failed to exist. However, Rundle's complaint that subtraction thought experiments do *nothing* to establish the logical and metaphysical possibility of there being nothing seems to be misplaced.

We have already conceded that our reflective intuitions in this area cannot be taken as infallible guides, merely as the best guides that we can have and thus *ceteris paribus* to be trusted, and our reflective intuitions in this area are, I suggest, that we can imagine and conceive of much more than Rundle allows. As well as imagining a world in which an iron lump had once existed and then stopped existing, one can equally well imagine a universe in which such an object had never existed in the first place and nor had any other. That is to say that as well as the standard subtraction thought experiment (where one imagines away a last object, such as an iron lump, leaving nothing at all behind in a previously-inhabited world), it is equally easy to imagine a world in which such a lump had not once existed and then stopped existing; rather, it had never existed in the first place. Furthermore, and also *contra* Rundle, it is possible to think away empty space. This author finds that he must concede to Rundle that it is hard for him to imagine away an iron lump, even imagine it away from all eternity, without forming a mental image which includes a residual empty space as a black background the part of which that was occluded by the lump being revealed by its departure in the initial thought experiment or having always been visible in the thought experiment where the lump is thought away from all eternity. However, someone who had been born blind would presumably *not* suffer from this sort of difficulty; not having any mental images at all, he or she would not have any mental image of a black background against which he or she would have been forming his or her image of the lump or considering its eternal absence. Surely though such a person could still be said to be able to imagine these things. In any case, a lack of literal 'imaginability' in the sense of image-ability does not prevent conceivability. I hazard that nobody can imagine, in the sense of picture in his or her mind's eye, the difference between a thousand-sided closed figure and a thousand-and-one-sided closed figure. Yet surely most can clearly conceive of it. Similarly, I suggest, one can conceive of there being nothing at all by in-the-end-total subtraction of objects, all of which one can do in the imagination, and finally subtraction of background, a final act which may take one out of the imagination proper and into pure conception, but which does not do anything more than the previous to arouse a logical or metaphysical repugnance. Again, one should be quick to stress that conceivability of this sort is no infallible guide to possibility; such thought experimentation does not provide conclusive proof that the situations we conceive of in it are logically or metaphysically possible. But it is some guide; it provides *prima facie* reason. So far then it looks as if Parfit is right to maintain that subtraction thought experiments, at least if adapted in the manner suggested in this paragraph and carefully followed through, give us good *prima facie* reason to suppose that it is logically and metaphysically possible that there have been nothing.[6]

A traditional theist might think that it is not metaphysically possible that there have been nothing for quite different reasons from those of Rundle. Theists may assert that whilst it is logically possible that there have been nothing, it is not metaphysically possible, for it is not metaphysically possible that there be no God. On this view we may say the following of subtraction thought experiments. When we imagine the logically possible world in which all that exists is a universe constituted by a single lump of iron, we have in fact strayed *outside* the realm of metaphysical possibility. The most similar metaphysically possible world is one in which there is God plus this single-iron-lump universe. We might not recognize a repugnance to our metaphysical imagination when we think the lump away and thus imagine nothing existing, but that is simply due to the epistemic uncertainty that surrounds the issue of God's existence in our minds. Special considerations – that is considerations of the sort that give us reason to think that the conceivable might not after all be a guide to the metaphysically possible in a particular area – do obtain here. When we follow Parfit and think what little physical stuff we have imagined into existence out of existence along with any background space (as is, *pace* Rundle, possible), we have thus conceived of the genuine logical possibility of nothing existing. But, on Theism, the most similar[7] metaphysically possible world to this is one in which God and nothing else exists. If we can consistently think God away too, then this just shows that there are logically possible worlds in which God does not exist and that God's nature as a metaphysically necessary being is not immediately obvious to us in such a way as to restrain our imaginations from wandering into them; it does nothing to threaten the fact that if God does exist, none of these logically possible worlds is metaphysically possible. So, according to such a Theist, Parfit has gone wrong too, but gone wrong for quite different reasons from those suggested by Rundle. Parfit was right to suggest that it is metaphysically possible that there have been nothing physical, but he was wrong to go on from this to suggest that it is metaphysically possible that there have been nothing at all. He forgot about God. God, of metaphysical necessity, could not but exist even if there were not anything physical. The nature of logic is such as to guarantee that one logically possible world be actual; the nature of God is such as to guarantee that whichever world is actual, it is one in which He exists, in which there is consequently something. Thus we have an answer to the question of why there is something rather than nothing. It is of course an answer which, pending an argument for Theism, one has no reason to suppose is the right one. But that one has in those circumstances no reason to suppose that it is the right answer does not undermine its rightness if it is right.

At this stage, someone who was enamoured of the point that the question of why there is anything at all is illegitimate because any answer to a question of why something exists must make mention of something that is already supposed to exist may feel his or her love for that point rekindled.

Has the Theist not just answered the question of why there is something rather than nothing by presupposing the existence of something, just as he or she had said any putative answer would (illegitimately) have to do? The Theist may accept that this is what he or she has done and simply deny the illegitimacy of having done it when offering an explanation in terms of something the essence of which entails existence (if not logically, then metaphysically). If there is a metaphysically necessary being, then that just does explain why there is anything as it is thus metaphysically impossible that there have been nothing; any putative principle of legitimacy in explanation that would render illegitimate an explanation of this sort for why there is anything shows itself, *ipso facto*, to be too restrictive. This is not Theistic special pleading; a thinker as uncongenial to Theism as Rundle would in fact need to accept it. The theist's claim is in essence similar to Rundle's. It adds to the claim that Rundle elsewhere presupposes, the claim that *if* there is something metaphysically necessary, then that explains why there is something rather than nothing, not Rundle's further claim that there is some such thing and it is physical stuff, but instead the claim that there is some such thing and it is God.

So I conclude that – pending a consideration of arguments for and against Theism – epistemically speaking, God could well be the right answer to the question of why there is something rather than nothing; metaphysically speaking, if God does exist, He must be the right answer. And what if God does not exist? Is there no hope of a satisfactory answer then? Of course, one might posit a non-theistic metaphysically necessary being – for example, physical stuff, in the manner of Rundle. But what if one does not do that? Surely then one must think that there could not be an explanation of why there is something rather than nothing, for having admitted that it is logically *and* metaphysically possible that there be nothing, the fact that there is something cannot then be claimed to be a logical or metaphysical necessity. However, before accepting this apparently inescapable conclusion, let us turn to consider an argument of Peter van Inwagen's, an argument which seems to come as close to calling it into question as makes only infinitesimal difference.[8]

As the totality of logically possible worlds is exhaustive of all ways the whole of reality could have been, so some logically possible world had to exist. Logic alone is sufficient to have guaranteed that. Further, as there can be nothing outside any logically possible world to raise or lower the probability of its existing relative to the probability of another existing instead, so the probability of each logically possible world existing must be equal. As there is only one logically possible world in which there is nothing at all and an infinite number in which there is at least something, so the probability of there being nothing at all is infinitesimally small. Thus we have as satisfactory an answer to the question of why there is something rather than nothing as we can legitimately hope for from the starting point of allowing that it is logically and metaphysically possible that there be nothing: there had to be a logically possible world (the putative alternative to that genuinely is a logical impossibility); there is only one logically possible world in which there is nothing; in every other logically possible world there is something; the probabilities of each world existing are the same; and thus the probability of there being nothing is infinitely small. That it be infinitely improbable that there be nothing is not its being logically impossible that there be nothing, but the difference is vanishingly small and logic alone assures us that there is no room for anything that could close whatever gap may remain. Thus someone thinking along van Inwagen's line has an explanation of why there is something rather than nothing too.

Against van Inwagen's argument, it might be suggested that there are in fact an infinite number of logically possible worlds in which there is nothing, what we might call 'empty worlds'. There is one where there is a universe in which Newton's Physics reigns; one where there is a universe in which Aristotelian Physics reigns; and so on.[9] Of course in none of these empty worlds or their component universes is there anything for these differing Physics to reign over; their universes are, after all, empty. But in each of them the obtaining of different laws makes different counterfactuals true.

This counter-argument to van Inwagen obviously relies on a particular conception of the laws of nature, one which holds that a law can be true in a universe even if there is no stuff in that universe of which it is true, and this conception could be questioned. Rundle, for example, would certainly question it.[10] As well as directly challenging this conception of laws of nature, he would say that if we think we can succeed in imagining one empty universe which obeys Newton's laws and another which obeys Aristotle's, we are unwittingly supposing that these different universes are, after all, not empty: there is different stuff – in his attenuated sense of 'stuff' – in these universes; there is space stuff which has different properties in each. So-called 'Just an Empty Newtonian Universe' World and 'Just an Empty Aristotelian Universe' World are not genuinely empty worlds after all. Even if that is right, there are other ways in which it might be suggested that there could be many empty worlds, other ways that, at least *prima facie*, seem equally damaging to van Inwagen's argument.

Only if S5 describes the logic of modality will it be the case that there are not world-specific possibilities. If there are world-specific possibilities, we cannot rule out there being some empty worlds in which speaking dogs popping into existence uncaused are possible and some empty worlds in which their popping into existence is not possible. A defence of S5 would of course take one outside the scope of this chapter, but it does strike many people as obviously irrefragable; this author, for one, finds no reason for van Inwagen to be troubled on this front. To him, a more worrying line of counter-argument is to suggest that different empty worlds might be distinguished by the differing probabilities that something will turn up uncaused in them and the differing probabilities that any uncaused things turning up in them will have certain properties. Perhaps one empty world is one in which it is more probable that a dog will turn up uncaused than a cat; another is an empty world in which it is more probable that a cat will turn up uncaused than a dog. Perhaps in one empty world it is more probable that any dog that does turn up will bark rather than speak and another empty world is one in which it is more probable that any dog that does turn up will speak rather than bark.[11] Of course there are ways to sweep these musings from the board too; one could ruthlessly employ an exclusively frequentist understanding of probability or a metaphysical necessity that there be nothing that is uncaused. But each of these ways seems not just *ad hoc*, but wrong; there just are notions of probability other than the frequentist one; uncaused things just do seem metaphysically possible (God, if He exists; the universe, if He does not).[12] And it has been suggested that empty worlds might differ in their ethical qualities too.[13]

One response that van Inwagen might make here, appealing in its generality, would be to argue that, even if we allow that there *are* an infinite number of empty worlds, his original argument is not in fact weakened at all. Even conceding all the points made against van Inwagen's argument so far, for each empty world with a given set of laws, possibilities, probabilities and ethics, there will be an infinite number of non-empty ones with the same laws, possibilities, probabilities and ethics, but each having some different set of things existent in them. That being so, one might draw a comparison between non-empty worlds and even numbers and empty ones and prime numbers. We may say that the frequency of prime numbers is less than that of even numbers; numerical space is less densely populated with prime numbers than with even. It follows from this that were an integer to be plucked at random from numerical space, the chances of its being a prime would be less than that of its being an even number. Indeed the chances of the number being a prime would be fantastically small as primes are not just infrequent, they diminish in frequency and without limit the higher up the number line one goes. One might even say then that with *all* of numerical space to select from, the chances of plucking a prime at random are infinitesimally small even though there are an infinite number of them that one might pluck. Similarly, one might suggest, were a logically possible world plucked at random (i.e. selected by logic alone to be actual), as must of course – of logical necessity – happen, the chances of it being one of the infinite number of empty worlds (if such a number of empty worlds has been admitted) is fantastically small. One might even maintain that it is infinitesimally small. It is thus as small as van Inwagen's original argument maintained.

Van Inwagen's argument assumes that all logically possible worlds are equally probable. He spends some time in a sophisticated defence of this claim.[14] However, it does not seem right; some logically possible worlds seem to be more probable than others. Consider this. There is a logically possible world with nothing but a universe in it that is like ours. Epistemically speaking (prior to a knowledge of God's existence), this logically possible world may be the actual world. There is also a logically possible world with nothing in it but a universe that is like ours except that every fundamental particle in that universe has written on it in Times Roman tiny-sized font, 'This particle created by the God of Classical Theism.' In this latter world, scientists have, let us further suppose, just discovered this message written on a large sample class of these particles, let us say 100,000, and made their results widely known. The latter world is surely immensely more unlikely than the former. If one were to maintain with van Inwagen that it was not more unlikely, one would have no way of explaining why it is that people living in the latter world, now that they have become aware of this unambiguous message purporting to be from the creator, have more reason than us to believe that there is a God.

Let us suppose then that van Inwagen concedes that not all logically possible worlds are equally probable. For example, the logically possible world in which there is this sort of message on every fundamental particle in the one and only universe it contains and yet no God is less probable than the logically possible world in which there is this sort of message on every fundamental particle in the one and only universe it contains and a God. The distribution of probabilities over logical space is uneven. Nevertheless, there is only a 'probability pie' of size one, as one might put it, to distribute and every logically possible world must have a slice of that pie; some may get thicker slices than others, but every world has to get at least a sliver. Still then, van Inwagen might maintain, given the relative infrequency of empty worlds amongst non-empty ones, the amount of pie that will remain to be divided between the, we may grant, infinite number of empty worlds will be infinitesimally small. Again, his original conclusion is not threatened.

Another objection to van Inwagen's argument would come from someone who maintained that the simplest logically possible world is one with nothing in it and that *a priori* we should expect the simplest to obtain. Thus the fact that there is something when there could have been nothing is surprising and thus our title question has a more pressing need for an answer than the seeming parallel question, 'Why is there nothing rather than something?'[15] as it would arise in an empty world. Leibniz thought along these lines and thus would presumably think that van Inwagen had gone wrong in divvying up the probabilities. The empty world (or empty worlds, if multiplicity has been allowed) should be apportioned greater than half the pie to start with, thus stopping his argument in its tracks. However, to suggest this is to suggest that simplicity is what Parfit would call a 'selector', something that explains why there is what there is.[16] But van Inwagen would surely be right to say that what selector operates (if any) is itself a feature that is only internal to logically possible worlds. In some logically possible worlds simplicity is a selector and in some it is not. Of course, by thus closing the front door to Leibniz in this manner, van Inwagen would have let in a multiplicity of empty worlds through the back door. He must be positing that there is more than one empty world, the world with nothing in it in which simplicity is a selector and the world with nothing in it in which it is not (it just being a brute inexplicable fact that there is nothing). But then again we have seen that there is scope for van Inwagen to defend himself even if he concedes a multiplicity of empty worlds.

These considerations, at least as they have so far been presented, are thus hardly conclusive, one way or the other. So at the moment we do best to say that pending an argument for or against Theism and pending a resolution to the just-mentioned issues faced by van Inwagen's argument, the Theistic and van Inwagen lines should strike one as more or less equally satisfactory as answers to the question of why there is anything at all. The 'more or less' features as one will of course have already reached some tentative conclusions about arguments for and against Theism and/or pertaining to the points raised in the last few paragraphs. If there is a difference in satisfactoriness between the Theistic and van Inwagen answers that is not generated in this way, then it is the tiniest of differences allowed for by the fact that taking the van Inwagen line only allows one to say that it is infinitely unlikely that there would have been nothing whereas taking the Theistic line allows one to say that it is strictly metaphysically impossible.

Finally, let us consider a putative alternative to both the Theistic and van Inwagen's answers to the question of why there is something rather than nothing. This is the view which occupies Parfit from about the stage in his thought where we left him, the view that he calls – following Leslie[17] – the Axiarchic view.

As Parfit points out, as well as the sort of metaphysical and logical modalities we have been considering so far, there are also value modalities. For example, if A reduces suffering more than B, then, *ceteris paribus*, A must be better than B. Value modalities form a recognizably distinct set (or subset) of modalities from those we have so far been considering and a set within which it has been suggested that one might find an answer to the question of why there is something rather than nothing.

> In its simplest form, [the Axiarchic view] makes three claims: (1) It would be best if reality were a certain way. (2) Reality is that way. (3) (1) explains (2). (1) is an ordinary evaluative claim, like the claim that it would be better if there was less suffering. . . . (2) is an ordinary empirical or scientific claim, though of a sweeping kind. What is distinctive in this view is claim (3).
>
> (Parfit, 1998, pp. 10–11)

According to the Axiarchic view, of all logically possible worlds, one is the best world that there could be and its being the actual world is explained in terms of its having that feature (which of course it does of logical necessity, so there is nothing needing explaining there) and there being a value modality 'selecting for actuality', as we might put it, between logically possible worlds, a value modality that ensures there is in fact no possibility of the best world not existing.

Now whilst some value modalities – suffering must be bad, for example – seem to be such that there is no logically possible world in which they are violated, the value modality that links what is of supreme value to what actually exists seems logically contingent. There are surely some logically possible worlds where that which would be best does not obtain and thus it cannot be a *logical* necessity that that the obtaining of which would best obtains because it is best that it obtains. The most credible way for the proponent of the Axiarchic view to make his or her case then is for him or her to suggest that the principle that the best be actualized is akin to a metaphysical necessity. (In Parfit's terminology, it is a selector.) Were it to be the case that such a necessity obtained, it could then – in principle – explain why there is something rather than nothing, if it would be best were there something rather than nothing. It could even explain why there is a universe rather than anything else, if it would be best were there a universe. And, finally, it could explain why the particular universe that does exist has the features it does, if these are the best features for a universe to have. However, as this train of thought starts to indicate, the Axiarchic view appears to generate a particularly striking variant of the Problem of Evil in that it has as a consequence that things must be as good as they could be. Thus if ever something happens that is less than the best that could happen, the Axiarchic view is proven false; surely then, someone might argue, it is proven false by almost every experience we have. However, this is too quick. We need to be in the business of judging 'integral wholes' here. If a painful experience results in a good which is inaccessible in any other way and the goodness of which outweighs the badness of the experience, one would have been rash (and quite possibly mistaken) to conclude from having had the experience that overall this was not in fact the best that could have happened. So the Axiarchic view is not proven false by almost every experience we have.

Someone might concede that the Axiarchic view is not proven false by almost every experience we have yet suggest that it is nonetheless very implausible given our experience; whilst not demonstrably false, it is very implausible to suggest that there are no gratuitous evils in the world. But even this is not obviously right. Remember, we should be considering the integral whole that is the world here, not just the possibly very minor part of the world that is our universe. The best possible world may well contain universes that have bad, even gratuitous from the point of view of those universes, things happen in them; these bad things just need to be not gratuitous from the point of view of the world. However, this thought does not seem enough to defuse the implausibility of the claim that our universe is a part of the best of all possible worlds. Take an evil that is seemingly gratuitous from the point of view of our universe at least. Consider, for example, the last headache that you had that was so mild that you did not bother mentioning it to anyone; did not bother doing anything about; and indeed the only effect of which you can think of is the painful sensation that constituted your having of it. Supposing the universe had been in all ways the same as it actually was but *sans* this headache thus seems to be supposing a better universe than this. It thus seems to be supposing a better world than this *unless* this headache was in fact a logically or metaphysically necessary condition of some greater good at the integrated world level. Whilst one cannot prove that it was not, there is no plausible contender for such a greater good. If this is right, we may then be tempted to consider whether it would be desirable to move to a less extreme Axiarchic view than that considered by Parfit, one along lines suggested by Rice.[18]

According to Rice, the universe exists not because it is best that it do so but merely because it is overall good that it does so. This is a milder suggestion then, but before we can use it as a basis from which to answer the question of why there is anything at all, we shall need to make it a bit less mild. We shall need to move from it to the bolder claim that everything the existence of which is overall good must exist. We shall need to move here as the less bold claim cannot really adequately explain why whatever it is that exists does exist (even if it can be assumed that whatever exists is overall good), as it cannot explain why all those things the existence of which would have been overall good yet do not exist. If it is not sufficient for being actual that something's existence would be overall good, then there is no necessity that anything which exists because it is overall good that it exists have actually existed and thus there is no explanation of why there is anything rather than nothing.

With the move to the bolder claim we might seem to have failed to leave any room between this Axiarchic view and the original Axiarchic view. One could contend with justification that the view is still committed to the claim that the best of all possible worlds exists and just characterizing that world as being that in which all and only that the existence of which would be overall good exists. But the proponent of this variant of the Axiarchic view could concede that and yet maintain that it is still the case that the notion of best that he or she employs is such as to face a weaker version of the Problem of Evil than the original Axiarchic view. That the universe is not overall good is far less obviously the case than that the universe contains some bad things that are gratuitous at the world level. The notion of best that this version of the Axiarchic view thus operates with, whereby the best of all possible worlds is one where all and only things that are overall good exist, may of course still have questions asked of it. One might think that there is no unique set of such things. One might also wonder whether the total amount of goodness in the world is all or even much of what one thinks of when one thinks of things being best. These are all pressing issues and they appear to be more pressing than the parallel issues that would be faced by the traditional Theistic answer to the question of why there is something rather than nothing, that answer not committing one to, for example, some totalizing version of Consequentialism. So let us register a preliminary preference for the Theistic story over the Axiarchic on these grounds and move on to consider whether the Axiarchic view is more or less appealing than Theism on other grounds. Against its being more appealing, one may initially be impressed by an argument such as that advanced against it by Swinburne.

Swinburne, in commenting on Parfit's entertaining the idea that value modalities might explain why there is something rather than nothing, says that

> there are no plausible examples of such principles at work in the world. When food appears on the tables of the hungry, it does not appear there because it is good that it should, but because some person (i.e. a substance) caused it to be there because he thought that it was good that it should.
>
> (Swinburne, 1998, p. 428)

For Swinburne, all acceptable explanations of why something obtains have to go through a substance and, if they involve value modalities, through that substance's beliefs about these value modalities.

Swinburne is surely correct in maintaining that in his example of food appearing on the table of the hungry, the right explanation will involve some substance – in particular, we suppose, some person – rather than the mere value necessity that it is good if hungry people get food. But how shall we explain the thought 'It is good if hungry people get food' as we may suppose it appears in the mind of the person who is responsible for putting the food on the table? At some stage we shall be forced to posit that some person has the belief – knowledge indeed, for surely we wish to claim some cases of the belief to be such – that it is good for those who are hungry to receive food without having got it from any other substance or person. How then shall we explain that?

The most natural explanation would be that this person knows that it is good for the hungry to be given food because he or she recognizes as true the relevant value modality. The explanation would not need to differ from that which we give of how people come to recognize logical or metaphysical modalities of the sorts we have already discussed. One just knows these things *a priori*. Of course knowing something *a priori* is quite compatible with one's awareness of that thing being initiated or heightened by *a posteriori* findings. If one lives in the relatively affluent West, then one's appreciation of the necessity that it is good if the hungry receive food will be somewhat less vivid than that of someone who works in refugee camps in famine-stricken parts of the world. In any case, one will have to admit that a change in the world – one's coming to the belief that this modality obtains – has been brought about by the modality's obtaining. *Contra* Swinburne then, not only *can* value modalities make a direct difference to the world, they *have to be* posited as making a direct difference for they have to be posited as directly explaining at least some of the knowledge of them that is had by agents. Of course it may be true that in everyday life we only have experience of value modalities making a direct difference to things – ourselves – that already exist: we do not have any experience of these modalities bringing substances (as opposed to some of the particular beliefs had by substances) into existence. And it is true that the value modality that links value and existence is not – as we have seen – one that can plausibly be regarded as a logical necessity. So if one perceives that such a modality does obtain in this world, one will be perceiving something that can only be on a par with the traditional Theistic answer. That it is necessary that that the existence of which would be overall good exist is no less a claim of necessity than that it is necessary that God exists. But it is no more a claim either. So on this score Theism and the Axiarchic view appear to be on a par.

Another worry that one might have with the Axiarchic view could arise from the thought that things can only be good or bad if they are good or bad for people who actually exist (have existed, do exist, or will exist). Such a view of value might seem to make value modalities unsuitable for answering the question of why there is anything at all and such a view of value has much plausibility to it. Let us accept for the sake of argument then that it is right. This does not in fact rule out a value modality of the sort we are considering explaining why there is anything at all, indeed doing more than that, explaining why there are people. If it is a necessary condition of anything's being good (or bad) that there be people, then the value necessity that that the existence of which would be overall good must exist will bring into existence the necessary conditions for its obtaining, *viz.* people. We may be tempted to ask at this stage, 'But for whom could it have been good that the necessity that that the existence of which would be overall good must exist obtain prior to that necessity bringing anyone into existence? The answer must be "nobody", but then how can things ever have got started?' But of course we should not be thinking of 'prior' or 'things starting' here. There are people, so there are subjects of the sort that are – *ex hypothesi* – necessary for it to be the case that that the existence of which would be overall good must exist. The Axiarchic view need not say that it would have been bad had there been nothing; it need only say that it is good that there is something. If it is a necessary condition of something being good that there be people for whom it is good, then it follows from its being good that there be something that it is good that there be people. Is such 'bootstrapping' acceptable? This author thinks that it is and that any unease we feel with it in this case is caused by our actually not accepting that it really is a necessity that that the existence of which would be overall good must exist. So, even if it is conceded then that things can only be good if there are actual people for whom they are good, the Axiarchic view can soldier on, although it will then generate in this bootstrapping way metaphysically necessary beings, people. I say 'people'; of course one person could do the job. Which makes one think...

Even without it being a necessary condition of things having value that there be people for whom they have the value, the Axiarchic view can be seen to necessitate the existence of any person the existence of whom would be overall good and there is one possible person who will obviously fit this bill, the best possible person; thus He will be actual on the Axiarchic view. In other words, the Axiarchic view entails Theism: on it, God exists because it is overall good that He exists. It does so on the assumption that such a being is not in fact logically or metaphysically impossible. But to attack that assumption would be to attack Theism. Thus we can see that judging the acceptability of the Axiarchic answer to the question of why there is something rather than nothing and whether or not its answer is a variant of the Theistic answer rather than a genuinely alternative answer waits on judging arguments for and against Theism. So where does all this leave us?

We have argued that the question 'Why is there anything at all?' makes sense and – epistemically at least – may well have an answer. We have, more or less favourably, assessed three contenders for the answer. There is the Theistic answer: God is a necessary being, so it is metaphysically impossible for there to be nothing. There is van Inwagen's answer: whilst not metaphysically impossible for there to be nothing, it is infinitely unlikely that there be nothing. And there is the Axiarchic answer: it would be overall good were there something rather than nothing and that which would be overall good has to obtain. If van Inwagen's line can be shown to be untenable, then, if there is any answer at all to our title question, there will have to be a metaphysically necessary being; this metaphysically necessary being cannot, *pace* Rundle, be physical stuff (we have seen that Parfit was right to suggest that there might not be any physical stuff), so it will have to be something very much like the God of Classical Theism. Knocking out van Inwagen's argument then is important for anyone who wishes to argue from the claim that there must be (or even that it is rational to suppose there to be) an answer to the question of why there is anything at all to the claim that there must be (or that it is rational to suppose there to be) a God. Alternatively, establishing on other grounds that there is a God would establish that He is the right answer to our question and thus render van Inwagen's concerns moot. We have raised more questions of van Inwagen's answer and the Axiarchic answer than we have of the Theistic answer, but none of the objections we have considered has been conclusive. We have also seen that which of these answers one has most reason to believe is the correct one depends ultimately on what reasons one has for or against Theism. At this stage then, if not before, the question of what sort of question it is that one is asking when one asks 'Why is there anything at all?' can be clearly seen to be first and foremost a question in the Philosophy of Religion.[19]

Notes

1. See Mawson (2005), part I, for a sustained exploration and defence of the claim that God, if He exists, is a person, indeed the best possible person.

   It follows from the comments in the main text that if it can be shown that God, were he to exist, would satisfy the Identity of Indiscernibles, then this is for it to be shown that failing to satisfy the Identity of Indiscernibles cannot be of the essence of concreteness, which in turn would run contrary to a suggested characterization of concreteness in Baldwin (1996). Sometimes concreteness is characterized in terms of having a spatiotemporal location; again, this may be shown to be incorrect merely by reflection on the fact that if it were right, were there a God, He would not be concrete. This pertinancity in taking God to be concrete and adjusting whatever else needs to be adjusted accordingly goes against a trend in the literature; see the papers on the subtraction argument referred to in a later note for how the discussion of that argument may go if one is less pertinacious.
2. See, for example, Leibniz (1956, p. 1038).
3. See Carlson and Olsson (2001) and the later discussion of what I call 'van Inwagen's argument' for suggestions of how such a presupposition might in any case be defended.
4. I owe my knowledge of this joke to Thomas Nagel who uses it in his review of Bede Rundle's *Why There is Something Rather Than Nothing* in *The Times Literary Supplement* (7 May 2004) and attributes it to Sidney Morgenbesser.
5. I call Parfit's and my thought experiments versions of the subtraction argument in favour of its being possible that there be nothing. The term comes from Baldwin (1996). Variants of this argument have been subject to sustained examination. In what follows in the main text I give a relatively informal version. For more detailed discussion, see G. Rodriguez-Pereya, 'There Might Be Nothing: The Subtraction Argument Improved', *Analysis* 57 (1996); G. Rodriguez-Pereya, 'Lowe's Argument against Nihilism', *Analysis* 60 (2000); E. J. Lowe, 'Metaphysical Nihilism and the Subtraction Argument', *Analysis* 62 (2002); A. Paseau, 'Why the Subtraction Argument Does Not Add up', *Analysis* 62 (2002); G. Rodriguez-Pereya, 'Metaphysical Nihilism Defended: Reply to Lowe and Paseau', *Analysis* 62 (2002); G. Coggins, 'World and Object: Metaphysical Nihilism and Three Accounts of Worlds', *Proceedings of the Aristotelian Society* 103 (2003); G. Rodriguez-Pereya, 'Modal Realism and Metaphysical Nihilism', *Mind* 113 (2004); D. Efird and T. Stoneham, 'The Subtraction Argument for Metaphysical Nihilism', *Journal of Philosophy* 102 (2005); R. Cameron, 'Much Ado About Nothing: A Study in Metaphysical Nihilism', *Erkenntnis* 64 (2006); A. Paseau, 'The Subtraction Argument(s)', *Dialectica* 60 (2006); and R. Cameron, 'Subtractability and Concreteness: Response to Efird and Stoneham on the Subtraction Argument', *The Philosophical Quarterly* 57 (2007).

6. It is a mistake to put too much weight on the subtraction argument as an argument against Rundle, rather than a picturesque articulation of the claim that he is mistaken. It is hard to see what imagination could be if it did not involve some presentation before a mind's eye, a mind's ear, a mind's... of something akin to a sensory experience, so the blind man discussed could still be argued to be imagining a wholly silent time, time then being lined-up to play the same role as space in Rundle's original argument. With a switch to someone born deaf and blind, perhaps they could be accused of imagining a wholly empty 'tactile space' or some such. With the move from imagining to conceiving, conceiving may simply collapse into describing without contradiction, in which case to appeal to it would simply be to deny what Rundle asserts without argument. (I am grateful to Brian Leftow for these points.) However, see the literature on the subtraction argument referred to in the previous note for further discussion.

7. Although see later note on how one need not think that any non-empty world is closer to an empty one than any other.

8. See van Inwagen (1996). I say the argument is van Inwagen's, but Nozick had earlier discussed it (Nozick, 1981, p. 127) and van Inwagen himself would not endorse all the details of the argument as it finds final articulation in the main text, for example, he does not think it makes sense to speak of choosing an object at random from a denumerably infinite set.

9. See Carroll (1994, p. 64).

10. So would van Inwagen himself; see van Inwagen (1995).

11. I owe the points about S5 and probabilities to Brian Leftow.

12. Of course this does not exhaust the options for removing these difficulties. van Inwagen has pointed out to me in discussion that it is hard to see how either of two non-empty worlds could be closer to an empty world than the other and that one could argue from this that – with minor qualifications – no counterfactuals about what sorts of things would exist, if anything existed, are true in any non-actual world. This would form a part of his argument for the existence of at most one empty world.

13. See Sorenson (2005). I am grateful to David Efird for drawing this to my attention.

14. This is well discussed and criticised in Carlson and Olsson, *op. cit.*

15. van Inwagen (1996) discusses this.

16. Or at least that is it is more likely to be a selector than not. (The overall force of the points that follow would be unaffected by this modification.)

17. See Leslie (1979).

18. See Rice (2000).

19. I am grateful for the comments of David Efird, Brian Leftow, Richard Swinburne and Peter van Inwagen on the drafts of this chapter.

References

T. Baldwin, 'There Might Have Been Nothing', *Analysis*, 65 (1996), 231–38.

E. Carlson and E. Olsson, 'The Presumption of Nothingness', *Ratio*, XIV (2001), 203–21.

J. Carroll, *Laws of Nature* (Cambridge: Cambridge University Press, 1994).

G. Leibniz, The Principles of Nature and Grace, Based on Reason. L. Loemker (trans. & ed.), *Philosophical Papers and Letters* (Chicago: University of Chicago Press, 1956).

J. Leslie, *Value and Existence* (Oxford: Blackwell, 1979).

T. J. Mawson, *Belief in God* (Oxford: Oxford University Press, 2005).

R. Nozick, *Philosophical Explanations* (Oxford: Oxford University Press, 1981).

D. Parfit, 'Why Anything? Why This?', *London Review of Books*, 20 (2) (22 January 1998), 24–27 and 20 (3) (5 February 1998), 22–25. The page references given in the notes are to the downloadable version (http:www.lrb.co.uk/v20/n03/parf01_html).

H. Rice, *God and Goodness* (Oxford: Oxford University Press, 2000).

B. Rundle, *Why There is Something Rather Than Nothing* (Oxford: Oxford University Press, 2004).

R. Sorenson, 'The Ethics of Empty Worlds', *Australasian Journal of Philosophy*, 83 (2005), 349–58.

R. Swinburne, 'Response to Derek Parfit', in D. Zimmerman and P. van Inwagen (eds), *Metaphysics: The Big Questions* (Oxford: Blackwell, 1998), pp. 427–29.

P. van Inwagen, 'The Place of Chance in a World Sustained by God', *God, Knowledge and Mystery* (Ithaca, NY: Cornell University Press 1995).

P. van Inwagen, 'Why is There Anything at All?', *Proceedings of the Aristotelian Society*, 70 (1996), 95–110.

4
Programs, Bugs, DNA and a Design Argument

Alexander R. Pruss

1 Introduction

Prima facie, there seems to be an analogical argument from the claims that DNA is like a computer program and that computer programs have programmers, to the claim that the DNA of an organism has a designer. This is a teleological argument. But unfortunately an unsound one: some computer programs do not have designers, but are themselves generated by other programs, perhaps via evolutionary methods. If it is countered that in these cases there is still a programmer behind the scenes who wrote the initial programs, then a different disanalogy can be pointed out: in the case of DNA we know of a process, namely neo-Darwinian evolution, that could be reasonably thought to produce the DNA without the intervention of an intelligent being, while we do not know of such a process in the case of a computer program.

I will argue, however, that the analogical argument can be rescued if one fleshes out the analogy further, by showing that if there were computer programs that were not themselves designed by intelligent agents, they would lack certain normative characteristics that designed computer programs have, and then by arguing that DNA exhibits these same normative characteristics. Moreover, these characteristics of designed computer programs are such that we do not know of any natural process that does not involve an intelligent agent which could produce a program with them. This strengthens the analogical argument. It will turn out, I expect, that the main question for further debate will be whether in fact DNA has the characteristics in question.

2 Bugs and features

I am on the development team for an open source software project, Plucker, implementing an e-text reader for PalmOS PDAs.[1] Periodically, we receive 'bug reports' and 'feature requests' from users.[2] A user making a request from the development team needs to describe the issue sufficiently clearly for us to understand and hopefully duplicate. Moreover, he/she needs to classify whether the request is a bug report, and of what severity, or a feature request. Once we receive the report, we may do several things. We might reclassify a bug report or feature request. We might immediately resolve a bug report, marking it as 'not a bug,' and explaining why. Or we might, immediately or later, fix the bug or add the requested feature.

The distinction between a bug report and a feature request is of practical relevance to the development team. For instance, the project goes through periodic feature freezes during which the focus is on fixing bugs rather than adding possibly buggy code that adds new features.

To see the distinctions at work, consider a particular case. User 'KYSoh' filed report #708 stating: 'Hires Plucker v20030611-am is displaying a black dot after I scroll to the end of a document on my Palm m515.' The user classified this as a major bug. Less than four hours later, user 'Belousov' posted a follow up: 'It's not bug, it's a feature! This dot is mark of bottom previous page.' An hour and a half later, I set the bug report status to 'resolved' with a resolution of 'Not a bug.' The issue was that when paging through a webpage, because the text on the last screen may have significant overlap with the data on the previous screen, a square is drawn in the margin to guide the reader's eye to new text. At the same time, I also noted in my resolution note that if the dot annoyed the user, the user was free to file a feature request to allow users to configure if they want the dot or not.

There are a couple of things worth noting here. First, there really is a distinction between a bug, something that should not be there in the program, and a feature. This is true even if the feature, like the black square in question, annoys some users. Second, the distinction is epistemically accessible, though fallibly, even to users like 'Belousov' who quite possibly did not have to look at the source code for the program, read the documentation (which unfortunately does not mention this feature), or talk to any of the developers, but who treated the program as a black box. User 'Belousov,' I am assuming, found that the square appearing on the margin served a useful purpose, and inferred that the square was a feature, not a bug. Nonetheless, this inference was ampliative. It could have been the case that the square appeared there due to a bug in the scrolling code, say, and simply *happened* to serve a useful purpose. My own inference that this was a feature was more reliable than one based on a black box type analysis, because I had seen the lines coding for the feature in the source code (I was not responsible for them myself), and thought, defeasibly but with great confidence, that these lines were deliberate and correct.

Distinct from the cases of a bug and a feature is the case of missing functionality. This is a case where a program fails to do something that a user would reasonably want it to do because the program was never designed to do this. We encourage users to file 'feature requests' in such cases, though sometimes a user mistakenly thinks the functionality was already supposed to be there and files a bug report instead of a feature request.

We thus have a threefold distinction, between bugs, features and missing functionality. The distinction is important to software development work and appears to be objective at least in the sense that one can be mistaken in one's classification. Note, too, that while bugs and missing functionality tend to have disvalue and features tend to have value, this is not sufficient to ground a distinction between features on the one hand and bugs or missing functionality on the other. After all, a feature can annoy the majority of users, and still be a feature, though a misguided one. For instance, an older version of Microsoft Word would guess if the user were typing a letter and annoyingly ask the user if he/she wanted help with writing a letter – many users resented this and Microsoft eventually removed the feature. Conversely, a particular bug might actually please some users, and it is conceivable that it could please the majority of users. For instance, if due to a bug in Microsoft Word the query about helping the user with writing a letter disappeared after three appearances, this might well have pleased the majority of users. Similarly, missing functionality might render a program smaller and faster, and if the user does not care about the functionality this might be an improvement.

Thus, the distinction, though a normative one, cannot be made solely in terms of the value that an aspect of the program has to the users. Nor can it be made in terms of the value that it has to the developers. A software development team, against its better judgment, may have to implement a feature requested by a boss, even though neither the team nor the user community likes the feature.

The existence of unclear cases does not undermine the existence of clear cases. The square on the margin really was a feature and not a bug. The failure of a program to take special advantage of the features of new hardware is typically a lack of functionality and not a bug.

Next, observe that a characteristic shared by two programs identical byte-by-byte can fall under one of the three descriptions 'bug,' 'feature' or 'an instance of missing functionality' in the case of one program and another one of the descriptions in the other case. Consider as a hypothetical case Plucker*, a program developed by a different team of programmers, but coincidentally byte-by-byte just like Plucker, but where the team never intended to implement a marginal square to mark the start of the last part of the text viewed. However, the team wrote a part of the Plucker* code by cutting and pasting lines of code from another project – a not uncommon procedure given appropriate copyright licenses – and accidentally included the code that in its new context produced the marginal square. Then, the square would be a bug in Plucker* and a feature in Plucker, despite the two programs being qualitatively identical byte-by-byte.

This example suggests that the way to figure out whether something is a bug, a feature or a piece of missing functionality is to look at the intentions of the developers. It may, however, be more complicated than that. There may, for instance, be an interaction between the intentions of the developers and social standards. Thus, there might be a reasonable expectation that a program should do something, for example, not crash a computer, and the fact that a sloppy developer just did not care whether his/her program would occasionally crash computers perhaps does not make the crashes be something other than bugs. However, even here the developer's intentions, or at least those of his/her employer, are *relevant*. There is specialized software that for testing purposes deliberately induces crashes, where the absence of a crash would be a bug.

All this makes highly plausible the claim that if a program appeared randomly on my computer with no programmers behind it at all, for example, due to random cosmic ray bombardment of my hard drive, then although I would be able to make a distinction between its doing what I want and its not doing what I want, I could not make the distinction between bugs, features and missing functionality. What is of greatest interest to me from now on is that I could not make a distinction between, on the one hand, a bug and, on the other, a feature or missing functionality. Given that a coincidentally byte-by-byte identical program can be buggy if produced by a programmer with one set of intentions and not buggy if produced by another with other intentions, it does not appear that there is any hope for figuring out what is a bug and what is not in the case of randomly generated software. I simply cannot tell if the system is correctly following a rule that it is undesirable for it to follow (a misguided feature or a piece of missing functionality) or if it is incorrectly following a rule that it would have been desirable for it to follow (a bug).

Observe, however, that in practice judgments can often be made about whether something is a bug without directly checking the intentions of the developers. Recall the case of the marginal square which a user figured out to be a feature, despite the developers having failed to document it as such, and which I then confirmed on the basis of internal features of the code. In the case of a program that was produced by cosmic rays, both the behavioral and the internal grounds would remain. Thus, it would be possible to make a distinction between a bug* and a feature*, where a bug* is something that looks behaviorally or internally like it would be a bug if the program came from a programmer, and a feature* is defined similarly. However, a bug* is not the same as a bug, since the assertibility grounds for judging something to be a bug are not the same as the truth grounds. Something may look to all users like a bug, and yet be a feature, and the code for it can look like buggy code even though it is perfectly correct, as we would find out if we queried that developer who actually wrote it. The assertibility grounds serve as evidence and make it possible to make judgments of bugginess without communicating with the developer, but the judgments will be fallible.

3   DNA and a designer

Like computer programs, DNA directs complex functioning in a system. Now, is DNA like computer programs *simpliciter*, or is it more specifically like *designed* computer programs? Designed computer programs, we have seen, have the normative characteristic that they are subject to evaluation for bugginess. I claim that the same is true of genetic material where we have the category of a 'genetic defect or disorder.'

A genetic defect or disorder is not an instance where something occurs in an organism contrary to the DNA. That indeed would not be akin to a software bug, but would be more like a 'hardware error.' In the case of a genetic disorder, the DNA codes for certain traits which in fact are produced, but these traits, such as two sides of the palate failing to meet, are undesirable. However, undesirability is insufficient to define a genetic disorder. If 'undesirable' is understood as 'socially undesired,' then we have the absurd conclusion that we could bring it about that there are no genetic disorders simply by changing our expectations.

On the other hand, if we are using an objective sense of 'undesirable,' as implying an objective badness, then there are *prima facie* counterexamples. Our DNA guides our development in such a way that we do not grow prehensile tails. The failure to grow prehensile tails is objectively undesirable, since it is *prima facie* objectively desirable that humans should have prehensile tails – they would enable them to better engage more easily in various activities that are now rather difficult, such as taking care of twins or using a computer mouse while typing with both hands. The desirability here is only *prima facie*. It may be that if I had a prehensile tail, I would find shoplifting too easy and hence too tempting to withstand or I might find life less challenging and hence less interesting, and therefore the net effect on me might be negative. But once one admits such *secunda facie* considerations, then it is no longer clear whether, say, different things that we class as 'disabilities' are really undesirable, since they can lead people who have them to develop various moral virtues, such as perseverance, humility and so on.

So just as software bugs cannot be defined in terms of desirability, neither can genetic disorders be. Some of our attitudes toward software bugs parallel our attitudes toward genetic disorders. It may be 'a pity' that a program lacks some functionality or that I not have a prehensile tail, but that this is so is not positively bad. But a bug or genetic disorder is intrinsically a bad thing for a program or organism to have. Of course the program or organism can be good *overall* despite the bug or defect. Moreover, it might sometimes be better that a program or organism should have a bug or defect – think of how good it is if a computer virus infecting your computer fails to work or if the tiger that is sneaking up on you is, due to a genetic disorder, lacking in claws and teeth (this is objectively overall good, because your welfare is objectively more important than a tiger's). In the case of an undesirable bug or an undesirable genetic disorder, we feel that something has gone wrong. In the case of an instance of missing functionality or of, say, an organism's innate inability to cope with certain environments, it is not so much a matter of something having gone badly, as of something not having gone well.

It seems deeply plausible, though this may be controversial, that there is an intrinsic difference between a doctor surgically treating cleft palate and a doctor attaching a prehensile tail to a person. Yet under certain circumstances, both could result in an equal improvement of quality of life. For instance, suppose that you live in a poor area where there is a very high unemployment rate, but having a prehensile tail would enable you to find a form of employment that keeps you from starving to death. One way to see the difference is that we would talk about surgical 'correction' of cleft palate, but we would not talk of the attachment of a prehensile tail as a 'correction.' The former is akin to a work-around for a bug, where the bug remains but a way is found for the software to still do what one wants it to, whereas the latter is like an extension to the software.

Conversely, there seems to be a *prima facie* badness in parents genetically modifying the egg and sperm in such a way as to bring it about that the resultant person should have cleft palate, which badness would not be shared in by, or would not be shared in the same way by, the actions of parents who found that their genes were such as to produce a child with a prehensile tail and who had the genetic material modified to remove this possibility. This is true even should it be the case that the community was such that the child and the community would be much better off with the child having the tail. For instance, imagine that local dress codes were such that the child and parents could ensure that no one would find out about the tail until the child grew up, thereby avoiding teasing, and that in adulthood the tail would greatly improve the child's quality of life and contribution to the community.

This suggests that there is an analogy not just between our DNA and computer programs, but between this DNA and those computer programs that support a distinction between bugs and non-bugs. But those computer programs that support such a distinction are precisely those that are *designed* by an intelligent agent. Hence, by analogy, our DNA is probably designed by an intelligent agent.

Insofar as the designer of our DNA would have to be a highly sophisticated intelligent agent, this is a teleological argument. Moreover, if one thinks that there is strong evidence that our DNA evolved under the guidance of apparently naturalistic processes from the DNA of an initial simple organism, then this intelligent agent has to be the sort of being that is capable of intentionally producing our DNA through such processes. Now while a pretty smart Tau Cetian *might* be able to design human DNA from scratch, to set things up so that human beings would arise through a billion years of apparently naturalistic processes *and yet* be the product of design would take more than just a pretty smart alien. If the processes behind evolution are in fact essentially deterministic, it would seem to require a being capable of predicting ahead of time the results of a billion years of such processes. If the processes essentially exhibit quantum randomness, then the being would have to be either capable of predicting how indeterministic processes would turn out, no mean feat, or of affecting the outcomes of quantum mechanical experiments, again a difficult task. Thus, the intelligent being would have to be quite powerful and/or intelligent indeed.

4   Some objections

i. 'The distinction between genetic disorders and non-defects is purely subjective.' This simply denies my basic intuitions here. If these are denied, then the argument indeed fails. But it is important to see the manifold consequences of such a view. It threatens, for instance, to undercut the distinction between a doctor's enhancing something and a doctor's correcting something, a distinction particularly important to HMOs and to societies with socialized medicine, and indeed one with far-reaching consequences in medical ethics. Likewise, it destroys the rational basis for our common social attitudes toward genetic disorders, attitudes that imply that there is a special badness in producing them. These attitudes, in fact, apply not just in the case of humans, but in the case of animals, though there, depending on our views on animal experimentation, we may not take the badness to imply indefeasible claims of moral illiceity.

ii. 'This argument for a designer is circular, because if the notion of a bug depends on the programmer's intentions, then the notion of a genetic disorder depends on the designer's intentions, and so we cannot know that something is a genetic disorder unless we already know that there is a designer.' This may be seen as a variant of the first objection, attempting to get out of my argument simply by denying or casting into doubt the obvious fact that there are genetic disorders. Moreover, this response neglects the lesson learned from the computer case that one can figure out that something is a bug *without* direct access to the programmer's intentions, on the evidential grounds that are not the same as the truth grounds.

iii. 'If the universe is created by God, why are there any genetic disorders? Are not genetic defects an argument against the existence of God?' This is not an argument against the conclusion of the argument I give in this chapter, namely that there is a designer, but an argument against what the reader may conjecture to be my ultimate concern – making plausible the existence of God. The question of why God permits there to be genetic disorders is only relevant to arguing against the conclusion of *this* chapter if there is a good argument from the claim that the species here on earth are designed by an intelligent being to the claim that there is a God.

But I will bite, since *in persona propria* I think there is a God and I suspect, though I do not so argue here, that an argument for the existence of God could be given if one combined the argument from analogy to designed programs with other theistic arguments.

One can expand on the worry about God and genetic defects in two different ways. First, that if defectiveness depends solely on God's intentions, then if God intends something to happen, it is not a defect. But if God is the creator of the universe, then he intends the features we call 'genetic defects or disorders' to be exemplified. Hence, they are not defects, and the argument is undercut. This argument, however, neglects the fact that intentions are an intensional phenomenon. One can intend something under one description and not under another. Thus, a programmer working under a deadline may release a buggy program, knowing it is buggy, and intending that this program be the one that is sold. The bugs are, nonetheless, bugs. The programmer's intention to release *this build of this program* does not filter through to an intention to release *this buggy build of this program*, which would make the bugs intentional and indeed endanger their status as bugs. Furthermore, as we saw, the relationship between the programmer's intentions and the notion of a bug is actually not as simple as it might seem at first sight.

Secondly, it may be argued that God does not operate under such limitations as programmers do, and hence has no excuse for non-intentionally present bugs. This leads to the second argument, namely what sort of excuse a perfectly good being would have for producing a world containing genetic defects. Conceptually, we might start by noting that having a genetic disorder is only *prima facie* bad, or that having such a disorder need not be a violation of any rights that the beings subject to these disorders have, and need not even be instances of God's being less than perfectly kind to creatures, especially if it could be argued that the beings would not have existed without these disorders.[3] If one is pressed further for the sorts of reasons that God would have for permitting such disorders, one is thereby pushed into the realm of theodicy. And for that, alas, there is no room in this chapter. All I can do is point toward what I consider to be the most plausible philosophical candidates for theodicies, the cumulative theodicy of Alston[4] and the Irenaean theodicy of Hick.[5]

iv. 'The distinction between genetic defects and non-defects is purely statistical.' But if so, then if Einstein's high intelligence is genetically grounded, it is a defect since it is statistically abnormal. If anything more needs to said about this absurdity, it is to point the reader to Kurt Vonnegut's story 'Harrison Bergeron' about a future where everyone who is above average at anything is handicapped to ensure average functioning.

v. 'Evolutionary natural selection gives us a way of distinguishing between genetic disorders and bugs. We can take a genotype as *correct* provided that it has been selected for through the selective benefits of its associated phenotype, and this notion of correctness is sufficient for underwriting judgments of genetic defectiveness or non-defectiveness.'

Unfortunately, this story, and ones like it, do not do justice to how we use terms like 'genetic disorder' or 'genetic abnormality' (Plantinga has made this point in the case of proper function[6]). For instance, suppose that Lucy has, for genetically grounded reasons, slightly sharper vision than any human being has ever had before, and we are considering Lucy before she has any children. The DNA code responsible for the incremental improvement in vision has *not* been selected for through the selective benefits of its associated phenotype, viz., the improvement in vision, because natural selection has not yet had a chance to work. At this point, then, it appears that we cannot say that the relevant parts of the DNA are correct.

One might try to remedy the problem by adverting to the future and saying that a genotype is correct if it *will* be selected for. However, it is implausible to suppose that judgments of genetic abnormality depend on contingent future events. Moreover, this solution has the even more implausible consequence that if Dr Evil deliberately forces people who exhibit something that we would all consider a genetic disorder – say, genetic coding producing congenital blindness – to reproduce while inhibiting the reproduction of others, then not only will this genotype *become* correct because it will be selected for, which itself may not be plausible, but it will *have been* correct even before Dr Evil embarked on his cacogenic project. If it is retorted that a distinction between artificial selection and natural selection must be made, and only genotypes selected for or about to be selected for via *natural* selection count as correct, then we get the implausible conclusion that dogs are genetically incorrect insofar as they differ from wolves. Moreover, one can replace Dr Evil with an unconscious and unintelligent robot that exhibits the behavior that Dr Evil in fact exhibited. Since the robot is unintelligent, it will not behave in all counterfactual situations the way Dr Evil does, but that should not matter unduly here as long as the robot is capable of ensuring the success of the cacogenic project.

Nor will it do to replace actual future natural selection with merely potential natural selection, by saying that the genotype is correct if it could be selected for, since any genotype that does not render the organism that has it utterly incapable of reproduction could be selected for – and kin selection effects might even allow for that.

But perhaps we can get around the counterexample of Lucy by saying that while the incremental improvement in the sharpness of her vision was not selected for, having sharp vision was naturally selected for, and the genetic basis of a quantitative improvement in a feature selected for by natural selection *also* counts as correct. The notion of 'improvement' here is perfectly straightforward: If a genotype g was selected for because it produced a phenotype *f* which aided the passing on of the genotype by fulfilling function *F*, where the function *F* is something that comes in degrees, like moving quickly or seeing sharply or thinking creatively, then we can talk of genotypes that lead to a quantitative improvement in *f*'s fulfilling *F*.

This does mean, however, that if Lucy had eyesight and none of her ancestors did, then because this would not be a merely quantitative improvement, Lucy's eyesight would still be genetically abnormal. Now, it would be very strange to call the eyesight genetically *defective*. But the defender of natural selection as definer of defectiveness can say that a genetic *disorder* is not just any genetic *abnormality*, but rather an abnormality that confers a selective disadvantage. This would imply that should there be a situation where cleft palate does not confer a selective disadvantage, it would not be a genetic disorder but only a genetic abnormality, no matter how much suffering it caused the individual, and this surely is not right. Nor will it do to say that a genetic disorder is a genetic abnormality that *would have* conferred a selective disadvantage had it occurred in an ancestral organism. For it may be that Lucy's ancestors, by chance unlike Lucy, lived in a dark area of the ocean where sight would only be a disadvantage – yet another thing that could go wrong and cause confusion.

vi. 'Perhaps, though, there is a *metaphysical* matter of fact about an organism or natural kind as to what is natural to members of that natural kind. Objectively, for instance, an organism might have an Aristotelian substantial form that does not merely supervene on the arrangement of matter in the organism, and that form could specify what is a defect and what is not. This does not conceptually require a designer and hence shows a disanalogy with the computer program case.'

This objection, however, while showing one disanalogy highlights a central part of the analogy, namely, the lack of supervenience of normative defect/bug claims on the descriptions of the stuff constituting the organism/program.

Furthermore, one would like there to be an explanation for why it is that at some point the descendants of two animals of one species should be of a different species, with different normative properties. At some point in the evolutionary history a transition was made from being the sort of organism in which *g* was abnormal to being the sort of organism in which *g* was normal. Saying that the claims about normalcy depend on deep Aristotelian metaphysical facts about the animals does not answer the question of how *these* metaphysical facts came about.

It may well be possible to explain why the DNA of the descendant organism was as it was. We can just cite the mutations and recombinations that led up to this. But to explain why that descendant organism had one kind of substantial form rather than another is surely beyond the competence of a science at all like ours. Yet, surely, it is also not a coincidence or a merely brute fact that change at the normative level – for example, change from one kind of form to another – accompanied the change in the molecular structure. This gives strong plausibility to supposing that there *is* an explanation of the change in the normative features, and that the explanation is not scientific in nature. But following an insight going back to Swinburne,[7] the only other kind of explanation than the scientific that we know of is explanation in terms of the agency of an intelligent person. Moreover, no ordinary person that we know of has the power to effect this kind of change at the objective normative level, for example, to bring it about that an organism has one substantial form rather than another. We can only bring about changes at the physical level, for example, in breeding, and then *somehow* changes at a normative level may follow (e.g., in the case of dogs descending from wolves). It seems like a radically different kind of being than us would be needed to instill substantial forms and set things up so that an organism would have one kind of substantial form rather than another.

Could one claim as an alternative that just as there are contingent laws of physics, so too there are contingent laws of the normative realm that have no further explanation? It seems to me that to stretch the idea of laws of nature to a realm as different as the normative is from the descriptive would seem quite a stretch indeed. Moreover, the coordination between the physical and normative laws, so that normative change would be appropriately correlated with physical change in DNA would also have to be explained, for once a species' physical DNA arrangement evolves into a very different DNA arrangement, we surely have reason to think that there has been a normative change, too.

5 Flourishing and genetic disorders

The basic conceptual difficulty seems to come from the fact that we have two different normative measures for genes of animals. On the one hand, there is the notion of natural selection, so that a gene counts as correct if it is selected for, or would be selected for, or will be selected for, or something like that. On the other hand, there is the notion of flourishing, and we might say that a gene is correct if it contributes to flourishing. It is clearest in the case of humans that the two notions need not go together, but this is also true in the case of non-human animals. Consider an animal that breeds poorly in captivity but is tasty to humans. If the animal develops in such a way as to be better capable of breeding in captivity, then it is likely to become the subject of factory farming, which will lead to large scale genetic success for the species. If, however, the animal continues to be incapable of breeding in captivity, its species may be genetically less successful. But at the same time, if one thinks that factory farming does not contribute to the flourishing of the animals thus farmed, at least with the animals considered in and of themselves,[8] this is a case where the same feature would detract from flourishing and yet be a selective advantage.

Moreover, it appears that our ordinary notion of genetic disorder is more closely tied to the notion of flourishing than to genetic success. Observe, for instance, how those who believe that homosexuality does not impede the living of a flourishing human life will also insist that even if homosexuality is genetically grounded it does not constitute a genetic disorder, and would insist on this even if in fact it were to turn out to impede genetic success. Of course, homosexuality might not impede genetic success once one accounts for kin selection effects and the like, but the judgment by those advocating gay rights that homosexuality is not a genetic disorder is not made on the basis of such empirical claims about genetic success, but on the basis of their (controversial) intuitions about human flourishing. Likewise, those who believe that homosexuality does impede a flourishing human life will conclude that if homosexuality is genetically grounded, then it is a genetic disorder.

Yet, nonetheless, it is not the case simply that a genetic disorder is a genetically grounded feature that fails to contribute to the flourishing of the organism. It is not a genetic disorder for me to lack wings or superhuman intelligence, even were it shown that I would flourish more were I to have wings or such intelligence. Nor will it do to respond to this example by saying that wings could not help me to flourish *humanly*. Plainly they could. In Hayao Miyazaki's anime film *Kiki's Delivery Service*, a 13-year-old witch starts a delivery service, flying errands on her broom. As we watch the film, we see how Kiki grows as a *human being* through how she deals with issues arising from her magical skill. If she had wings instead of magic, much the same plot could be used. One can grow and flourish humanly with the help of features not normal to humanity.

Nor can we set some 'standard' level of flourishing for an organism and say that a genetic disorder is a genetically grounded feature that moves one below that level. After all, one can have a genetic disorder and stay far above any 'standard' level of flourishing.

But perhaps we can define a genetic disorder as a feature that in its *direct* effect decreases our human flourishing. My not having wings does not directly decrease my flourishing, though it may indirectly do so. However, even this is not so plausible. For instance, the *direct* effect of our having a pain center in the brain, no doubt a genetically grounded feature, is our feeling pain, and it is plausible that feeling pain directly decreases human flourishing, even though it perhaps remotely increases flourishing by informing us about damage to our bodies, and even more remotely does so by making possible aspects of virtues such as courage. And yet our having a pain center is surely a *normal* feature of us, not a bug. Likewise, the direct effects of my heartbeat are (a) movement of blood through the heart, which does not contribute to my flourishing directly but only indirectly once the blood moves through the rest of my body, as well as (b) the using up of energy, which perhaps contributes negatively to my flourishing. It does not appear possible to separate out the direct and the indirect effect in a way that makes for a viable distinction between the normal and abnormal.

So defining the notion of a genetic disorder or defect purely in terms of our flourishing also fails, just as defining bugs in terms of the good that computer programs achieve failed. The analogy between DNA and designed programs, then, is quite tight. In fact, one can argue that in experiments – which have been done – where computer programs arise purely through simulated natural selection processes, precisely the same conceptual issues arise for the notion of a 'bug' as we saw coming up for a natural selection account of a genetic disorder or defect. It would seem that in such contexts, the notion of a bug or disorder would be inapplicable, unless perhaps it is defined in terms of the intentions of the experimenters who set up the virtual evolutionary system.

If in fact the notion of a genetic disorder *is* applicable to us and other species – and a significant part of our normative reasoning about medicine depends on this in our case – we do have a tight analogical argument for the species on earth being designed. And hence there is a designer. What is this designer like? No doubt highly intelligent and, if the Aristotelian account of teleology holds, very different ontologically from us. What more can we say? That would be the subject for another paper. And is the idea of a designer compatible with the empirical data we have in favor of evolution? That depends on whether one construes evolution in such a way as to make it be incompatible with the existence of design behind the process.[9]

Notes

1. www.plkr.org
2. See bugs.plkr.org
3. Cf. Robert M. Adams, 'Must God Create the Best?', *Philosophical Review* **81** (1972), pp. 317–32.
4. William P. Alston, 'The Inductive Argument from Evil and the Human Cognitive Condition', *Philosophical Perspectives* **5** (1991), pp. 29–67.
5. *Evil and the God of Love*, revised version (New York: Harper and Row, 1978).
6. Alvin Plantinga, *Warrant and Proper Function* (New York: Oxford University Press, 1993).
7. 'The Argument From Design,' *Philosophy* **43**, (1968) pp. 199–212
8. Certain theists think that the *telos* of non-human animals is to serve humans, and so in some sense the flourishing of the animals may be promoted through factory farming.
9. Cf. my 'How Not to Reconcile the Creation of Human Beings with Evolution,' *Philosophia Christi*, **9** (2007), pp. 145–163.

5
The 'Why Design?' Question

Neil A. Manson

Given all of the attention the design argument has received both from philosophers and the general public, the idea that a key premise of it usually escapes scrutiny seems incredible. Yet typically the claim that the evidence of design is highly probable given the design hypothesis is both taken for granted by defenders of the design argument and unchallenged by critics of the design argument. Instead, the debate focuses on whether the alleged evidence of design is real or bogus and on whether there are or are not plausible alternative naturalistic explanations of that alleged evidence. But even assuming a designer exists, why should that lead us to expect the evidence of design in the first place? Why think the designer would design anything? Let us refer to this as the 'Why design?' question. As the import of the 'Why design?' question emerges in the course of this chapter, we will see how and why it is neglected in the literature on the design argument and consider what can be done to remedy the situation.

1 Bayesian design arguments and how the 'why design?' question arises for them

Although in centuries past David Hume (1970 [1779]) and William Paley (1963 [1802]) framed the design argument as an argument from analogy, nowadays design arguments are almost always fit within some probabilistic inferential structure. This is true of both of the leading current versions of the design argument: the argument from alleged cases of irreducible complexity in biology and the argument from the apparent fine-tuning for life of the fundamental parameters of physics. The exact nature of the inference underlying any one of these probability-based design arguments is a matter of considerable debate, however, with a choice amongst three types of inference: Bayesian, likelihood, and classical statistical.[1] The solid consensus within the professional philosophy literature on the design argument is that the inference underlying the design argument is Bayesian. As it turns out, it is only for Bayesian versions that the 'Why design?' question is pressing.

To see the differences amongst the three types of inference, the following notation will prove helpful. Let the conditional probability of some proposition A on some other proposition B be expressed as P(A|B). Let (E) stand for some proposition regarding the alleged evidence of design. Let (K) stand for some proposition summing up the background knowledge relevant to assessing that evidence. Finally, let (D) stand for the hypothesis that there exists a supernatural intelligent designer. With this notation in place, we can distinguish Bayesian, likelihood, and classical statistical design arguments in terms of the claims about conditional probability asserted in them.

The proponent of a Bayesian design argument makes three claims about conditional probability and then draws a conclusion. (1) If there is no designer, the probability of the evidence of design is very low given our background knowledge. (2) If there is a designer, the probability of the evidence of design is quite high given our background knowledge. (3) The prior probability of there being a designer is considerably higher than the probability of the evidence of design conditional on there being no designer and given our background knowledge. So, given the evidence of design, and our background knowledge, the probability that there is a designer is quite high. We can represent this argument generically as follows.

The Generic Bayesian Design Argument

(1) $P(E|K \& \sim D) \approx 0$
(2) $P(E|K \& D) >> 0$
(3) $P(D|K) >> P(E|K \& \sim D)$
∴ $P(D|K \& E) >> 0$

On the likelihood version, the conclusion is more modest – not that a designer probably exists, but that whatever one's personal probability was for there being a designer prior to discovering the evidence of design, one should revise one's personal probability upward in light of the new evidence.[2] That is, on the likelihood version, premises (1) and (2) of the generic Bayesian version are effectively conjoined to form an inequality: $P(E|K \& D) >> P(E|K \& \sim D)$. Meanwhile, premise (3) is not asserted, and the conclusion is simply that $P(D|K \& E) >> P(D|K)$.

Lastly, classical statistical versions of the design argument attempt to rule out non-design hypotheses on the grounds that the probability of the evidence conditional on any of them is extremely low. In effect, the sole premise retained from the generic Bayesian design argument is (1). The conclusion that a designer exists supposedly follows simply from the fact that the design hypothesis D is the only remaining alternative – the last hypothesis standing. We can make this inference, according to proponents of this version, without any formal reference whatsoever to $P(E|K \& D)$.[3]

How do these points connect with the 'Why design?' question? Well, the question 'What is the probability of E given K and D?' is answered differently depending on which form of inference is used in a given design argument. With Bayesian versions, the answer is 'high.' With likelihood versions, the answer is 'higher than the probability of E given K and the denial of D.' And with classical statistical versions, no answer needs to be given. But the 'Why design?' question just is the question of why we should believe that the probability of E given K and D is high. Since only on Bayesian versions is it asserted that the probability of E given K and D is high, it is only Bayesian versions of the design argument that interest us in this chapter. The 'Why design?' question simply does not arise for classical statistical versions of the design argument.

The 'Why design?' question also does not arise for likelihood versions, but for a more subtle reason. Someone advancing a likelihood version of the design argument can always dodge the 'Why design?' question by simply stipulating without further argument that among the putative designer's characteristics is a set of desires guaranteed to render probable the particular evidence of design on offer. Graham Oppy nicely articulates the problem with this approach in the following comments on the Bayesian design argument from cosmic fine-tuning for life.

> [I]t is not immediately obvious to me that the probability adverted to in the second premise [P(E|K & D)] should be said to be 'quite high.' Given only the hypothesis that there is an intelligent designer of a universe – and given no further assumptions about the *preferences* of that designer – it is not clear to me that there is very much that one can conclude about the kind of universe that the designer is likely to produce. Moreover, it is not obvious that one can meet this alleged problem by 'bulking up' the hypothesis of design, that is, by adding claims about the preferences of the designer to the hypothesis that there is an intelligent designer, since, at least *prima facie*, it seems plausible to suppose that any such additions will drive down the *a priori* probability that the hypothesis in question is true.
>
> (Oppy, 2006, p. 207)

Oppy is pointing to a basic dilemma facing any Bayesian version of the design argument. Attributing, without any justification, the property 'having a desire to design' to the designer drives down the prior probability of the design hypothesis and thus puts pressure on premise (3) of the generic Bayesian design argument. Not attributing the property 'having a desire to design' to the designer drives down the conditional probability of the evidence of design on the design hypothesis and thus puts pressure on premise (2). It is this basic dilemma that makes the 'Why design?' question so pressing for the proponents of any Bayesian design argument.

This dilemma, however, will not confront any likelihood version of the design argument, since such a version does not include premise (3).

Remember, likelihood versions only try to get us to revise our beliefs in light of the evidence of design. They merely tell us that the probability we assign to D ought to be higher than it was before we considered E, not that it should be high. What the prior probability, and hence the posterior probability, for D should be is not something with which proponents of the likelihood version are concerned. Nothing intrinsic to likelihood versions forbids the 'bulking up' move mentioned by Oppy, and so the 'Why design?' question is not forced upon those advancing likelihood design arguments.[4] Only on Bayesian versions does the 'Why design?' question force itself.[5]

Before we proceed, a note is in order about the design argument and the design hypothesis as they are typically presented by contemporary philosophers. The 'official' story of the design argument – the story philosophers typically give when covering arguments for the existence of God in their introductory textbooks – has it that the design argument is only the first stage in a two-stage argument to the existence of God. Call these stages 'the existence stage' and 'the identification stage.' In the existence stage, arguments are given for the existence of an otherwise-unspecified supernatural intelligent designer. In the identification stage, further arguments are given for identifying that designer with God.[6] Other classic arguments for the existence of God – for example, the cosmological argument and the moral argument – also supposedly follow this two-stage process. In all three cases, the 'official' strategy is first to prove the existence of a being partially matching the standard description of God ('first cause of the universe,' 'necessarily existing concrete being,' or 'ultimate standard of morality') and then to mount further arguments for thinking any being meeting that description would be God. It is this first step that is the design argument proper, or the cosmological argument proper, or the moral argument proper. As we will see, however, deviation from the 'official' script is rampant in the literature on the design argument.

2 Non-philosophers on the 'why design?' question

Most of that literature was not written by trained philosophers. Physicists, biologists, theologians, lawyers, journalists, and even economists have entered the fray. Indeed, in terms of books sold, articles read, television programs viewed, radio programs heard, and Internet sites visited, the non-philosophers surely dominate the market. Thus if the 'Why design?' question is largely ignored, this can perhaps be attributed to a general lack of philosophical sophistication amongst the bulk of contributors to the literature. Still, a few of the non-philosophers address the 'Why design?' question in their work.[7] What do they say?

In a three-page chapter entitled 'The Expectations,' physicist Stephen Barr (2003) sets up the question of which set of expectations – the atheist's or the theist's – current science supports, with the next chapter showing that the evidence of fine-tuning confirms the theist's expectations and disconfirms the atheist's. In most of 'The Expectations' Barr documents the claim that atheists expect a pointless universe in which humans are unimportant. He spends just one paragraph (the first) discussing what kind of universe we would expect if God existed. He concludes that paragraph by saying 'from the religious perspective, it can be said that it was partly for the sake of the existence of rational, free creatures such as ourselves that God created the universe' (Barr, 2003, p. 115). But in that same paragraph, he equates 'the religious perspective' with the perspective of Jews and Christians. The question of why, exactly, we should expect a universe with rational, free creatures from God – aside from the fact that this is what Jews and Christians traditionally believe – is never taken up. Barr simply presupposes Judeo-Christian theology in answering the 'Why design?' question.

Kenneth Miller does the same. Miller, a cell biologist, addresses the question of what kind of world we might expect God to create. His focus, however, is really on the more specific question of whether we might expect God to create a world in which evolution operates given that God wants to create a world in which free, rational creatures exist.

> All of the Western monotheistic religions maintain that God brought the universe into being, that He intended to create creatures deserving of a soul, and that He wished that universe to be a place in which those creatures had a truly free choice between good and evil, God and darkness. Given those theological basics, let's see where we can go.
>
> (Miller, 1999, p. 249)

Miller's 'theological basics' are essentially the same as Barr's. Like Barr, Miller never seriously questions them.

Rodney Holder, formerly an astrophysicist and now an ordained minister in the Church of England, addresses the question of the probability of the evidence (E_1) that a fine-tuned universe exists on the hypothesis (H_3) that there is a designer, assumed for the sake of argument to be something like the Christian God (Holder, 2004, p. 93). Note that the notations E_1 and H_3 are Holder's, not mine. He consciously frames the design argument from fine-tuning as a Bayesian inference, and so is no doubt aware of how crucial it is to support the claim that would be premise (3) of a Bayesian design argument: $P(E_1|H_3) >> 0$. Here is what he says.

> It is harder to judge, given a designer, what the probability is that he would create a fine-tuned universe. But if the designer is something like the Christian God, we would expect him to exercise his creativity, and we would expect him to do so by creating as 'interesting' a universe as possible, so most likely a universe with life – a universe containing life might

well be a good which God would will to bring about. The probability of E_1 given H_3 will then be high, let us say $P(E_1|H_3) = 0.9$.

(Holder, 2004, p. 99)

Here Holder's answer to the 'Why design?' seems a bit less orthodox than that of Barr and Miller. For Holder, the creation of a fine-tuned universe is to be expected from any designer like God, not specifically because a fine-tuned universe is a prerequisite for the existence of free, rational beings, but more generally because a fine-tuned universe is as 'interesting' a universe as possible and God would want such a universe to exist. Holder presumes a universe containing life is very 'interesting' and so concludes God would probably create a life-friendly universe. Why we should expect God to be interested in creating an 'interesting' universe is never explained.

Lastly, paleontologist and noted science essayist Stephen Jay Gould raises the 'Why design?' question, but only to respond to it with a host of other questions – his point being that there is no way to answer them.

If disembodied mind does exist (and I'll be damned if I know any source of scientific evidence for or against such an idea), must it prefer a universe that will generate our earth's style of life, rather than a cosmos filled with diprotons? What can we say against diprotons as markers of preexisting intelligence except that such a universe would lack any chroniclers among its physical objects? Must all conceivable intelligence possess an uncontrollable desire to incarnate itself eventually in the universe of its choice?

(Gould, 1998, p. 190)

Notice the general skepticism about the very idea of disembodied mind. This is a theme that will emerge from the philosophers critical of the design argument. Notice also the skepticism regarding the value judgment of Barr and Miller that, other things being equal, it is much better for a universe to have intelligent observers in it than not.

In each case, the passage quoted represents the maximal engagement of the author with the 'Why design?' question. In each case, this maximal engagement is only a paragraph. And these were the only cases I could find of non-philosophers engaging with the 'Why design?' question in any way. Since I do not know that the authors in my sample represent the entirety of non-philosophers writing on the design argument, the following suggestions are only tentative. First, amongst non-philosophers, the 'Why design?' question is largely overlooked by both proponents and critics of the design argument. Second, the answer to the 'Why design?' question is taken by non-philosophers writing in favor of the design argument to be a theological question – a question about God in particular rather than supernatural designers in general. Only Gould, the skeptic in this case, treats the design hypothesis to be about 'disembodied mind' in general rather than God in particular. Apparently the non-philosophers are just not interested in the 'official' script for the design argument, because they almost all present the inference from design in nature to God as direct. Third, the non-philosopher proponents of the design argument regard the answer to the theological question 'Why would God design a world like ours?' as obvious enough that it needs little or no reply. A wave of the hand to 'theological basics' is sufficient to dispense with the question. These 'theological basics,' moreover, seem to be drawn from revealed – as opposed to philosophical or 'natural' – theology; Barr refers to 'the religious perspective,' Miller to 'the Western monotheistic religions,' and Holder to our conception of the Christian God. This is in violation of the rule that no design argument should presuppose the truth of any particular scripture or religion (on the grounds that to do so would beg the question). Finally, the non-philosopher critics of the design argument regard theological questions such as 'Why would God design a world like ours?' as beyond their competence at best and meaningless at worst, and find the very idea of a disembodied mind's acting in or on this world to be very strange, if not incoherent. This explains why such critics typically just move on to other questions and issues when criticizing the design argument.[8]

3   Philosophers critical of the design argument on the 'why design?' question

When we turn to the writings of professional philosophers, we find a slightly different pattern. With one notable exception (Richard Swinburne), those promoting the design argument tend to offer no more in answer to the 'Why design?' question than do their non-philosopher counterparts. On the other hand, those critical of the design argument do raise the question, but only to argue that we humans have no way to answer it. Their answer to the 'Why design?' question is that $P(E|K \& D)$ is inscrutable, not that it is low. As with my conclusions about the non-philosophers, I do not know whether my sample of philosophers is representative, so the generalizations I draw in the two sections below are advanced only tentatively. Since it is the philosophers critical of the design argument who most often engage the 'Why design?' question, let us begin with them.

The thrust of Jan Narveson's argument for the unanswerability of the 'Why design?' question is that the lack of limits on putative universe-designers – 'bodiless minded super-creators,' he calls them (Narveson, 2003, p. 99) – removes any basis we might normally have for answering questions about an agent's methods and motivations. For example, he regards William Paley's famous 'watchmaker' analogy as flawed because humans have an obvious need to tell time, but a designer has no obvious need for a universe. 'In the absence of any possible use for a watch, the hypothesis that humans must have invented them is not plausible,' he argues (Narveson, 2003, p. 92). 'In the absence of any motive for creating a universe, we likewise have no explanation of the Universe in the hypothesis of a creator.'

In response, the proponent of the design argument may argue that we surely have *some* insight into the motives of a putative designer because we know some designers – namely, ourselves. We can infer human design without knowing exactly what the human designer's motives were, so we can do the same with supernatural designers. Narveson anticipates this response, claiming that behind the inference to human design is considerable knowledge about humans, but that we have no such knowledge of supernatural designers and no way of getting it. '[W]e have, again by hypothesis, no independent mode of verification or source of information,' he says (Narveson, 2003, p. 95). 'The inference to gods is pure, in the sense that there is no independent way of observing the entities being invoked, nor any processes by which their motives or ways of doing things may be understood.' In this position, the 'Why design?' question is unanswerable.

> . . . . . in order for the [design] explanation to have any content, we need to know something that is not often addressed: *why* is this being supposed to have done this? Consider that a being of this type already knows everything there is to know, so he can hardly have created the world to satisfy his curiosity. And since he has no body, no senses, and no needs in any usual sense of the word, where are we to get the psychological premises we would require in order to make an inference to his creative activity plausible?
>
> (Narveson, 2003, p. 96)

Narveson goes so far as to suggest that the design hypothesis is consistent with the existence of any possible universe. 'No matter what the Universe is like, it could have been created by a super-creator who, for some utterly unknowable reason, just wanted to create one of those, precisely the way it is' (Narveson, 2003, p. 97).

Elliott Sober gives essentially the same argument for thinking the 'Why design?' question is unanswerable (Sober, 2003, pp. 38–41). We need evidence of 'the goals and abilities of the putative designer' for the design argument to work. In order for the argument not to be question-begging, this evidence must be independent of the assumption that the allegedly designed feature of the world (for example, the vertebrate eye) was in fact designed and is thus 'special' in some way. But, by the nature of the case, we can have no such evidence.

> When we behold the watch on the heath, we know that the watch's features are not particularly improbable on the hypothesis that the watch was produced by a designer who has the sorts of *human* goals and abilities

with which we are familiar. This is the deep and nonobvious disanalogy between the watchmaker and the putative maker of organisms and universes. We are invited, in the latter case, to imagine a designer who is radically different from the human craftsmen we know about. But if this designer is so different, why are we so sure that he would build the vertebrate eye in the form in which we find it?

(Sober, 2003, pp. 38–9)

One specific disanalogy between the inference to a human designer on the one hand and the inference to a supernatural designer on the other is that human designers are biological beings. Knowing that some minded being is a material thing produced by an evolutionary process, Sober suggests, actually provides us with a background of knowledge from which we can estimate the probabilities of various bits of evidence conditional on the existence of that minded being. This is the point of Sober's discussion of SETI, the Search for Extraterrestrial Intelligence (Sober, 2003, pp. 39–41).

I suspect that SETI engineers are on much firmer ground than theologians. If extraterrestrials evolved by the same type of evolutionary process that produced human intelligence, that may provide useful constraints on conjectures about the minds they have. No theologian, to my knowledge, thinks that God is the result of biological processes. Indeed God is usually thought of as a *super*natural being who is radically different from the things we observe *in* nature. The problem of extraterrestrial intelligence is therefore an intermediate case, lying somewhere between the watch found on the heath and the God who purportedly shaped the vertebrate eye (but much closer to the first). The upshot of this point for Paley's design argument is this: *Design arguments for the existence of human (and human-like) watchmakers are often unproblematic; it is design arguments for the existence of God that leave us at sea.*

(Sober, 2003, pp. 40–1)

Note that in this passage Sober switches to talking about God and theologians rather than otherwise-unspecified designers and the psychology of them. Sober himself acknowledges this (Sober, 2003, p. 41). This supports the claim that, even amongst philosophers, not many follow the 'official' script for the design argument throughout their discussions.

Other philosophers critical of the design argument go a bit farther even than Narveson and Sober, arguing that we not only cannot know the preferences of a supernatural designer, but that the very idea of a supernatural designer is incoherent. For example, Niall Shanks says that before we even consider evidence in favor of the design hypothesis, 'we must minimally ensure that the claim is meaningful' – which it is not, he thinks. Shanks suggests the idea of a supernatural mind affecting the natural world is 'incoherent babble,' as meaningful as a science fiction story according to which 'Captain Shanks . . . . hit the accelerator on the snagglefarg drive, thus warping his ship into Jabberwocky space' (Shanks, 2004, pp. 213–4). Presumably, Shanks thinks the idea is incoherent for all the standard Philosophy 101 reasons materialists think dualistic interactionism is incoherent. However, Shanks also advances the weaker claim of Narveson and Sober against the design argument – that the design hypothesis just does not predict anything. 'In the case of supernatural intelligent designers of unknown constitution using unknown methods and materials to unknown ends,' he says (Shanks, 2004, pp. 170–1), 'we have neither independent evidential warrant nor even mere explanatory utility.' Again, 'Postulating a supernatural designer (assuming it even makes sense to do so) requires the introduction of a new type of object and causality into science: supernatural causes and supernatural objects,' he says (Shanks, 2004, p. 219). 'These latter are matters we know absolutely nothing about.' Shanks thinks his brief against the design argument gets by on the weaker claim that the empirical consequences of the design hypothesis are inscrutable. The claim that the design hypothesis is incoherent is icing on the cake.

Generalizing from the cases of Narveson, Sober, and Shanks, we can say first that philosophers who are critical of the design argument and who take up the 'Why design?' question (not that there are many such philosophers) typically presuppose a naturalist or materialist theory of mind and lean toward the position that substance dualism is incoherent. They just cannot make sense of the idea of a being's having beliefs, desires, goals, and preferences apart from its existing embodied and navigating a physical environment. This is why, for example, Narveson (2003, p. 99) says 'bodiless minded super-creators are a category that is way, way out of control,' whereas Sober (2003, p. 41) thinks even the mere fact of their being material things that were produced by an evolutionary process constrains our expectations of extraterrestrials. Second, these critical philosophers assume the design hypothesis has substance dualism built into it. Narveson, Sober, and Shanks (as well as Gould) all think the designer being argued about has to be a disembodied mind to do the explanatory job it is supposed to do. Third, setting aside whether the design hypothesis is even coherent, they just do not see any reason to think a supernatural intelligent designer would create a universe like ours or create specific structures within the universe.

4 Philosophers promoting the design argument on the 'why design?' question

Let us now turn to philosophers who promote the design argument, beginning with Robin Collins. He formulates the fine-tuning design argument as a likelihood argument. The conclusion is merely that 'the fine-tuning data provide strong evidence to favor the design hypothesis over the atheistic single-universe hypothesis' (Collins, 1999, p. 53), not that the design hypothesis is probably true. Still, his argument is of interest here because the first premise of it is that 'the existence of the fine-tuning is not improbable under theism' (Collins, 1999, p. 53). What is his support for this premise – the premise that P(E|K & D) is much greater than zero? He addresses this question in a section of the paper entitled 'Support for the Premises.'

> Premise (1) is easy to support and fairly uncontroversial. One major argument in support of it can be simply stated as follows: *since God is an all good being, and it is good for intelligent, conscious beings to exist, it is not surprising or improbable that God would create a world that could support intelligent life.* Thus, the fine-tuning is not improbable under theism, as premise (1) asserts.
>
> (Collins, 1999, p. 54)

This is all Collins has to say about the matter. We see here the same pattern in Collins that we saw with the non-philosopher supporters of the design argument. The design argument is actually treated as an argument in support of theism, and so the 'Why design?' question is a question about what God would be expected to do. Furthermore, the answer to it is 'easy to support and fairly uncontroversial' – indeed, so uncontroversial that the answer only runs one sentence.

William Dembski is also a philosopher by training. In the very last section of (Dembski, 1999) he gives an answer to the 'Why design?' question. As with Collins and almost all of the non-philosophers who advance the design argument, he treats this as a question about what God would be expected to do.

> In closing this chapter I want to ask an obvious question. Why create? Why does God create? Why do we create? Although creation is always an intelligent act, it is much more than an intelligent act. The impulse behind creation is always to offer oneself as a gift. Creation is a gift. What's more, it is a gift of the most important thing we possess – ourselves. Indeed creation is the means by which a creator – human, divine, or otherwise – gives oneself in self-revelation. Creation is not the neurotic, forced self-revelation offered on the psychoanalyst's couch. Nor is it the facile self-revelation of idle chatter. Creation invests the creator's life in the thing created. When God creates humans, he breathes into them the breath of life – God's own life. At the end of the six days of creation God is tired – he has to rest. Creation is exhausting work. It is drawing oneself out of oneself and then imprinting oneself on the other.
>
> (Dembski, 1999, p. 234)

Theological questions abound. If God is omnipotent, then how can he ever get tired and need rest? And how is it a gift to make a person exists (rather than to give something to a person who already exists)? The silence makes the point. The author treats the 'Why design?' question as an afterthought – something to be tacked on at the end of the book rather than addressed at the very beginning.

It is somewhat misleading to characterize philosopher John Leslie as advancing the design argument, for the conclusion he favors drawing from the evidence of fine-tuning is that there exist 'creative ethical requirements' – platonic entities that nonetheless have quasi-causal efficacy – responsible for the existence of the universe. Leslie prefers a neoplatonic picture (one whereby the universe exists simply because it is good that the universe exists) over the traditional design picture (one whereby the universe exists because a person, possibly God, selects the universe for creation after recognizing that it is good that the universe exists). Indeed, Leslie suggests identifying God with the creative ethical requirement, meaning God is just our name for an abstract entity.[9] Nonetheless, in various writings of his Leslie does address the question of why God would design a universe. Here is a representative answer.

> The argument from design is really an argument *to* divine design from alleged signs of it. The idea is that the cosmos, as we can see by examining it, was selected for creation to serve a divine purpose, a purpose at least partially understandable because it is good. Leibnizian richness does enter into most people's thoughts about goodness. It is believed that a cosmos serving a divine purpose would have beauty, grandeur, etc.; but more basic, typically, is the belief that the cosmos would be good *through containing intelligent living beings*. I think that makes excellent sense.
>
> (Leslie, 2003, pp. 55–6)

Leslie devotes the rest of the paragraph to defending the claim that a universe displaying Leibnizian richness is intrinsically good, but only if that goodness is experienced from the inside – only if there are intelligent beings within that universe. Given the (unstated) premise that any divine being can be expected to create the good, we can conclude that God would be quite likely to create a universe well suited for the existence of intelligent observers.

Notice, however, that Leslie only comes up with an answer to the 'Why design?' question by assuming that the designer of interest is divine and that a divine being can be expected to create the good. I suspect Leslie allows his neoplatonism to seep in here when making the second assumption. If 'God' is just our name for the creative ethical requirement, and creative ethical requirements are truly requirements, then God *must* create the good, and so *a fortiori* God can be expected to create the good. But that argument is never really spelled out by Leslie, nor does he give reasons why God should be expected to create the good if the existence of intelligent living beings is not ethically required. Notice also that Leslie only comes up with an answer to the 'Why design?' question by assuming that the designer is divine rather than merely supernatural, very intelligent, and very powerful. Once again we see a philosopher indicating by his response that he thinks the only way to answer the 'Why design?' question is to depart from the 'official' script for the design argument by equating the design hypothesis with theism.

Lastly, we have Richard Swinburne, who gives a detailed Bayesian design argument (Swinburne, 2003), where E is the evidence of cosmic fine-tuning for life and D is the hypothesis that God exists.[10] He takes up the 'Why design?' question in an eight-page section entitled 'Why a world with human bodies is likely if God exists.' The short version of his argument is this: (i) it follows from God's nature that He will try to bring about a great amount of the greatest sort of good; (ii) bringing about a great amount of the greatest sort of good requires bringing about the existence of free beings; (iii) free beings need an arena in which to develop morally and inter- act socially; and (iv) this arena requires the creation of a fine-tuned and law-governed universe. Let us focus here on premise (i). A key move in his argument for this premise actually occurs in an endnote (Note 8), so both the passage and the endnote are included below.

> So our question must be – in so far as it is logically possible for God to determine what sort of a world there shall be, what sort of a world will He bring about?(8) A perfectly good being will try to realize goodness as much as He can. So in so far as there is a unique best possible world, God will surely make it. If there is no one best of all possible worlds but a number of incompatible equal best worlds, He will surely make one of them. But if every possible world is less good than some other incompat- ible possible world, all that He can do in virtue of His perfect goodness is to create a very good world.
>
> (Swinburne, 2003, pp. 107–8)

(8) In Plantinga's terminology, the question is what kind of a world God will 'strongly actualize' (Plantinga, 1974, p. 173). I use the word 'world' to include all that exists apart from God, and its way of behaving – whether (in part or totally) indeterministic or determined by its intrinsic powers and liabilities to act codified in natural laws. A world may or may not include many universes. Possible worlds are, however, to be individuated, as stated in the text, only by those features which it is logically possible for an omnipotent being to bring about. In this terminology (which is not standard) a world counts as a possible world if God given only His omnipotence and not His other properties could bring it about.

> (Swinburne, 2003, p. 121)

Swinburne's argument rests on the claim that a perfectly good being will try to bring about the most good it can. In God's case, bringing about the good means actualizing a possible world. But notice how Swinburne defines 'possible world' – as including 'all that exists apart from God.' Swinburne admits that this terminology is not standard, and indeed it is not. On the standard definition of 'possible world,' possible worlds *include* God. They are maximal states of affairs, including necessary states of affairs as well as contingent ones (Plantinga, 1974, pp 44–5). Indeed, this conception of possible worlds is indispensable for the standard theological account of what it is for God to exist necessarily.[11] So Swinburne's argument that P(E|K & D) is high – that we can expect God to create a universe that is fine-tuned for the existence of intelligent life – depends on the non-standard definition of 'possible world' as 'possible divine creation' rather than 'possible maximal state of affairs.' Allowing Swinburne this move, the rest of his argument relies on standard theological claims: that God is perfectly good, that a perfectly good being would create the best possible world it could, and that having free, embodied beings in it is part of what makes the best world (or any of the best worlds) a very good world. Almost alone amongst philosophers defending the design argument, Swinburne clearly recognizes the importance of the 'Why design?' question and works hard to answer it.[12]

Generalizing from the cases of Collins, Dembski, Leslie, and Swinburne, it seems that, in practice, even philosophers who advance the design argument and take on the 'Why design?' question (not that there are many such philosophers) do not follow the 'official' script. They do not think of the design argument as an argument for an otherwise-unspecified designer. They think of it as an argument for theism. Perhaps they think this because they think the only way to answer the 'Why design?' question is to make it a theological question. If this is what they think, however, then it is curious that they do not invoke the literature in philosophical theology addressing the questions of why God would create anything at all and of why God would create a world like the one we observe. Even Swinburne, in the section 'Why a world with human bodies is likely if God exists' (Swinburne, 2003, pp. 107–14), makes no reference to this literature. Overall, it seems that most philosophers advancing the design argument simply fail to take the 'Why design?' question seriously.

5 How to address the 'why design?' question more profitably

The preceding literature survey reveals that a crucial premise in the Bayesian version of the design argument is generally neglected by all sides. How to remedy this situation? To make sure the 'Why design?' question comes up, it would help if anyone either advancing or criticizing a Bayesian version of the design argument were to address the following set of clarifying questions.

1   Does the design argument in question follow the 'official' script?

If so, proceed to question 2. If not, then the design argument in question is presumably a direct argument for the existence of God, and since God is immaterial, it is an argument that requires that substance dualism be coherent. In that case, skip ahead to question 4.

2   Is the design hypothesis being advanced exclusively about supernatural beings?

As we originally stated it the design hypothesis is the hypothesis that there exists a *supernatural* intelligent designer. However, according to some authors, the design hypothesis would be true if it turned out that some other material beings were responsible for the evidence of design. Michael Behe suggests as possible designers 'space aliens from Alpha Centauri,' for example (Behe, 2003, p. 277). The hypothesis of the existence of such a 'natural' designer might explain the evidence of design when that evidence is not some fact about the universe as a whole (for example, that its fundamental physical parameters are fine-tuned for life) but rather some particular fact about the arrangement of matter within the local part of the universe (for example, that certain organisms on this planet are 'irreducibly complex'). An example of such a hypothesis is the 'directed panspermia' idea of Francis Crick and Leslie Orgel – 'the theory that organisms were deliberately transmitted to the earth by intelligent beings on another planet' (Crick and Orgel, 1973, p. 341).

If natural designers are an option for the design argument, we could perhaps gain independent insight into their preferences and motives for the reasons Sober gave in connection with SETI, and so we might have a way to answer the 'Why design?' question. The possibility of a natural designer generally gets neglected in the literature on the design argument, however, and rightly so. On the 'official,' two-stage version of the design argument, it must at least be possible for the designer inferred at the first stage to be identified with God at the second stage, but that seems impossible if the designer is a natural, embodied entity and God is an immaterial spirit. In the context of the 'official' design argument, then, it seems right to proceed on the assumption that the designer in question is a supernatural being.

3   Does the design argument require that substance dualism be coherent?

It may seem obvious that substance dualism would have to be true for the supernatural design hypothesis to be true. Some precision is in order here, however. To say that a supernatural intelligent designer exists is just to say that there exists an intelligent designer that is outside *this* order of nature, outside of *this* universe. Might a supernatural intelligent designer occupy its own natural order and be a natural mind within that natural order rather than be a pure spirit? This possibility has in fact been suggested by several physicists. They think we might create a black hole in the laboratory and thereby create another universe (Krulwich, 2006), and they entertain the thought that our universe might itself be the product of an experiment by some scientist from another universe (Holt, 2004). Such a scientist would seem to count as a supernatural intelligent designer, though a material one. This scenario is consistent with the denial of substance dualism. There would be one kind of stuff – matter – and minds would necessarily be material things. Yet minds in one universe could give rise to other material universes. [Philosophers will have grave problems with causal interactions between universes, but the physicists do not seem to be bothered by the idea.] Whether those creations would subsequently be inaccessible to their creators is an open question. Andrei Linde (Krulwich, 2006) worries that the creator would be unable to communicate with the inhabitants of the universe it created, but he also suggests (Holt, 2004) that making the created universe just right for life ('manipulating the cosmic seed in just the right way') could itself count as a communication to certain of its inhabitants – namely, the physicists!

The physicists who broach this idea almost always raise the 'Why design?' question, although in this case the question they ask is not 'Why would a designer make our universe?' but 'Why would *we* design *some other* universe?' Maybe the 'Why design?' question arises more naturally when we put ourselves in the role of the creator, or maybe physicists are more prone to ask obvious philosophical questions than philosophers are. In any case, the problem with the hypothesis of a supernatural material designer is the same as the problem with the hypothesis of a this-worldly natural designer. Insofar as the supernatural physicist is a material being living in a world with laboratory instruments such as particle accelerators, it cannot be identified with God. Thus the possibility of supernatural material designers cannot be considered within the first stage of any 'official' design argument. The design hypothesis will have to be the hypothesis that a supernatural *immaterial* intelligent designer exists. In order for that hypothesis even to be capable of confirmation, substance dualism will have to be coherent.

4 Assuming the design argument requires the coherence of substance dualism, is substance dualism in fact coherent?

Would-be critics of the design argument who answer 'yes' or 'maybe' should move on to (5). But those who answer 'no' would greatly help the discussion of the design argument – both in the academic arena and in the public arena – if they would just come out and say that the design argument is a non-starter. As we saw in section III of this chapter, design critics such as Shanks believe that substance dualism is incoherent and that only naturalistic theories of mind make sense. If they believe this, they should just announce that the design argument is an argument to an impossible conclusion and be done with it. Their refutations of the design argument would only be a matter of a few paragraphs. Perhaps this is what most of the critics *do* think. It would explain their impatience with the design argument – an impatience that shines through the writing of Shanks, Narveson, Gould, and many others.

Why do design critics not respond in this way? Here are two possible reasons. First, they might worry that it would be a very bad public relations move. Typically books seeking to refute the design argument are directed towards the general public – rightly so, since much of social and political consequence hangs on the success or failure of the design argument. Yet most ordinary citizens are dualists. Resting one's objections to the design argument on a contrary theory of mind is a guarantee of poor book sales and a recipe for defeat in the raging battles over 'intelligent design.' Second, presupposing the incoherence of substance dualism is just not very satisfactory philosophically. It makes the status of the design argument hang on a much deeper debate – a debate that itself divides philosophers in a way that somewhat overlaps with the pro-design/anti-design split. So even if the only concern of the critics is to address the philosophical community, resting their case on the incoherence of substance dualism is unlikely to change any minds. 'Better I show flaws in the evidence, or alternative explanations of the evidence,' think critics to themselves, 'than rely on a view of mind that turns off the general public and already divides philosophers into hardened camps.'

5   What basis is there for attributing the relevant desires and preferences for designing to an otherwise-unspecified supernatural immaterial intelligent designer?

For design critics Oppy, Gould, Narveson, Sober, and Shanks, the answer is 'none.' Design proponents, meanwhile, always seem to address (6) rather than (5). The basic problem is that answering (5) requires 'bulking up' the design hypothesis, yet the 'bulking up' strategy confronts any Bayesian design argument with the dilemma mentioned in section I of this chapter. This is an intractable problem for any Bayesian design argument and therefore a good reason to give up on the 'official' script for one. A key lesson of this chapter is that the design hypothesis needs to be the hypothesis that the most perfect being exists for any Bayesian design argument even to get off the ground. From the concept of a perfect being, we can deduce the properties of moral perfection and omniscience. Starting with the concept of a being that is morally perfect and omniscient gives us at least some prospect of figuring out what that being is apt to do. This approach does not beg the question so long as those engaged in it fill out their concept of the most perfect being with the help of philosophical or 'natural' theology rather than revealed theology.

6   Why think the most perfect being would design? What could the purpose be?

Spinoza thought the answer was 'none,' arguing that the idea of an abso-lutely perfect being's having preferences and desires is incoherent. He claimed that 'if God acts with an end in view, he must necessarily be seek-ing something that he lacks' (Spinoza, 1982 [1677], p. 59). If an allegedly perfect being acts to fulfill a goal or purpose, the being must be incomplete and, thus, imperfect. Other philosophers skeptical of the design argument are more modest. Tim Mawson accepts the coherence of the idea of God's designing something but claims to see no reason why God would do so.

> [W]hat reason *could* God have to create anything (a lifeless universe; a uni-verse fine-tuned for life; a set of non-physical angelic beings; anything)? Being God, it's not as if any of these things could fulfil some previously unsatisfied need of His and their not existing prior to His creating them means that they themselves could hardly be said to have previous require-ments met by their being created.....This is not to suggest that God could not have created the World because it would have been positively *un*reasonable for Him to do so. Sometimes, we do things for no reason at all and this doesn't make our doing them *un*reasonable. But it is to suggest that the best account on Theism might well be that whilst God's free choice explains why this universe exists, that God made this choice, rather than another, is something for which there is no explanation.
>
> (Mawson, 2005, p. 149)[13]

In support of Mawson's point, observe that, contrary to Swinburne, pos-sible worlds are not the same things as possible creations. Possible worlds include God, whereas possible creations are simply possible worlds consid-ered apart from all of the necessary beings (concrete or abstract) existing in them. A world consisting of God alone (plus universals/abstract objects such as sets, propositions, and so on) seems to be a possible world. Indeed, Chris-tian theists are committed to the idea that a world consisting of God alone is a possible world, given that they believe God is the free creator *ex nihilo* of all contingent concrete entities. To say that God might not have created anything is just to say that there is a possible world consisting of God alone. What would be wrong with that world? Nothing, apparently. Indeed, it is quite plausible to think that if God is the greatest conceivable being, then a world consisting of God alone is the best of all possible worlds (with no other worlds even tied for the best). If Swinburne is right that 'in so far as there is a unique best possible world, God will surely make it' (Swinburne, 2003, p. 107), God will make it be the case that nothing but God exists. God will design nothing and create nothing. And assuming it is unreasonable for God to do anything less than the best, then (contrary to Mawson) it would indeed be positively unreasonable for God to create.[14] Even if we do not go this far, however, it is hard to see how a world consisting of God alone could be in anything less than a first-place tie for the title 'best possible world.' That, in itself, is enough to think there is no good answer to (6).

However, the proponent of a Bayesian design argument decides to respond to (6), that answer should be developed in light of the relevant literature in philosophical theology. Two strands of discussion seem particularly relevant. The first (and smaller) strand addresses the questions of whether God should be expected to create anything at all and, if so, why God would create a world like this one. The richest contributions to these questions in the literature are from Norman Kretzmann (Kretzmann, 1991a, 1991b, 1999), who addresses them from a Thomistic perspective. Other philosophers who have tackled the question of why God would create anything at all include (Teske, 1988) and (Nozick, 1989, pp. 217–35). The second, larger strand addresses the questions of whether there is or is not a best of all possible worlds and what implications the answer to this question has for traditional doctrines such as divine moral perfection and divine freedom. The seminal paper in this area is Adams (1972). It has given rise to a host of replies; the bibliography in Rowe (2004) gives a thorough and up-to-date catalogue of the relevant literature.[15] Both strands involve tackling profound philosophical questions regarding the nature of the good as well as the conflict between freedom and necessity. For various reasons, almost all of the participants in the current debate over the design argument dodge these profound philosophical questions. I hope this chapter serves as a call to action for philosophers addressing the design argument: start doing theology.[16]

Notes

1. In earlier work I described the last sort of inference as 'Fisherian' or as a 'significance test' inference. The description 'classical statistical' is due to Graham Oppy. For explication of all three of these options, see Manson (2003, pp. 5–8) and Oppy (2006, pp. 202–16).
2. For a full presentation of the likelihood version, see Sober (2003). See also Oppy (2006, pp. 208–9) for criticism of the likelihood version.
3. For a defense of the classical statistical approach, see Dembski (1998). For a particularly trenchant criticism of the classical statistical approach, see Fitelson, Stephens, and Sober (1999). See also Oppy (2006, pp. 211–16).
4. Oppy talks of 'bulking up' the design hypothesis; Sober talks of conjoining various specific claims about the goals and abilities of a designer with the generic hypothesis that there exists an intelligent designer. Sober criticizes this tactic (Sober, 2003, pp. 41–2) for leading to argumentative dead ends and for violating the injunction that, when evaluating scientific hypotheses, we should break apart conjunctions and scrutinize the conjuncts separately. Since these considerations against the 'bulking up' move seem extrinsic to the likelihood approach, however, I stick by my claim that likelihood versions of the design argument do not confront the dilemma Oppy points to.

5. Readers can judge whether this is a virtue or a vice of Bayesian versions of the design argument.

6. One example of this 'official' account of the design argument is Peter van Inwagen's presentation of the design argument from cosmic fine-tuning for life (van Inwagen, 1993, pp. 132–3). The two-stage strategy is also illustrated in Alexander Pruss's contribution to this volume. See his reply to objection (iii) in section 4 of 'Programs, Bugs, DNA, and a Design Argument,' where Pruss makes clear that the conclusion of his argument is not that God exists, but just that a designer exists.

7. My sample of works by non-philosophers on the design argument consists of books in my private collection. None were purchased or copied with an eye towards their contribution to the points I am about to make. The sample includes works by physicists promoting the design argument (Barr, 2003), physicists hostile to the design argument (Stenger, 2003; Edis, 2002), biologists advancing the design argument from irreducible complexity (Behe, 1996), biologists critical of the design argument from irreducible complexity but supportive of the design argument from fine-tuning (Miller, 1999), paleontologists opposed to any version of the design argument (Gould, 1998), pro-design lawyers (Overman, 1997) and journalists (Glynn, 1997), and even pro-design economists (Greenhut and Greenhut, 2002). The list of recent popular books on the design argument could surely be lengthened tenfold, especially given the rate of production of such books since the controversy over 'intelligent design theory' burst into the U.S. national spotlight in 2005 with the *Kitzmiller v. Dover* case. Miller is an interesting case. Even though the main purpose of his book is to rebut thoroughly the design argument from irreducible complexity in biology, he endorses the design argument from cosmic fine-tuning for life later in the book in a section entitled 'Stacking the Deck?' (Miller, 1999, pp. 226–32).

8. Design critic Victor Stenger does engage with theology substantially in his work (Stenger, 2003, Chapter 11), but for the sake of drawing out the conflicts between (and amongst) theistic evolutionists and traditional theists, not for the sake of claiming there is no reason at all for God to create a world.

9. Leslie develops this neoplatonic picture in a host of his works, but the picture is directly connected with the design argument from fine-tuning in Leslie (1989).

10. Unlike the other pro-design philosophers we have seen, Swinburne justifies his neglect of non-theistic design hypotheses on the grounds that all of them are more complicated than, and so have lower prior probabilities than, the hypothesis that God exists (Swinburne, 2003, p. 107).

11. The standard account of the claim that God exists necessarily is that God exists in every possible world. However, some philosophers argue that God's necessary existence is merely the impossibility of being either caused to exist or caused to cease to exist – a property sometimes referred to as 'causally necessary existence.' The most notable proponent of the view that God's necessary existence is best understood as causally necessary existence and not logically necessary existence is John Hick (Hick, 1967).

12. Another such philosopher is Tim Mawson, who devotes several pages to the question 'Why think that a universe fine tuned for life would be more likely on the hypothesis that there is a God than it would be on the hypothesis that there is not?' (Mawson, 2005, p. 146).

13. I did not know of Mawson's recent work until he called it to my attention in comments on the penultimate version of this chapter. In those comments, he

agrees that there just is no adequate response to the 'Why design?' question in the literature. His second professional opinion supports the claim that the 'Why design?' question is largely neglected in the literature on the design argument.

14. Tim Chappell develops an argument on these very lines for the conclusion that if the God of orthodox Christianity exists, then no consequentialist ethical theory is true (Chappell, 1993). Leon Pearl thinks Chappell's argument suggests an argument for the non-existence of God from the existence of concrete contingent entities, and takes this result as a *reductio* of Chappell's argument (Pearl, 1994). Interestingly, Pearl concludes that, contrary to traditional Christian theism, God *must* create because if He does not, then He will not be able to express all of the virtues that a perfect being should possess.

15. Rowe's book itself is a testimony to the lasting interest in Adams's question amongst philosophers of religion. Rowe argues, controversially, that if there is just one best of all possible worlds, then God does not create freely, while if there is an infinite series of better and better worlds, then if God creates any world, God cannot be morally perfect.

16. I thank Tim Mawson and Robert Westmoreland for numerous helpful comments on the drafts of this chapter. I also thank Yujin Nagasawa and Erik Wielenberg for inviting me to contribute to this volume.

References

R. M. Adams, 'Must God Create the Best?,' *The Philosophical Review* 81 (1972), 317–32

S. M. Barr, *Modern Physics and Ancient Faith* (Notre Dame, Indiana: University of Notre Dame Press, 2003)

M. J. Behe, *Darwin's Black Box: The Biochemical Challenge to Evolution* (New York: Simon & Schuster, 1996)

M. J. Behe, 'The Modern Intelligent Design Hypothesis: Breaking Rules,' in N. A. Manson, ed., *God and Design: The Teleological Argument and Modern Science* (London: Routledge, 2003), 277–91

T. D. J. Chappell, 'Why God is Not a Consequentialist,' *Religious Studies* 29 (1993), 239–43

R. Collins, 'A Scientific Argument for the Existence of God: The Fine-Tuning Design Argument,' in M. Murray, ed., *Reason for the Hope Within* (Grand Rapids, Michigan: Eerdmans, 1999), 47–75

F. H. C. Crick and L.E. Orgel, 'Directed Panspermia,' *Icarus* 19 (1973), 341–6

W. A. Dembski, *The Design Inference: Eliminating Chance Through Small Probabilities* (Cambridge: Cambridge University Press, 1998)

W. A. Dembski, *Intelligent Design: The Bridge between Science & Theology* (Downers Grove, Illinois: InterVarsity Press, 1999)

T. Edis, *The Ghost in the Universe: God in Light of Modern Science* (Amherst, New York: Prometheus Books, 2002)

B. Fitelson, C. Stephens, and E. Sober, 'How Not to Detect Design – Critical Notice: William A. Dembski, *The Design Inference*,' *Philosophy of Science* 66 (1999), 472–88

P. Glynn, *God: The Evidence* (Rocklin, California: Prima Publishing, 1997)

S. J. Gould, 'Mind and Supermind,' in J. Leslie, ed., *Modern Cosmology and Philosophy* (Amherst, New York: Prometheus Books, 1998), 187–94

M. L. Greenhut and J. G. Greenhut, *Science & God: Our Amazing Physical and Economic Universe – Accidental or God Created?* (Lanham, Maryland: University Press of America, 2002)

J. Hick, 'A Critique of the "Second Argument",' in J. Hick and A. McGill, eds, *The Many-Faced Argument* (New York: MacMillan, 1967), 341–56

R. D. Holder, *God, the Multiverse, and Everything: Modern Cosmology and the Argument from Design* (Hampshire, England: Ashgate, 2004)

J. Holt, 'The Big Lab Experiment: Was Our Universe Created by Design?,' *Slate*, posted Wednesday, May 19, 2004 at 10:59 AM EST (http://www.slate.com/id/2100715)

D. Hume, *Dialogues Concerning Natural Religion* (Indianapolis: Bobbs-Merrill Educational Publishing, 1970 [1779])

N. Kretzmann, 'A General Problem of Creation: Why Would God Create Anything at All?,' in S. MacDonald, ed., *Being and Goodness: The Concept of the Good in Metaphysics and Philosophical Theology* (Ithaca, New York: Cornell University Press, 1991a), 208–28

N. Kretzmann, 'A Particular Problem of Creation: Why Would God Create This World?,' in S. MacDonald, ed., *Being and Goodness: The Concept of the Good in Metaphysics and Philosophical Theology* (Ithaca, New York: Cornell University Press, 1991b), 229–49

N. Kretzmann, *The Metaphysics of Creation: Aquinas's Natural Theology in Summa contra gentiles II* (Oxford: Clarendon Press, 1999)

R. Krulwich, 'Build Your Own Universe,' broadcast on National Public Radio's 'All Things Considered,' November 27, 2006 (http://www.npr.org/templates/story/story.php?storyId=6545246)

J. Leslie, *Universes* (London: Routledge, 1989)

J. Leslie, 'The Meaning of Design,' in N. A. Manson, ed., *God and Design: The Teleological Argument and Modern Science* (London: Routledge, 2003), 55–65

N. A. Manson, 'Introduction,' in N.A. Manson, ed., *God and Design: The Teleological Argument and Modern Science* (London: Routledge, 2003), 1–23

T. J. Mawson, *Belief in God: An Introduction to the Philosophy of Religion* (Oxford: Clarendon Press, 2005)

K. R. Miller, *Finding Darwin's God: A Scientist's Search for Common Ground between God and Evolution* (New York: HarperCollins, 1999)

J. Narveson, 'God by Design?,' in N. A. Manson, ed., *God and Design: The Teleological Argument and Modern Science* (London: Routledge, 2003), 88–104

R. Nozick, *The Examined Life* (New York: Simon & Schuster, 1989)

G. Oppy, *Arguing About Gods* (Cambridge: Cambridge University Press, 2006)

D. L. Overman, *A Case against Accident and Self-Organization* (Lanham, Maryland: Rowman & Littlefield Publishers Inc., 1997)

W. Paley, *Natural Theology* (Indianapolis: Bobbs-Merrill Educational Publishing, 1963 [1802])

L. Pearl, 'God Had to Create the World,' *Religious Studies* 30 (1994), 331–3

A. Plantinga, *The Nature of Necessity* (Oxford: Clarendon Press, 1974)

W. L. Rowe, *Can God Be Free?* (Oxford: Oxford University Press, 2004)

N. Shanks, *God, the Devil, and Darwin: A Critique of Intelligent Design Theory* (Oxford: Oxford University Press, 2004)

E. Sober, 'The Design Argument,' in N. A. Manson, ed., *God and Design: The Teleological Argument and Modern Science* (London: Routledge, 2003), 27–54

B. Spinoza, *The Ethics*, in S. Shirley, trans. and S. Feldman, ed., *The Ethics and Selected Letters* (Indianapolis: Hackett, 1982 [1677])

V. J. Stenger, *Has Science Found God? The Latest Results in the Search for Purpose in the Universe* (Amherst, New York: Prometheus Books, 2003)

R. Swinburne, 'The Argument to God from Fine-Tuning Reassessed,' in N. A. Manson, ed., *God and Design: The Teleological Argument and Modern Science* (London: Routledge, 2003), 105–23

R. J. Teske, 'The Motive for Creation According to Saint Augustine,' *The Modern Schoolman* LXV (1988), 245–53

P. van Inwagen, *Metaphysics* (Boulder, Colorado: Westview Press, 1993)

6
Divine Command Theory and the Semantics of Quantified Modal Logic

David Efird

In this chapter, I consider divine command theory (DCT) as a theory of the nature of the properties of moral rightness and of moral wrongness.[1] As such, DCT gives a metaphysical analysis of these properties: what it is to be morally right is to be commanded by God, and what it is to be morally wrong is to be forbidden by God.[2,3] This analysis then generates the following universally quantified strict biconditionals:

(RIGHT) $\qquad\qquad\qquad\qquad \forall\varphi\Box(R\varphi \equiv Cg\varphi)$

(WRONG) $\qquad\qquad\qquad\qquad \forall\varphi\Box(W\varphi \equiv Cg \sim \varphi)$

where 'φ' ranges over actions, such as going to fight at the front, and '$\sim \varphi$' stands for 'refraining from φ',[4] 'R' stands for the predicate '—— is morally right', 'W' stands for the predicate '—— is morally wrong', 'C' stands for the relation '—— commands ——', where the first term of the relation stands for an agent and the second term stands for an action type, 'g' is a singular term standing for God, and 'x forbids φ' is true just in case 'x commands $\sim \varphi$'. RIGHT and WRONG are the central axioms of DCT considered as a theory of the nature of moral rightness and wrongness. In order to fill out DCT as an axiomatic theory, it is necessary to supplement RIGHT and WRONG with further axioms concerned with, among other things, what God can command. In this essay, I offer a series of axiomatic formalizations of DCT motivated by certain methodological considerations. Given these considerations, I present what I take to be the best axiomatization of DCT, an axiomatization which requires a non-standard semantics for quantified modal logic.

1 The basic theory: DCT1

To begin, in order for DCT to be substantial and to have at least some plausibility, the theory must entail that there are some things which are right and some things which are wrong. In order to secure this entailment, we need an axiom to the effect that there are some things which God commands and some things which he forbids.

(COM&) $(\exists\varphi Cg\varphi \ \& \ \exists\varphi Cg\sim\varphi)$

Given that RIGHT and WRONG are modal claims, we should consider the modal status of COM, that is whether COM is necessarily true

(□COM&) $\Box(\exists\varphi Cg\varphi \ \& \ \exists\varphi Cg\sim\varphi)$

or COM is merely contingently true.

(CONTCOM&) $[(\exists\varphi Cg\varphi \ \& \ \exists\varphi Cg\sim\varphi) \ \& \sim \Box(\exists\varphi Cg\varphi \ \& \ \exists\varphi Cg\sim\varphi)]$

When the theorist is faced with this choice, it is methodologically desirable to maintain CONTCOM& rather than □COM&. The methodological principle which tells in favour of this choice is what might be termed 'Hume's Razor':

(HR)   Do not multiply necessities beyond necessity.[5]

'Beyond necessity' here means: more than is required in order to construct an adequate theory. An adequate theory is one which satisfies sufficiently many and sufficiently well all instruments of theory choice, such as Hume's Razor. Now it is unlikely that any theory will satisfy all such instruments sufficiently well. Consequently, we will have to make comparative judgements among theories which satisfy different instruments of theory choice differently well. So, we will have to judge that some instruments of theory choice are 'trumped' by others. For example, in selecting the best axiomatization of DCT, we might judge that satisfying Hume's Razor is trumped by satisfying some other instrument of theory choice, and we could, for instance, be driven to affirm □COM&. But with only Hume's Razor on the table, when faced with choosing between □COM& and CONTCOM&, we should choose the latter. A similar argument tells in favour of accepting the contingency of God's commanding at all

(CONTCOM∨) $[(\exists\varphi Cg\varphi \lor \exists\varphi Cg\sim\varphi) \ \& \sim \Box(\exists\varphi Cg\varphi \lor \exists\varphi Cg\sim\varphi)]$

over the necessity of his commanding.

(□COM∨) $\Box(\exists\varphi Cg\varphi \lor \exists\varphi Cg\sim\varphi)$

Given these arguments, it seems that we should accept initially that there are some things which God commands and some things which he forbids, but it is not necessary that he commands or forbids anything at all.

(CONTCOM&∨) $[(\exists\varphi Cg\varphi \ \& \ \exists\varphi Cg\sim\varphi) \ \& \sim \Box(\exists\varphi Cg\varphi \lor \exists\varphi Cg\sim\varphi)]$

Now there are two ways in which it is possible that there are no commands: when God remains silent and when God does not exist, given that commanding strictly implies existing.

$$(\Box\text{COMGOD}) \qquad \forall\varphi\Box\big[(Cg\varphi \vee Cg\sim\varphi) \to E!g\big]$$

Given these two ways in which there might have been no commands, the same methodological reasons which favour CONTCOM& and CONTCOM$\vee$ favour affirming that it need not have been that if God exists, he issues commands, and that though God does exist, he might not have done so.

$$(\sim\Box\,\text{GODCOM}) \quad \sim\Box\big[E!g \to (\exists\varphi Cg\varphi \vee \exists\varphi Cg\sim\varphi)\big]$$

$$(\text{CONTGOD}) \qquad E!g \,\&\sim\Box E!g$$

Given $\Box$COMGOD, we can bring CONTCOM, $\sim\Box$GODCOM, and CONTGOD together into one axiom:

$$(\text{CONTCOM+}) \quad \big[(\exists\varphi Cg\varphi \,\&\, \exists\varphi Cg\sim\varphi) \,\&\, (\sim\Box\big[E!g \to (\exists\varphi Cg\varphi \vee \exists\varphi Cg\sim\varphi)\big] \,\&$$
$$\sim\Box E!g)\big]$$

It may be that we will end up denying CONTCOM+ because we are driven to accept $\Box$COM by other instruments of theory choice. But as CONTCOM+ is favoured by Hume's Razor, we should incorporate CONTCOM+ into the initial axiomatization of DCT. Similar considerations favour denying that there are any necessities concerning what God commands and what he does not command.

$$(\text{COMMANDS}) \quad \forall\varphi\big[(\Diamond\sim Cg\varphi \,\&\, \Diamond\sim Cg\sim\varphi) \,\&\, (\Diamond Cg\varphi \,\&\, \Diamond Cg\sim\varphi)\big]$$

Again, it may be that there is no adequate DCT which incorporates COMMANDS because any such theory generates theorems which offend other instruments of theory choice too egregiously. But, as Hume's Razor favours each of the conjuncts of COMMANDS, we should incorporate COMMANDS into the axioms. So to summarize, the axioms of the theory to be considered are:

$$(\text{RIGHT}) \qquad\qquad \forall\varphi\Box(R\varphi \equiv Cg\varphi)$$

$$(\text{WRONG}) \qquad\qquad \forall\varphi\Box(W\varphi \equiv Cg\sim\varphi)$$

$$(\text{COMGOD}) \qquad\qquad \forall\varphi\Box\big[(Cg\varphi \vee Cg\sim\varphi) \to E!g\big]$$

$$(\text{CONTCOM+}) \qquad \big[(\exists\varphi Cg\varphi \,\&\, \exists\varphi Cg\sim\varphi) \,\&\, (\sim\Box\big[E!g \to (\exists\varphi Cg\varphi \vee \exists\varphi Cg\sim\varphi)\big]$$
$$\&\sim\Box E!g)\big]$$

$$(\text{COMMANDS}) \qquad \forall\varphi\big[(\Diamond\sim Cg\varphi \,\&\, \Diamond\sim Cg\sim\varphi) \,\&\, (\Diamond Cg\varphi \,\&\, \Diamond Cg\sim\varphi)\big]$$

From these axioms we can derive two theorems which say, respectively, (i) that anything might have been right or not right, or wrong or not wrong, and (ii) that it might have been that nothing is either right or wrong:

(MORALCONT) $\qquad\qquad\forall\varphi\left[(\Diamond R\varphi \ \& \ \Diamond\sim R\varphi) \ \& \ (\Diamond W\varphi \ \& \ \Diamond\sim W\varphi)\right]$[6,7]

(MORALNIHIL) $\qquad\qquad\qquad\Diamond\forall\varphi(\sim R\varphi \ \& \sim W\varphi)$[8]

Let us call the theory characterized by the above axioms and the above two theorems 'DCT1'.

I take it that both of MORALCONT and MORALNIHIL are counter-intuitive; indeed, each conjunct of MORALCONT is counter-intuitive. It seems then, that in satisfying Hume's Razor, DCT1 offends another instrument of theory choice, an instrument which might be termed 'Moore's Razor':

(MR)   Do not contradict common sense beyond necessity.

We have already made use of Moore's Razor at the start of this section when we determined that in order for DCT to have any plausibility, it must entail that some things are right and some things are wrong, so we added COM& to the theory. Now in order to assess whether DCT1 really does contradict common sense beyond necessity, we need to consider other axiomatizations of DCT which do not entail MORALCONT and MORALNIHIL, and then judge the merits and demerits of these theories against each other. In what follows, I give four further axiomatizations of DCT, and I argue that the final axiomatization constitutes the best of the five DCTs.[9]

2   Brutally restricting what god can command: DCT2

If MORALNIHIL and each conjunct of MORALCONT are counter-intuitive, then it seems that in satisfying Hume's Razor we have done so at the expense of Moore's Razor. A straightforward way to reverse this situation is to preserve RIGHT, WRONG, and COMMGOD while denying each conjunct of COMMANDS[10] and also the second and third conjuncts of CONTCOM+. This theory is then:

(RIGHT) $\qquad\qquad\qquad\forall\varphi\Box(R\varphi \ \equiv Cg\varphi)$

(WRONG) $\qquad\qquad\qquad\forall\varphi\Box(W\varphi \ \equiv Cg\sim\varphi)$

$(\sim\&\text{COMMANDS})$ $\left[(\exists\varphi\Box Cg\varphi \ \& \ \exists\varphi\Box Cg\sim\varphi) \ \& \ (\exists\varphi\Box\sim Cg\varphi \ \& \ \exists\varphi\Box\sim Cg\sim\varphi)\right]$

From this theory, we can deduce the following theorems, which say, respectively, (i) that there are some moral necessities, that is some things which are necessarily right, some things which are necessarily not right, some things which are necessarily wrong, and some things which are necessarily not wrong; and (ii) that morality exists necessarily, that is that it is necessary that there is something that is right or something that is wrong:

(MORALNEC) $\qquad [(\exists\varphi\Box R\varphi\,\&\,\exists\varphi\Box\sim R\varphi)\,\&\,(\exists\varphi\Box W\varphi\,\&\,\exists\varphi\Box\sim W\varphi)]$[11]

(□MORALEX) $\qquad\qquad\qquad \Box(\exists\varphi R\varphi \lor \exists\varphi W\varphi)$[12]

These two theorems are the denials of MORALCONT and MORALNIHIL, respectively. Let us then call the theory characterized by these axioms and these two theorems 'DCT2'. DCT2 brutally restricts what God can command because it offers no ground for this restriction. In Dummett's (1991) terminology the facts,[13] assuming they are facts, that there are restrictions on what God can and cannot command are not 'reducible' to any other facts or set of facts in that they are not true in virtue of any other facts or set of facts; rather, they are 'barely' true. Now other things being equal, it would be desirable that these facts were not barely true because they limit what God can do. A strategy commonly employed to render plausible what seem to be limitations on God's power, for example his inability to create a stone which he cannot lift, is to appeal to God's nature and explain that these supposed limitations follow from his nature and therefore do not constitute limits on his power. Following this strategy, I present a DCT on which the facts, if they are facts, that there are restrictions on what God can and cannot command are reducible to, that is true in virtue of, facts about God's nature, in particular, being loving, and what it is to be loving.

3 Restricting what God can command by the nature of God: DCT3 and DCT4

In order to ground MORALNEC and □MORALEX, we will assume that God is necessarily loving, and that if someone is loving then that strictly implies that there are some things he must command, some things which he must forbid, some things which he cannot command, and some things he cannot forbid.[14] The axioms incorporating these assumptions would be:

(□LOVGOD) $\qquad\qquad\qquad\qquad \Box Lg$

(LOVCOM) $\qquad \Box\forall x(Lx \rightarrow \big[(\exists\varphi\Box Cx\varphi\,\&\,\exists\varphi\Box Cx\sim\varphi)\,\&\,(\exists\varphi\Box\sim Cx\varphi\,\&$

$\qquad\qquad \exists\varphi\Box\sim Cx\sim\varphi)\big])$

where 'L' stands for '—— is loving'. Now if we combine the above axioms with RIGHT and WRONG, we have the following axiomatization of DCT:

(RIGHT) $\qquad\qquad\qquad \forall\varphi\Box(R\varphi \equiv Cg\varphi)$

(WRONG) $\qquad\qquad\qquad \forall\varphi\Box(W\varphi \equiv Cg\sim\varphi)$

$$(\Box\text{LOVGOD}) \qquad\qquad \Box Lg$$

$$(\text{LOVCOM}) \qquad \Box\forall x(Lx \to [(\exists\varphi\Box Cx\varphi \;\&\; \exists\varphi\Box Cx\sim\varphi) \;\&\; (\exists\varphi\Box\sim Cx\varphi \;\&\;$$
$$\exists\varphi\Box\sim Cx\sim\varphi)])$$

From these axioms, we can deduce MORALNEC[15] and $\Box$MORALEX,[16] and so these claims are true in virtue of these axioms. Let us then call the theory characterized by these axioms and these two theorems 'DCT3'. DCT3 is clearly preferable to DCT2 because DCT3 grounds the limitations on God's power in God's nature and the nature of loving. Now is DCT3 preferable to DCT1? It is a difficult question as the virtues and vices of the two theories are equal and opposite. Whereas DCT1 entails MORALCONT and MORALNIHIL, which seem contrary to common sense, DCT3 does not, rather entailing their denials; whereas DCT3 contains necessities additional to RIGHT and WRONG, DCT3 does not. It is hard to say which is to be preferred, a theory which entails counter-intuitive consequences or one which has additional necessities. It would therefore be useful to have some further axiomatizations of DCT to consider.

4   Restricting what it is to be morally right and wrong by the nature of God: DCT4

Instead of restricting what God can command by his nature, one might instead restrict the metaphysical analysis of what it is to be right and wrong by his nature, in particular, by his being loving. On this account, we would have:

$$(\text{RIGHTLOV}) \qquad \forall\varphi\Box[R\varphi \equiv (Cg\varphi \;\&\; Lg)]$$

$$(\text{WRONGLOV}) \qquad \forall\varphi\Box[W\varphi \equiv (Cg\sim\varphi \;\&\; Lg)]$$

By adding to the theory the claim that being loving strictly implies that there are some things he must command, some things which he must forbid, some things which he cannot command, and some things he cannot forbid

$$(\text{LOVCOM}) \qquad \Box\forall x(Lx \to [(\exists\varphi\Box Cx\varphi \;\&\; \exists\varphi\Box Cx\sim\varphi) \;\&\; (\exists\varphi\Box\sim Cx\varphi \;\&\;$$
$$\exists\varphi\Box\sim Cx\sim\varphi)]$$

we can deduce

$$(\text{RIGHTCOM}) \qquad \forall\varphi\Box[R\varphi \equiv (Cg\varphi \;\&\; [(\exists\varphi\Box Cx\varphi \;\&\; \exists\varphi\Box Cx\sim\varphi) \;\&\; (\exists\varphi\Box\sim Cx\varphi \;\&\;$$
$$\exists\varphi\Box\sim Cx\sim\varphi)])]$$

$$(\text{WRONGCOM}) \qquad \forall\varphi\Box[W\varphi \equiv (Cg\Box\sim\varphi \;\&\; [(\exists\varphi\Box Cx\varphi \;\&\; \exists\varphi\Box Cx\sim\varphi) \;\&\; (\exists\varphi\Box\sim Cx\varphi \;\&\;$$
$$\exists\varphi\Box\sim Cx\sim\varphi)])]$$

Though the theory also does not entail MORALNEC, if we can take the necessities of the second conjunct of RIGHTCOM and WRONGCOM to correspond to what we would intuitively think would be necessarily right or wrong, then it seems we can avoid offending Moore's Razor here.

Difficulty arises, though, when we attempt to deal with the derivation of MORALNIHIL. It seems that the only way to deal with this difficulty is for the theory to entail $\Box$MORALEX. In order to do this, the most plausible move to make is to include in the theory the axiom that God is necessarily loving, and this then entails that he issues commands. So to summarize we have:

(RIGHTLOV) $\qquad\qquad\qquad\quad \forall\varphi\Box\big[R\varphi \equiv (Cg\varphi\ \&\ Lg)\big]$

(WRONGLOV) $\qquad\qquad\qquad\quad \forall\varphi\Box\big[W\varphi \equiv (Cg\sim\varphi\ \&\ Lg)\big]$

($\Box$LOVGOD) $\qquad\qquad\qquad\qquad\quad \Box Lg$

(LOVCOM) $\qquad \Box\forall x(Lx \rightarrow \big[(\exists\varphi\Box Cx\varphi\ \&\ \exists\varphi\Box Cx\sim\varphi)\ \&\ (\exists\varphi\Box\sim Cx\varphi\ \&$

$\qquad\qquad\qquad \exists\varphi\Box\sim Cx\sim\varphi)\big]$

Let us call this axiomatization 'DCT4'. But now given $\Box$LOVGOD, the restriction we built into the metaphysical analysis, namely, what it is to be morally right and morally wrong is determined not only by what God commands and forbids but also that he is loving, is otiose since God is necessarily loving. Consequently, DCT4 has no advantage over DCT3; rather, it is unnecessarily complicated in comparison with DCT3. Therefore, by Quine's Razor,

(QR)   Do not complicate theory beyond necessity.

DCT3 is to be preferred over DCT4. So, it seems we are still left with the choice between DCT1 and DCT3, a choice which is difficult to make since their virtues and vices seem to be equal and opposite.

There is, though, a way through this impasse. When faced with the choice between two theories whose virtues are equal and opposite, it is desirable to examine what assumptions are forcing this choice, and then to determine whether one of these assumptions can be denied plausibly in order to open up further possible theories for consideration. One such assumption forcing the choice between DCT1 and DCT3 is the assumption that the semantics we should employ to interpret the axiomatization of DCT is the standard, Kripkean semantics for quantified modal logic. There are, however, alternative semantics, in particular a Priorian semantics, which we can exploit in order to restrict the metaphysical analysis, thereby blocking the derivations of MORALCONT and MORALNIHIL, and so securing an advantage over DCT1 regarding Moore's Razor, but positing fewer necessities than DCT3, thereby securing an advantage over DCT3 regarding Hume's Razor.

5   The semantics of quantified modal logic: Kripkean and Priorian

On the standard, Kripkean (1963) semantics for quantified modal logic,

> □Fa is true iff Fa is true in all possible worlds.
> ◇Fa is true iff Fa is true in some possible world.

On this semantics, (i) for every possible world w, Fa has a truth value in w, regardless of whether a exists in w, (ii) the modal operators are duals,

(DUALS) $\Box Fa \equiv \sim \Diamond \sim Fa$

and (iii) the rule of necessitation,

(RN)   If A is a theorem, then so is □A.

is valid. This semantics validates a normal modal logic.

There is, though, an alternative, Priorian (1957), semantics for '□' which validates a non-normal modal logic, namely, Q.[17] On this Priorian semantics, we have

> □Fa is true iff Fa is true in every possible world and a exists in every possible world.
> $\sim \Diamond \sim$Fa is true iff Fa is true in every possible world in which a exists.
> ◇Fa is true iff Fa is true in some possible world in which a exists.

These clauses differ from the Kripkean clauses only on the assumption that a is a contingent existent. In explicating the differences between the Kripkean and Priorian semantics, we will therefore make this assumption. On the Priorian semantics, (i) Fa does not have a truth value in every possible world, in particular, Fa has no truth value in worlds in which a does not exist; (ii) given that a has some of its properties essentially, the modal operators are not duals since $\sim \Diamond \sim$Fa is true but □Fa is false; and (iii) given that there are logical truths about contingent existents, the rule of necessitation is not valid since there are no necessary truths whatsoever about contingent existents.

6   Restricting moral claims having truth-value by the nature of God: DCT5

Up to this point, we have been employing the standard, Kripkean semantics for interpreting the various axiomatizations of DCT proposed so far. So,

> □Rφ is true iff 'φ is morally right' is true in all possible worlds.
> ◇Rφ is true iff 'φ is morally wrong' is true in some possible world.

On this semantics, (i) for every φ and for every possible world w, Rφ has a truth value with respect to w, regardless of whether God exists, God commands, or God is loving in w; (ii) the modal operators are duals, such that $\Box R\varphi \equiv {\sim}\Diamond{\sim}R\varphi$; and (iv) the rule of necessitation is valid for formulas containing the predicates standing for '——— is morally right' and '——— is morally wrong'. In sum, the modal logic governing reasoning about moral rightness and wrongness is a normal modal logic, and its semantics is the standard Kripkean semantics.

As a way through the impasse of having to choose between DCT1 and DCT3, I propose replacing the standard Kripkean semantics with a suitably modified Priorian semantics which will suggest an axiomatization of DCT which seems to be preferable to both DCT1 and DCT3. In most general terms, the Priorian semantics has the following clauses:

> $\Box A$ is true iff A is true in every possible world and the presuppositions of A are true in every possible world.
> ${\sim}\Diamond{\sim}A$ is true iff A is true in every possible world in which the presuppositions of A are true.
> $\Diamond A$ is true iff A is true in some possible world in which the presupposition of A is true.

Following Adams (1973),[18] let us suppose that 'φ is morally right' and 'φ is morally wrong' presuppose that God is loving. Consequently, on a Priorian semantics for sentences containing the predicate '——— is morally right', we have the following clauses:

> $\Box R\varphi$ is true iff $R\varphi$ is true in all possible worlds and God is loving in every possible world.
> ${\sim}\Diamond{\sim}R\varphi$ is true iff $R\varphi$ is true in all possible worlds in which God is loving.
> $\Diamond R\varphi$ is true iff $R\varphi$ is true in some possible world in which God is loving.

and similarly for sentences containing the predicate '——— is morally wrong'. These clauses differ from the Kripkean clauses only on the assumption God is not necessarily loving. In explicating the differences between the Kripkean and Priorian semantics, we will therefore make this assumption. On the Priorian semantics, (i) $R\varphi$ does not have a truth value in every possible world, in particular, $R\varphi$ has no truth value in worlds in which God is not loving and consequently no truth value in worlds in which God does not exist;[19] (ii) given that some actions are essentially morally right, the modal operators are not duals since ${\sim}\Diamond{\sim}R\varphi$ is true but $\Box R\varphi$ is false; and (iii) given that there are logical truths about what is morally right, the rule of necessitation is not valid since there are no necessary truths whatsoever about what is morally right.

We can now explore some consequences of this semantics for the axiomatization of DCT. Given these semantics, we have:

$$(\sim\Box\text{MORAL}) \qquad \forall\varphi\big[(\sim\Box R\varphi\ \&\ \sim\Box\sim R\varphi)\ \&\ (\sim\Box W\varphi\ \&\ \sim\Box\sim W\varphi)\big]$$

but $\sim \Box$MORAL is not equivalent to MORALCONT on the Priorian semantics we are employing as it is on the Kripkean semantics. Indeed $\sim \Box$MORAL is consistent with there being some things which are essentially right, some things which are not possibly right, some things which are essentially wrong, and some things which are not possibly wrong:

(MORALESS) $[(\exists\varphi \sim \Diamond \sim R\varphi \ \& \ \exists\varphi \sim \Diamond R\varphi) \ \& \ (\exists\varphi \sim \Diamond \sim W\varphi \ \& \ \exists\varphi \sim \Diamond W\varphi)]$

Because MORALESS is intuitive, it seems the axiomatization of DCT should entail it. Similarly, on this theory, we have that it is not necessary that there is anything morally right or wrong

$(\sim \Box$MORALEX$)$ $\sim \Box(\exists\varphi R\varphi \lor \exists\varphi W\varphi)$

but $\sim \Box$MORALEX is not equivalent to MORALNIHIL on the Priorian semantics. Indeed, $\sim \Box$MORALEX is consistent with

(MORALESSEX) $\sim \Diamond \sim (\exists\varphi R\varphi \lor \exists\varphi W\varphi)$

MORALESSEX is also intuitive, so it too should be entailed by the axiomatization.

In order to secure MORALESS and MORALESSEX on this semantics, we need the following axioms:

(RIGHT) $\forall\varphi \sim \Diamond \sim (R\varphi \equiv Cg\varphi)$

(WRONG) $\forall\varphi \sim \Diamond \sim (W\varphi \equiv Cg \sim \varphi)$

(LOVCOM-) $\Box\forall x(Lx \to [(\sim Cx\varphi_{1\ldots j} \ \& \ \sim Cx \sim \varphi_{1\ldots k}) \ \& \ (Cx\varphi_{1\ldots m} \ \& \ Cx \sim \varphi_{1\ldots n})])$

where '$Cx\varphi_{1\ldots j}$ abbreviates '$Cx\varphi_1 \ \& \ Cx\varphi_2 \ \& \ldots Cx\varphi_j$', and these actions correspond to what we would intuitively would think that a loving being commands, and similarly for the other clauses.[20] Given this semantics and these axioms, secure MORALESS and MORALESSEX follow.

Before we complete this axiomatization, we should consider the semantics for modal sentences about God, which we should assume, is a contingent existent. We should, it seems, give a Priorian semantics for such sentences with the following clauses

> $\Box$Fg is true iff God satisfies '—— is F' in every possible world and God exists in every possible world.
> $\sim \Diamond \sim$Fg is true iff God satisfies '—— is F' in every possible world in which God exists.
> $\Diamond$Fg is true iff God satisfies '—— is F' in some possible world in which God exists.

where 'F' stands for a predicate of any adicy clauses. These clauses have the now usual consequences.

We can now complete the axiomatization, of DCT, which we will call 'DCT5':

(RIGHT) $\forall \varphi \sim \Diamond \sim (R\varphi \equiv Cg\varphi)$

(WRONG) $\forall \varphi \sim \Diamond \sim (W\varphi \equiv Cg \sim \varphi)$

(CONTLOV) $(Lg \mathbin{\&} \Diamond \sim Lg)$

(CONTGOD) $E!g \mathbin{\&} \sim \Box E!g$

(LOVCOM-) $\Box \forall x(Lx \to [(\sim Cx\varphi_{1\ldots j} \mathbin{\&} \sim Cx \sim \varphi_{1\ldots k}) \mathbin{\&} (Cx\varphi_{1\ldots m} \mathbin{\&} Cx \sim \varphi_{1\ldots n})])$

(CONTCOM&$\vee$) $\left[(\exists \varphi Cg\varphi \mathbin{\&} \exists \varphi Cg \sim \varphi) \mathbin{\&} \Diamond \sim (\exists \varphi Cg\varphi \vee \exists \varphi Cg \sim \varphi)\right]$

(COMMANDS) $\forall \varphi \left[(\Diamond \sim Cg\varphi \mathbin{\&} \Diamond \sim Cg \sim \varphi) \mathbin{\&} (\Diamond Cg\varphi \mathbin{\&} \Diamond Cg \sim \varphi)\right]$

The benefit of the semantics is now apparent. The restriction it places on the metaphysical analysis allows us to allow for contingency concerning God's existence and his nature along with his commands. This axiomatization, DCT5, together with the Priorian semantics is preferable to both DCT1 and DCT3 because DCT5 is consistent with Moore's Razor by entailing MORALESS and MORALESSEX at a cost of only one additional necessity, namely, LOVCOM-. Therefore, DCT5 together with a Priorian semantics for interpreting modal sentences about God, moral rightness, and moral wrongness is the best way of understanding divine command theory as a metaphysical analysis of the properties of moral rightness and of moral wrongness.

Acknowledgements

I wish to thank Greg Restall for very helpful comments on a previous draft of this essay.

Notes

1. This understanding of DCT is pioneered by Adams (1979) and developed further in Adams (1999).
2. For the notion of metaphysical analysis, see Dorr (2005, pp. 261–2). This notion should be contrasted with that of conceptual analysis, a kind of analysis which DCT does not plausibly provide.
3. I will pass over in silence the issue of whether the theory should be formulated in terms of the commands or the will of God and simply assume the former. For the purposes of this essay, nothing depends on this choice.
4. I take both of the following contexts, '——— is right' and 'God commands ———' to be intensional.
5. If our modal logic is S5, this will have to be restricted to the necessitations of non-modal claims, because in S5 p entails that it is necessarily possible that p.
6. Proof. From RIGHT, we have $\forall \varphi \Box (Cg\varphi \to R\varphi)$, which entails $\forall \varphi (\Diamond Cg\varphi \to \Diamond R\varphi)$. From COMMANDS, we have: $\forall \varphi \Diamond Cg\varphi$. We can then conclude $\forall \varphi \Diamond R\varphi$. From

RIGHT, we have $\forall\varphi\Box(R\varphi \to C\varphi g)$, which entails $\forall\varphi(\Box R\varphi \to \Box C\varphi g)$. From COMMANDS, we have $\forall\varphi\sim\Box C\varphi g$. We can then conclude $\forall\varphi\sim\Box R\varphi$, which is equivalent to $\forall\varphi \Diamond \sim R\varphi$. Similar reasoning yields $\forall\varphi \Diamond W\varphi$ and $\forall\varphi \Diamond \sim W\varphi$. We can then conclude $[(\forall\varphi \Diamond R\varphi \ \& \ \forall\varphi \Diamond \sim R\varphi) \ \& \ (\forall\varphi \Diamond W\varphi \ \& \ \forall\varphi \Diamond \sim W\varphi)]$, which entails $\forall\varphi[(\Diamond R\varphi \ \& \ \Diamond \sim R\varphi) \ \& \ (\Diamond W\varphi \ \& \ \Diamond \sim W\varphi))]$.

7. MORALCONT is, in effect, a formalization of Cudworth's (1996) objections to DCT, namely, that DCT entails that there are no necessary truths about moral rightness and wrongness and that any action might have been morally right or morally wrong. Two much discussed special cases of this objection are: If DCT is true, then it might have been right, and not wrong, for Abraham to have killed his son, Isaac, and it might have been wrong, and not right, for Abraham to refrain from killing his son, Isaac, similarly for torturing innocent children. RIGHT, WRONG, and COMMANDS make precise what is needed to derive this consequence; MORALCONT generalizes it.

8. Corresponding to the two ways in which there might have been no commands, there are two proofs for MORALNIHIL. Proof A. From CONTCOM+ we have $\Diamond[E!g \ \& \ \forall\varphi(\sim CG\varphi \ \& \ \sim Cg \sim \varphi)]$. Because '$\varphi$' ranges over action types, we can assume a constant domain semantics. Consequently, we can permute the quantifier and necessity operator, so from RIGHT we have $\Box\forall\varphi(R\varphi \to Cg\varphi)$ and from WRONG we have $\Box\forall\varphi(W\varphi \to Cg \sim \varphi)$. From these claims, we can now conclude $\Diamond\forall\varphi(\sim R\varphi \ \& \ \sim W\varphi)$. Proof B. From RIGHT, we have $\forall\varphi\Box(R\varphi \to c\varphi g)$. From COMGOD, we have $\forall\varphi\Box(C\varphi g \to E!g)$. Together these then entail $\forall\varphi\Box(R\varphi \to E!g)$. Because '$\varphi$' ranges over action types, we can assume a constant domain semantics for φ. Consequently, we can permute the quantifier and necessity operator, so we have $\Box\forall\varphi(R\varphi \to E!g)$. Similar reasoning yields $\Box\forall\varphi(W\varphi \to E!g)$. We can then conclude $\Box\forall\varphi[R\varphi \lor W\varphi) \to E!g)]$. This then entails $\Box[\exists\varphi(R\varphi \lor W\varphi) \to \Box E!g]$, from which we can conclude $[\Box\exists\varphi(R\varphi \lor W\varphi) \to E!g]$. From CONTCOM+, we have $\sim \Box E!g$. We can then conclude $\sim \Box\exists\varphi(R\varphi \lor W\varphi)$, which is equivalent to $\Diamond\forall\varphi(\sim R\varphi \ \& \ \sim W\varphi)$.

9. There are a very large number of alternative theories that could be constructed in the light of this tension between Hume's and Moore's Razors. I select the alternatives I judge to shed the most light on the dialectic.

10. For simplicity, I will not consider less radical alternatives which deny fewer than all of the conjuncts of COMMANDS. I do this because it seems that all of the conjuncts of MORALCONT stand or fall together, and if they are all to fall, then each conjunct of COMMANDS must be denied. If, however, one disagrees with this verdict, it is straightforward how to modify what follows in the light of this disagreement.

11. Proof. From $\sim$&COMMANDS, we have $(\exists\varphi\Box Cg\varphi \ \& \ \exists\varphi\Box \sim Cg\varphi)$, which, together with RIGHT, entails $(\exists\varphi\Box R\varphi \ \& \ \exists\varphi\Box \sim R\varphi)$. Similarly, from $\sim$&COMMANDS we have $(\exists\varphi\Box Cg \sim \varphi \ \& \ \exists\varphi\Box \sim Cg \sim \varphi)$, which, together with WRONG, entails $(\exists\varphi\Box W\varphi \ \& \ \exists\varphi\Box \sim W\varphi)$. We can therefore conclude $[(\exists\varphi\Box R\varphi \ \& \ \exists\varphi\Box \sim R\varphi) \ \& \ (\exists\varphi\Box W\varphi \ \& \ \exists\varphi\Box \sim W\varphi)]$.

12. Proof. In note 11, we derived MORALNEC which entails $(\exists\varphi\Box R\varphi \ \& \ \exists\varphi\Box W\varphi)$. Because '$\varphi$' ranges over action types, we can assume a constant domain semantics for φ. Consequently, Buridan's Formula, $(\exists x\Box Fx \to \Box\exists xFx)$ is valid. So, from $(\exists\varphi\Box R\varphi \ \& \ \exists\varphi\Box W\varphi)$, we can then conclude $(\Box\exists\varphi R\varphi \ \& \ \Box\exists\varphi W\varphi)$. This then entails $\Box(\exists\varphi R\varphi \ \& \ \exists\varphi W\varphi)$, from which we can conclude $\Box(\exists\varphi R\varphi \lor \exists\varphi W\varphi)$.

13. Here I am using 'fact' as synonymous with 'true proposition'.

14. Adams (1973) introduced the idea that God's being loving might be employed to deal with the derivation of MORALCONT, though he put the idea to a different effect.

15. Proof. From □LOVGOD, we can conclude Lg. Then, by LOVCOM, we can conclude $[(\exists\varphi\Box Cx\varphi$ & $\exists\varphi\Box Cx\sim\varphi)$ & $(\exists\varphi\Box\sim Cx\varphi$ & $\exists\varphi\Box\sim Cx\sim\varphi)]$, which, together with RIGHT and WRONG entail $[(\exists\varphi\Box R\varphi$ & $\exists\varphi\Box\sim R\varphi)$ & $(\exists\varphi\Box W\varphi$ & $\exists\varphi\Box\sim W\varphi)]$.
16. The proof for this claim is found in note 12.
17. This semantics is derived from Prior (1957) rather than being taken explicitly from this work. Q is given explicitly.
18. According to Adams

> the statement that something is ethically wrong (or permitted) says something about the will or commands of God, but not about his love. Every such statement, however, *presupposes* that certain conditions for the applicability of the believer's concepts of ethical right and wrong are satisfied. Among these conditions is that God does not command cruelty for its own sake – or more generally, that God loves his human creatures. (1973/1987, pp. 101–2; emphasis in the original)

19. This consequence formalizes the dependence of morality on the commands and nature of God in a way more radical than has yet been considered, in particular, in a way more radical than that codified in the previous axiomatizations of DCT. On the previous axiomatizations of DCT, we could derive a claim which Quinn (1978, p. 30) has termed 'Karamazov's Theorem': If God did not exist, then everything would be permitted. If we take it that 'φ is permitted' is true just in case 'φ is not morally wrong' we can formalize Karamazov's Thesis thusly:

$$\text{(KT)} \quad \Box(\sim E!g \to \forall\varphi\sim W\varphi)$$

Given that God might not have existed, which DCT1 assumes, KT is entailed by MORALNIHIL. Now Quinn (1980/2006, p. 47) takes it that Karamazov's Thesis 'ought to be a consequence of any divine command theory worthy of the name'. The motivation for accepting Karamazov's Thesis, presumably, is that if what it is to be morally wrong is determined by God's commands, when there are no commands, it seems there should be nothing morally wrong. On the present approach, however, Karamazov's Theorem is not true since in worlds in which God does not exist, he is not loving, and so there are no truths at all in such worlds about moral rightness and moral wrongness, including $(\sim E!g \to \forall\varphi\sim W\varphi)$, and so we have $\sim\Box(\sim E!g \to \forall\varphi\sim W\varphi)$. We do, however, have $\sim\Diamond\sim(\sim E!g \to \forall\varphi\sim W\varphi)$.

On the present approach, we can think of God's loving his children as bestowing moral value on the world; consequently, in worlds in which God does not love his children, there is no moral value at all in these worlds, that is, there are no true claims concerning moral rightness and wrongness. This is why the present approach still provides a metaphysical analysis of moral rightness and wrongness for it specifies the extension of moral rightness and wrongness in every world in which there is moral rightness and wrongness.

20. This axiom formalizes and generalizes Adams's insight quoted in note 18.

References

Adams, R. M. (1973) 'A Divine Command Theory of Ethical Wrongness', in G. Outka and J. P. Reeder, Jr. (eds) *Religion and Morality: A Collection of Essays* (New York: Doubleday). Reprinted in Adams 1987. All page references to the reprinted edition.

Adams, R. M. (1979) 'Divine Command Metaethics Modified Again', *The Journal of Religious Ethics*, 7, 66–79.

Adams, R. M. (1987) *The Virtue of Faith and Other Essays in Philosophical Theology* (New York and Oxford: Oxford University Press).

Adams, R. M. (1999) *Finite and Infinite Goods: A Framework for Ethics* (Oxford: Oxford University Press).

Cudworth, R. (1996) *A Treatise Concerning Eternal and Immutable Morality*, in S. Hutton (ed.) (Cambridge: Cambridge University Press).

Dorr, C. (2005) 'What We Disagree About When We Disagree About Ontology', in M. E. Kalderon (ed.) *Fictionalism in Metaphysics* (Oxford: Clarendon Press).

Dummett, M. (1991) *The Logical Basis of Metaphysics* (Cambridge, MA: Harvard University Press).

Kripke, S. (1963) 'Semantical Considerations on Modal Logic', *Acta Philosophical Fennica*, 16, 83–94.

Prior, A. N. (1957) *Time and Modality* (Oxford: Clarendon Press).

Quinn, P. L. (1978) *Divine Commands and Moral Requirements* (Oxford: Clarendon Press).

Quinn, P. L. (1980) 'Divine Command Ethics: A Causal Theory', in J. M. Idziak (ed.) *Divine Command Morality: Historical and Contemporary Readings* (New York: Edwin Mellen Press). Reprinted in Quinn (2006). All page references to the reprinted edition.

Quinn, P. L. (2006) *Essays in the Philosophy of Religion*, C. B. Miller. (ed.) (Oxford: Clarendon Press).

7
Divine Desire Theory and Obligation

Christian B. Miller

Thanks largely to the work of Robert Adams and Philip Quinn, the second half of the twentieth century witnessed a resurgence of interest in divine command theory as a viable position in normative theory and meta-ethics. More recently, however, there has been some dissatisfaction with divine command theory even among those philosophers who claim that normative properties are grounded in God, and as a result alternative views have begun to emerge, most notably divine intention theory (Murphy, Quinn) and divine motivation theory (Zagzebski). My goal here is to outline a distinct theory, divine desire theory, and suggest that, even if it is not clearly superior to these extant views, it is at least worthy of serious consideration.[1]

As far as this chapter is concerned, the discussion will be limited just to the deontic status of actions (obligatory, permissible, forbidden), and so no attempt will be made to also account for axiological properties such as goodness or evil. In order to get oriented to the range of deontological views in this area, consider the following three rough characterizations:

Divine Command Theory: Deontological properties are metaphysically grounded in God's relevant commands.[2]

Divine Intention Theory: Deontological properties are metaphysically grounded in God's relevant intentions.[3]

Divine Desire Theory: Deontological properties are metaphysically grounded in God's relevant desires.

For divine command theory, God's mental states give rise to his commands, but it is the commands themselves which determine the deontic status of actions. The other two views acknowledge that God's commands play an important *epistemic* role in communicating how human beings are to behave, but it is certain prior mental states themselves, intentions in the one case and desires in the other, which are the metaphysical basis for deontic properties.[4]

Does anything hang on the outcome of the debate between advocates of these three views? While a proper treatment of this question would require a paper in its own right, it seems apparent that a great deal does depend on this outcome. Both divine intention and divine desire theory avoid certain serious objections to divine command theory,[5] and elsewhere I have argued that grounding obligations in divine intentions is also seriously problematic.[6] Thus divine desire theory may be the most promising place to look of these three views if the theist wants to claim that God is the basis for deontic properties.

Given limitations of space, however, my concern here is not with carrying out a comparative evaluation of the costs and benefits associated with these three positions. Rather, I first simply outline divine desire theory in section one, and then attempt to respond to what will likely be some of the leading objections in section two.

One final note, though, before we begin. This chapter is a contribution to an intramural debate among philosophers who accept, if only for the sake of argument, that two central claims are true – a theistic God exists, and such a God is the metaphysical ground of deontic properties. Thus divine desire theory, like the other leading theories mentioned above, should have no appeal to anyone who does not accept one or both of these assumptions.

1   Divine desire theory

Imagine that you are considering whether you are required to perform action A in circumstances C. You have been contemplating this for some time, and really cannot decide whether A is obligatory or not. A friend of yours, Smith, knows about your plight and offers to help. He considers all the reasons for and against your A-ing in C that he can think of, and ultimately wants you to indeed perform A. Does Smith's desire for you to A in C serve as any kind of metaphysical basis for your being obligated to A in C? Clearly not. For, among other things, Smith might not be aware of stronger additional reasons for not performing A in C. And the reasons he *is* aware of might not count in favor of A-ing to nearly the degree that Smith thinks they do.

So let us replace your friend Smith with a virtuous human being, someone like Gandhi or Mother Teresa. And now suppose that this person again contemplates the merits of your A-ing in the relevant circumstances, and wants you to A in C. Does the fact that this person is virtuous suffice to allow her desire to ground an obligation for you to A in C? Again, clearly not. For while this person might assess the reasons she is aware of correctly, she is still a fallible human being, and may be unaware of a host of additional considerations against your A-ing in C. Given these epistemic limitations, it is hard to take seriously the idea that her desires could be the final metaphysical word about your obligations in C.

Suppose, finally, that we replace the desires of a human being with the desires of God, where God is the familiar omnipotent, omniscience, and omnibenevolent theistic deity. God now contemplates what he takes to be the reasons for and against your A-ing in C, and on the basis of his evaluation of what those reasons indicate and their comparative strengths, he comes to desire that you freely A in C. Indeed, of all the actions you could perform in C, this is the *only* action which he desires that you perform. Could *this* desire that you A in C ground an obligation for you to do so?

There are several reasons for thinking that it could. For one thing, there can be no question about the reasons involved in forming the desire. Being omniscient, God would not be ignorant of any relevant factual considerations, and being perfect, he would assign them their valences and their weights in a way which is consistent with his nature. From there he could determine what action of yours they favor overall.

Furthermore, God is the creator of the universe, including the free creatures in it, and has strong desires about their behavior in various circumstances. It is reasonable to think of those desires as grounding his expectations for the behavior of his creatures, expectations which are often not met but which in God's mind are *supposed* to be met. In other words, if God desires that his free creatures not kill other innocent human beings, then they are supposed to not do so, and failure to meet this expectation will likely foster God's disappointment in the creatures. This desire, then, looks like it would be the basis for a standard of behavior for those creatures when it comes to killing, and violation of that standard would be wrong.

There is a close analogy here to parents and their children. A mother might desire that her son clean his room, and because of this she tells him to do so before he can play video games. This desire has created an expectation in the mother's mind as to her son's behavior. The child might ask why he has to do it, at which point the mother's most immediate answer might just be – because I want you to. If the child persists, the mother might go on to elaborate some of the reasons for why she formed the desire – because people are coming over to look at buying the house, or because we are having a party tonight, or because it is a mess, and so on. This is where the analogy can become misleading, as we might then think that the mother's expression of her desire serves a merely epistemic function of communicating to the child the good reasons for cleaning his room, reasons which would have continued to exist even if the mother were not around. As we will see in section two, however, when it comes to God, his desires play a far more robust role of serving as the actual metaphysical ground for obligations, rather than just as the epistemic intermediaries for what we have most reason to do.[7]

Looking to divine desires as the ground for deontic properties also begins to appear more promising once we note the lack of plausible alternative divine mental states from which to choose. Cognitive mental states such as beliefs seem ill-suited to the job since they have the wrong direction of fit to the world; they aim to fit the world, and are true when their intentional object is the case. But this picture would have God's beliefs being formed as a result of deontological properties which exist either apart from God altogether, or which depend on some other facet of God such as his desires. In either case, God's beliefs would not be the immediate ground of those properties. Instead of cognitive mental states, then, we can look to God's intentions. But as I have already suggested, this alternative is not promising either.[8]

Thus we have some initial, albeit far from conclusive reasons to say that God's desires could ground an obligation for a human being to A in C. Or so, at least, is the claim of divine desire theory (hereafter 'DDT'). More generally, DDT is committed to the following claim about obligation:

(O)   Human agent S's performing action A in circumstances C is obligatory if and only if, after considering all the reasons relevant to S's freely A-ing in C, God desires that S freely A in C. Furthermore, what directly grounds S's obligation to A in C is this desire.[9]

Suppose, for example, that it is obligatory for me as I walk past a shallow pond to rush in and save a drowning child. Then according to (O), what grounds this obligation is God's desire toward my saving the child. Indeed we can suppose that given the circumstances, he is also averse toward my doing anything else that I could freely do at that moment, although strictly speaking according to (O) that aversion does not serve as the basis for the obligation.

It is important to note that (O) is not intended as a thesis specifically about *moral* obligations, although the chapter will draw heavily on examples of obligations which are clearly moral. Part of my hesitancy about restricting (O) just to moral obligation is that I do not know of any precise way of delimiting moral from non-moral obligations, and the same is true of moral versus non-moral reasons. Hence I want to leave it open as to the kinds of reasons and desires that God might have; in some cases, he might form a desire that I perform an action on the basis of purely prudential reasons (such as his desire that I call the hospital when I am having a heart attack), while in other cases he might form a desire that I act in a certain way based solely on moral considerations (such as his desire that I save the drowning child). But I have nothing to offer in order to restrict the reasons, desires, and obligations in (O) in some meaningful way only to the moral domain.

Clearly, (O) will need some additional explication. Let us take the central concepts in turn.

1.1   Reasons

The reasons in question are *motivating reasons*, or considerations in light of which an agent deliberates, decides, and intentionally acts.[10] From the first person perspective, motivating reasons are taken by an agent to be *good* reasons for action, and by the agent's own lights they can serve to justify not only the performance of an action, but also the formation of the mental states deemed necessary for so acting. On my view, and following a common theme in the recent literature, a person's motivating reasons are to be found in the contents of intentional mental states had by him or her. By 'mental states' I mean pairs of mental attitudes and contents such as my belief that *p*, your desire that *q*, and her wish that *r*. Believing, desiring, wishing, and the like are mental attitudes directed at intentional mental contents, in this case *p*, *q*, and *r*. So on this view, an agent's motivating reasons are not his beliefs, desires, wishes, or mental states more generally, but rather the *contents* of at least some of those mental states, which are intentional mental representations of putative facts in the world, representations which are typically propositional in form.[11] So if I believe that there is widespread starvation in Iceland, one of my motivating reasons for donating to famine relief in Iceland can be the propositional content of that belief, namely *there is widespread starvation in Iceland*, even if this belief is *false* and there is in fact almost no starvation in Iceland.

Arguing for this view would take us too far afield, and fortunately others have already done so persuasively.[12] So let us assume that something like this rough picture of motivating reasons is true in the human case. Now it is always a danger to extrapolate from facts about human psychology to putative facts about God's mind; indeed it is not even clear that God forms mental states or acts for reasons in any way resembling our doing so. However, since all the rival views to DDT mentioned at the start of this chapter also freely appeal to claims about God's psychological life, DDT at least will not be any worse off in this respect. So returning to (O), the assumption is that some if not all of God's desires are formed for reasons.[13] Suppose, for example, that God strongly desires that I do not torture a dog. Some of his motivating reasons could be the contents of divine beliefs, such as *that action would cause pain to the dog* or *there are many other free actions he could perform that do not involve torture*. Other reasons might be the objects of prior divine desires, such as *that there be less pain in the world* or *that animals not suffer*. And still other motivating reasons could be the contents of divine emotions, such as *that action is not loveable* or *that action is cruel*.

It is worth considering in a bit more detail what is involved in the reasons God uses in forming a desire about a particular action I might perform. These reasons have three main properties: they are factual considerations, they have valences, and they have weights. First, given God's omniscience, he would know all the factual considerations relevant to my action, such as exactly how much pain would be caused to the dog if I tortured it. These facts may themselves be non-normative,[14] but on the basis of his character, God would assign a *valence* to each fact such that it is either a reason *for* the action, a reason *against* the action, or a fact that is neutral with respect to the action. Finally and again on the basis of his character, he would assign different *weights* or degrees of importance to different considerations. The consideration *that the action would cause the dog to suffer* would be a fact with a far more negative valence, presumably, than the fact *that the action would cause my character to become more vicious*. So when formed on the basis of reasons, a divine desire about a particular human action will always appropriately reflect all the factual considerations God deems to be relevant, as well as the valences and weights he assigns to those facts.

1.2 Desires

As we have seen, according to DDT what grounds an obligation for a human being to act in a certain way is a particular divine *desire* formed on the basis of the relevant reasons. For our purposes here, we can just treat 'desires' in (O) as the folk psychological states with a world-to-mind direction of fit which are to be understood narrowly as being distinct from intentions, wishes, and emotions.[15]

A question that naturally arises about (O) is what we should make of the possibility that, for a particular agent and a given set of circumstances, God has multiple desires directed at different free actions. Perhaps God desires that I volunteer at a church, but perhaps he also desires that in those same circumstances I make a donation to charity. If such a state of affairs is possible, (O) is in trouble, since then I would have multiple obligations which are impossible for me to fulfill simultaneously in the circumstances, and so performing either of these actions, or any other for that matter, would be wrong.[16]

In response, I want to suggest that when it comes to the divine desires which ground a human being's obligations, it is plausible to think that God forms only *one* such desire about a certain action for me to perform in circumstances C, provided that he is not indifferent toward any of the actions I could freely carry out in C.[17] To see this, I first assume that the following principle is true:

(R)   Only God's desires concerning free human actions which are formed on the basis of his assessment of *all* (rather than just *some*) of the relevant reasons for action in the circumstances can ground deontic properties pertaining to those actions.[18] For instance, if God's desire that S freely A in C grounds his obligation to do so, then that desire is based on God's assessment of all the reasons relevant to S's freely A-ing in C.

Now suppose one of my free actions, such as donating to charity, is favored more so by the balance of reasons than any other of my potential actions in C. And suppose that God as a result desires that I freely make the donation, thereby rendering it obligatory. It follows from (O) that my volunteering at a church in the same circumstances would only be obligatory as well if it were grounded in God's desire that I do so. But given (R), such a desire would have to be based on God's assessment of the very same reasons used in forming the first desire. And so why would God also form this all-things considered desire that I volunteer, since by hypothesis making the donation is the action in C that is *best* supported by the reasons? In other words, why would God also want me to do something in C which is such that, were I to do it, I would be objectively irrational for doing so?[19]

1.3 Freely

It is plausible to think that given God's omnipotence, for any state of affairs not involving free actions, if God desires that it obtain, then it will obtain. Indeed, such a claim is likely to be necessarily true. But clearly if *all* of God's desires were like this, then there would never be noncompliance with any obligations, which is absurd. Hence by specifying that God desires that S *freely* A in C, thesis (O) implies that God's desire will only be satisfied in the event of this particular creature's exercising his or her own free will in choosing A.

1.4 Grounds

Thus far little has been said about the sense in which divine desires might 'ground' deontological properties. This is intentional, as there are a number of proposals one could make, and advocates of DDT can plausibly develop the view in a variety of directions. More specifically, we can distinguish at least four different proposals:

> *Meaning Equivalence*: The best conceptual analysis of 'A is obligatory for me' is 'God desires that I A.'
>
> *Casual Grounding*: God desires that I A is a causally necessary and sufficient condition for A's being obligatory for me.
>
> *Identity*: Its being obligatory for me to do A is identical to God's desiring that I A.
>
> *Non-Reductive Constitution*: A's being obligatory for me is constituted by but not identical to God's desiring that I A. There is an asymmetrical dependency relation between the two.[20, 21]

It is important to note that merely postulating a bi-conditional between obligation and divine desires (as is done in the first sentence of (O)) is not sufficient for rendering DDT a distinctive position, as nothing would thereby be indicated about the dependence relation between the two. Indeed, an advocate of divine *command* theory could accept this claim and still hold that what actually ground obligations are divine commands not divine desires. Hence a fully developed version of DDT also needs an account of the grounding relation between the relevant divine desires and deontological properties, and relations of causal dependence, identity, or non-reductive constitution are likely going to be the most popular options. Meaning equivalence proposals, on the other hand, since they are not making metaphysical but rather just conceptual claims, are not directly relevant to the concerns of this chapter.

Finally, (O) specifies that God's desire 'directly' grounds S's obligation. This is intended to block the possibility that God's desire that S freely A in C might cause the formation of something else, such as an intention or belief, which itself is the immediate and direct ground of S's obligation in C.[22]

Let us end this section by further developing DDT to include forbidden and permissible actions as well:

(F) Human agent S's performing action A in circumstances C is forbidden if and only if, after considering all the reasons relevant to S's freely A-ing in C, God desires that S refrain from freely A-ing in C. Furthermore, what directly grounds S's obligation to refrain from A-ing in C is this desire.

(P) Human agent S's performing action A in circumstances C is permissible if and only if, after considering all the reasons relevant to S's freely A-ing in C, God neither desires that S freely A in C nor desires that S refrain from freely A-ing in C.

Here the permissible is treated as exclusive of both the obligatory and the forbidden, rather than just as the set of those actions which are not forbidden. If an action is one about which God is indifferent, neither desiring that I perform it nor that I refrain from performing it, then according to (P) it is merely permissible.[23]

2 Objections to divine desire theory

According to DDT, our obligations to behave in certain ways are grounded in what God desires that we do in those circumstances. Such a claim is likely to give rise to a number of objections, some of which I hope to head off in this section. In doing so, we can also further refine the theory in the process.

2.1 Prima facie obligations

The first objection claims that DDT does not have a way of distinguishing between *prima facie* and *ultima facie* obligations. (O), even if correct, seems to be an account of the latter, and yet we ordinarily would think that I still had a *prima facie* obligation to keep my promise to meet my friend for lunch even if I broke that promise in order to take a stranger to the hospital in an emergency.

Borrowing a move from Mark Murphy, the advocate of DDT can account for *prima facie* obligations in the following way (Murphy, 1998, p. 20). The desires in (O) are formed based on the reasons that God considers relevant to the circumstances as a whole, and so let us instead consider a different set of divine desires which are based just on a proper subset of these circumstances.

Thus in the above example, God can consider the circumstances apart from anything having to do with the stranger in need of medical assistance, and so in this case God might desire that I meet my friend for lunch. This desire, based only on a selective set of circumstances, would directly ground a *prima facie* obligation to keep the promise.

2.2 Independent moral obligations

A familiar complaint one finds in the literature on divine command theory can also be used against DDT. According to this worry, either God's commands are based on reasons or they are not. If they are not, then they are arbitrary. If instead they are based on reasons, then those reasons would appeal to an external morality apart from God, and so God would not be the basis of morality after all. Either way, so the objection goes, the divine command theorist is in trouble.[24]

I doubt that this is a real problem for divine command theory, and the corresponding version of the dilemma certainly need not be one for DDT. We have already seen how according to DDT, the desires which ground obligations are those based on reasons, and so the resultant obligations will not be arbitrary. But neither need such reasons appeal to an external morality. Admittedly, a specific desire about what action a particular person freely performs might be based in part on an inference from a more general obligation applying to all people. But this more general obligation will in turn be grounded in a prior desire God has concerning how people behave in those circumstances, a desire which itself is based on its own set of reasons. What one will not find, according to DDT, is a divine desire based on an obligation which itself is not grounded in some prior divine desire. Instead, all obligations will be ultimately based on a host of different kinds of reasons such as, to use our previous example, reasons with only descriptive content like:

> *The stranger will live with Miller's help.*
> *Miller has made a promise.*

as well as reasons with normative content such as:

> *The stranger's surviving would be a good thing.*
> *Miller's helping would be valuable.*

Recall that DDT is only a theory of the grounding of deontological properties. Like most versions of divine intention and divine command theory, it will have to appeal to a separate account of axiological and characterological properties.[25] But at no point does it need to appeal to deontological properties which are not ultimately grounded in divine desires.

2.3 God's irrelevance

This discussion of reasons for God's desires leads immediately to a more serious worry that DDT makes God ultimately irrelevant as the source of deontological properties. The divine desires grounding obligation, according to DDT, are supposed to be based upon all the relevant reasons pertaining to the circumstances and the people involved. But then it seems as if we are ultimately basing obligation on what there is most reason to do, and it is not clear whether God and his desires really have a significant grounding role to play in the theory.[26]

A quick response simply notes that, even if this objection is sound, it also applies equally well against the rival positions to DDT. Divine intention theory, for instance, maintains that obligation is grounded in certain divine intentions which are based on reasons. Similarly, proponents of divine command theory acknowledge that God's commands are expressions of divine mental states which are formed for reasons. So at least the advocate of DDT can take comfort in the fact that her view is no *worse* off when it comes to this objection than are the leading contenders in this discussion.

However, it would also be nice to be able to address the objection directly. And it looks like DDT can do so since the objection neglects the different respects in which God plays a central role in the view: (i) in selecting the relevant factual considerations, (ii) in establishing their valence, (iii) in fixing their strength, and (iv) in assessing them collectively. First of all, God determines which considerations are to factor into evaluations of the relevant circumstances. In our earlier example, he might deem considerations like *the stranger will live with Miller's help* and *Miller made a promise* as relevant, whereas others such as *Miller is wearing long pants* or *Miller's friend is drinking water at the restaurant* are treated as irrelevant. Such a selection process will be largely based on God's character – his loving nature, for example, could make the death of the stranger highly salient.[27]

We have already noted that God's character will determine the valence he assigns to the relevant considerations. Because of God's love, for instance, he might treat the consideration *the stranger will live with Miller's help* as a reason in favor of my helping, whereas his justice might treat *Miller will have to break a promise to help the stranger* as a reason again. Similarly, we also said that God assigns weights to these considerations as well. We can suppose, for instance, that the first consideration would be a very strong reason in favor of helping, whereas the second, although a reason against helping, would not be so to a similar extent.

While these points so far might show why God and his character in particular do in fact have an important role to play in DDT, they have yet to explain the importance of the *desires* formed on the basis of these reasons. Hence we come to the fourth point, namely that for DDT these desires are the conclusions reached as a result of assessing the relevant reasons. The number of reasons pertaining to the different possible free actions the agent could perform in a given set of circumstances might be vast, and we should not assume that God simply weighs together all of their valences and strengths as part of a simple overall calculation. In fact, given recent work on reasons for action, we should assume just the opposite. For some of the reasons could belong to one or more of the following kinds:

2.3.1   Purely justificatory reasons

It is common to think of practical reasons as playing only one role, namely that of requiring actions. But recently there have been a number of arguments for the claim that some reasons can play a purely justificatory role such that we are not required to act on them but for which we would not be irrational if we do not follow them.[28] For example, altruistic reasons in favor of certain very demanding actions such as making large donations to charity may be only justificatory and not rationally requiring reasons. If there are such purely justificatory reasons, then God's arriving at desires for my behavior will be a more complex matter than just adding up the strengths of the various reasons along one scale of evaluation. Instead, for each action that I could freely perform in the circumstances, he will often have to assess both the justifying and the requiring strengths of the reasons separately, and then make a comparative evaluation.[29]

2.3.2   Incommensurable reasons

Another view of reasons has it that there is widespread incommensurability between reasons favoring many incompatible actions.[30] As a result, agents cannot comparatively assess these reasons, but provided they act on one of them, their action would be rationally permissible. Hence even for God the adjudication of reasons on this view cannot in principle be carried out by merely comparing their strengths.

2.3.3   Exclusionary reasons

These are second-order reasons which allow some or all first-order reasons to be excluded which otherwise would rationally require (or forbid) that an action be performed.[31] Thus there might be overwhelming first-order reasons to do something altruistic, but an exclusionary permission permits those reasons to be excluded in favor of a self-interested action. One may still perform the altruistic action, but one is not required to do so. Thus if such reasons exist, then God would have to evaluate both first- and second-order reasons before forming a desire as to my behavior in the relevant circumstances, and such an evaluation would not be carried out only by comparing their strengths (Raz, 1975, p. 168).

2.3.4   *Equally strong opposing reasons*

In rare cases of human deliberation, ties emerge in which the available reasons equally support two incompatible courses of action. Relying on these reasons alone, the agent is paralyzed. But the agent also strongly desires that *some* action be performed, and so may form a desire to carry out one of the actions just by way of ending the stalemate. I see no reason why the same situation could not arise for God's deliberation, and so by arriving at a desire that the agent perform action A as opposed to equally well-supported action B, God arrives at a decision as to how he wants the agent to behave.[32]

Stepping back from these specific claims about reasons for action,[33] the central point is this: according to DDT, God's desire that a person A in C may be the conclusion of a process of assessing a wide array of reasons for and against doing so. Precisely how that assessment is carried out will depend on the nature of the reasons in question and the makeup of God's character, but our interest is not in trying to outline this process but rather in noting the fact that by forming this desire, God brings the process of assessment to a close and reaches a final determination as to what he wants the person to do in the circumstances.[34] For DDT, this determination grounds his obligation to perform that particular action.[35]

Let me say this on behalf of the objection, though. As an *epistemic* point there is certainly something to it. Suppose I have not been told by God what he desires me to do with my lunch promise once I come across the stranger in need, and so I try to determine this based on what the reasons relevant to the circumstance seem to militate in favor of doing. Thus in this case God's desire seems to be epistemically irrelevant. But rather than being a flaw of the theory, the fact that we can potentially discover our obligations using our rational capacities for assessing reasons seems to me a mark in its favor on practical grounds, especially given that the process of assessing reasons is one we already carry out on a daily basis to begin with. To be sure, though, if DDT is correct then the best way to carry out this process when we are ignorant of God's desires is not to simply think about what the relevant considerations are by *our* lights, but rather to think about what the considerations are that would factor into this decision process by *God's* lights given his nature.

2.4   Supererogation

Finally we come to what is perhaps the most forceful objection to divine desire theory, namely that it does not seem to allow any room for supererogation.[36] Ordinary morality suggests that there are actions – jumping on a grenade, donating a tremendous amount to charity, running into a burning building – which are neither forbidden nor obligatory but which seem to go beyond the merely obligatory and deserve our praise and esteem. According to the objection, God surely would desire that I freely perform such an action if I can in the relevant circumstances – after all, he would not be indifferent about the matter or desire that I not perform it. But if he does have such a desire, then according to DDT the action would be obligatory. Thus the supererogatory is really just a proper subset of the obligatory. In the remainder of this section, I propose several different strategies for responding to this worry.

2.4.1 Denial

The first strategy is the one toward which I am most sympathetic, namely denying outright that from a theistic perspective there are any supererogatory acts. No doubt this would involve a departure from ordinary morality, but perhaps not one that theists should seriously mind.

There is both a historical and a theoretical reason for this denial. The historical reason is that the scriptures of the leading theistic religions contain numerous statements which seem incompatible with supererogation. Focusing here just on the Christian scriptures for the sake of brevity, we find statements such as this:

> Love your neighbor as yourself. Love does no harm to its neighbor.
>
> (Romans 13:9–10)

This claim is clearly presented as an obligation,[37] and yet it is hard to think of what acts could go above and beyond such a demanding standard in the way that supererogatory actions allegedly do. Similarly, we find demands such as:

> Be perfect, therefore, as your heavenly Father is perfect.
>
> (Matthew 5:48)

> Do everything in love.
>
> (1 Corinthians 16:14)

> Finally, all of you, live in harmony with one another; be sympathetic, love as brothers, be compassionate and humble.
>
> (1 Peter 3: 8)

For Christian theists at least, there seems to be no obvious textual evidence that God considers certain actions to be supererogatory. Instead, given the demandingness of these claims, the New Testament authors are moved to stress the importance of forgiveness and grace since no one will ever live up to their obligations on their own, much less go beyond them.

The theoretical justification for denying supererogation from a theistic perspective goes as follows. Consider again my action A in circumstances C. Suppose, after considering all the reasons which he deems relevant to the various actions I could perform in C, God determines that my A-ing in C is the action favored by those reasons. Surely, then, God would desire that I A in C, and according to DDT, it is obligatory that I do so. But then it follows that refraining from A-ing in C is not favored by the same reasons, and so given his perfect rationality, God would never form a desire that I refrain from A-ing in C and instead perform some other action. Yet if one of these other actions that I could freely do is supposed to be supererogatory, then it follows that God would not desire that I perform it. Indeed, in failing to A in C and instead doing this other action, I would not be doing what I have most reason to do, and would be directly contravening what God desires me to do. So it seems as if my action would not be praiseworthy but rather blameworthy, which contradicts the nature of supererogatory actions. Thus, although this argument needs to be developed more fully than it can be here, there is at least some initial reason to doubt that theists who want to ground deontological properties in God's desires should accept supererogation.[38]

2.4.2   Desire and aversion

Another approach suggests that obligatory actions would be directly grounded in two psychological states of God – both his desire that I perform the action *and* his aversion to my refraining from performing it. Superogatory actions, on the other hand, are such that God has only the first mental state, but is not averse to my not performing the action. Thus without this aversion, he would not be inclined to criticize or punish me for not performing it, which aligns with our intuitions about such acts. (O) would then be revised as follows:

(OA)   Human agent S's performing action A in circumstances C is obligatory if and only if, after considering all the reasons relevant to S's freely A-ing in C, God desires that S freely A in C and God desires that S not refrain from A-ing in C. Furthermore, what directly grounds S's obligation to A in C is only both desires.

However, there might be something difficult to accept about the idea that, for instance, God would be indifferent to my not donating $10,000 to Oxfam which would have saved a 1,000 children from pneumonia.

2.4.3   Blame and guilt

It is common to find accounts of obligation tied closely to one or more of the following notions: responsibility, punishment, guilt, or shame.[39] These concepts could be used to modify (O) in a variety of ways so as to open the door for supererogation, such as the following:

(OG)   Human agent S's performing action A in circumstances C is obligatory if and only if, after considering all the reasons relevant to S's
freely A-ing in C, God desires that S freely A in C and that S feel guilt
(or shame) if S does not A in C. Furthermore, what directly grounds
S's obligation to A in C is this desire.

Clearly, then, supererogatory acts are ones that God also desires be freely
performed but for which he does not desire that the relevant agents feel
guilt (or shame) if they do not perform them in the circumstances.[40]

2.4.4   Purely justificatory reasons and exclusionary permissions

Using the views of reasons for action we saw in addressing the previous
objection, we can arrive at an account of obligation which, for instance,
respects the justificatory role of reasons:

(OE)   Human agent S's performing action A in circumstances C is obligatory
if and only if, after considering all the reasons relevant to S's freely
A-ing in C, God desires that S freely A in C and the reasons for S
freely A-ing in C do not have much more justifying strength than
requiring strength. Furthermore, what directly grounds S's obligation
to A in C is this desire.

S freely A-ing in C could instead be supererogatory if God also desires
that S perform it but the reasons for doing so have much more justifying
strength than requiring strength.[41] Similarly, using the idea of exclusionary
permissions, we get:

(OP)   Human agent S's performing action A in circumstances C is obligatory
if and only if, after considering all the first-order reasons relevant to
S's freely A-ing in C, God desires that S freely A in C and there is not
an exclusionary permission that makes it rationally permissible for S
to not A in C. Furthermore, what directly grounds S's obligation to A
in C is this desire.

Supererogatory actions could then be those where God forms the same desire
but second-order reasons allow the exclusion of some or all of these first-
order reasons requiring S to A.[42]

Again my preference is for the first strategy of simply denying that there
are any supererogatory actions at least according to the major theistic religions, thereby eliminating the need for DDT to have to accommodate these
actions from the start. Hopefully, though, one of the other strategies above
(or a combination of them) has some plausibility for those who do not share
this preference.

3 Conclusion

I have tried to suggest that divine desire theory is an interesting and viable alternative to the leading views which attempt to ground deontological properties in God. Of them, it bears the closest similarity to divine intention theory, but replaces what I suggest elsewhere is the problematic focus on intentions with divine desires. Clearly, though, much more needs to be done in explicating and defending the view.[43]

Notes

1. Divine desire theory is not a new theory; indeed something like this view has been gestured at in the literature for some time but never developed at length. See, for example, Brody (1981) and Wierenga (1983, p. 390).
2. See Quinn (1978) and Adams (1979, 1999, 2002).
3. See Murphy (1998) and Quinn (2000, 2002).
4. Given space limitations, I have omitted discussion of divine motivation theory here. For what I consider to be the central difficulty with the view, see my 2008a.
5. Divine intention theorists such as Murphy and Quinn have been especially critical of divine command theory in recent years, and I have nothing to offer here in addition to their objections. Rather, I want to only make one important point, namely that their central objections – such as Murphy's trilemma or his 'objectionable contingency' charge – give us good reason to reject divine command theory, but *not* to favor divine intention theory over divine desire theory. In other words, advocates of divine desire theory can readily help themselves to these objections. This includes what I consider to be the simplest and most intuitively compelling concern of all, namely that 'it is at the deepest level God's will, and not his commands, *which merely express his will*, that determines the deontological status of actions' (Quinn, 1990, p. 293, emphasis mine.)

    For Murphy's trilemma, see Murphy (2002a, 2002b, pp. 82–92), and (2004) and the discussion in Almeida (2004) and Wainwright (2005, p. 89). For the objectionable contingency charge, see Murphy (1998, pp. 4–7).
6. See Miller (2008c).
7. Thanks to Tim Bayne for pointing out the potentially misleading nature of the analogy.
8. See my (2008c). Another option would be divine emotions, and this is the strategy that advocates of divine motivation theory adopt (Zagzebski, 2004). A more detailed discussion would certainly have to consider this approach as well, but given limitations of space I leave that discussion to my (2008a).
9. Note that (O) is stated in terms of God's desire that an agent perform a particular action, and not in terms of God's desire that *it be morally obligatory that* the agent perform the action. For reasons in favor of rejecting the latter option, see Murphy (1998, pp. 10–16).
10. For a similar characterization, see Dancy (2000, p. 1) and Setiya (2003, pp. 346–347).
11. 'Typically' because there may be intentional mental states with non-propositional intentional objects. Searle, for example, thinks that this is true for states of love. See his *Intentionality: An Essay in the Philosophy of Mind* (1983, pp. 6–7) and (2001, p. 36).

12. I develop the view at length in Miller (2008b). See also Dancy (2000), Setiya (2003), and Davis (2005).
13. Linda Zagzebski has argued that some of God's desires might not be based on reasons. See her (2004, pp. 267–268).
14. But they need not be. The fact *that causing this amount of pain to the dog is bad*, is a fact with moral content.
15. It has become customary in the action theory literature to distinguish between wide and narrow conceptions of desire. For more, see Smith (1994) and Schueler (1995).
16. Note that this example is not intended to be a special case which we might be tempted on independent grounds to understand as a moral dilemma (such as Sophie's choice or Abraham's sacrifice). If it were a special case, then perhaps such a consequence of (O) would not be troublesome. But the example is intended to be an ordinary case in which we would never think that all of the actions would be wrong. For a related concern, see Murphy (1998, p. 17).
17. This claim is compatible with God's forming multiple desires pertaining to which actions to *not* perform in C. It is also a claim about *unconditional* desires, and so is compatible with God's forming multiple conditional desires pertaining to the same agent and circumstances, i.e., that the agent perform certain acts as opposed to others if he happens to not perform the action that God unconditionally desires for him to do.
18. The deontic properties here are intended to only be *ultima facie* rather than *prima facie* properties. We shall take up this distinction at greater length in the next section.
19. Note that two actions could be favored to the *same* extent by the relevant reasons, and more so than any other actions I could do in C. But this does not militate in favor of God's forming two desires; rather, he could for instance just form the desire that I *either* freely make a donation in C or freely volunteer at a church in C.
20. Simply calling this relation a supervenience relation would not be sufficient to properly distinguish the view since identity is also a supervenience relation. For this point in the context of discussing divine command theory, see Almeida (2004).
21. These four characterizations are just intended to be crude initial statements of the proposals. For similar surveys of such options for both divine command and divine intention theories, see Wierenga (1983), Quinn (2000, pp. 54–55), and Murphy (2002b, chapter four).
22. In order to simplify the presentation, I have omitted other properties of this grounding relation, such as totality, exclusivity, activity, and necessity. For a discussion of these properties, see Quinn (2000, p. 55).
23. Whether there actually *are* any such actions is, in my view, rather doubtful when we turn to the putative obligations of specific theistic religions such as Christianity. We shall return to this issue in the next section when examining supererogation.
24. For discussion, see Wierenga (1983, pp. 400–401), Sullivan (1993), and Timmons (2002, p. 29), among many others.
25. For divine intention theory as only a deontological theory, see Murphy (1998) and Quinn (2000). For divine command theory as only a deontological theory, see Adams (1999). For a similar point in response to this objection, see Wainwright (2005, p. 117).
26. For a related discussion of this objection, see Wierenga (1983, pp. 396–397).

27. For more on the saliency of some facts as opposed to others in practical reasoning, see Wiggins (1978) and Dancy (1988).
28. See in particular Gert (2004). Gert characterizes a justifying reason in part as 'making it rationally permissible to do actions that would, without it, be irrational' (p. 80). See also Raz (1999, pp. 101–102).
29. If there are such purely justificatory reasons, and if there are cases in which their strength can outweigh the strength of the relevant requiring reasons, then the desires which God forms in those cases may render certain actions supererogatory rather than obligatory. This in turn would mean that I have to revise the response I give to the next objection, as I suggest there that theists should reject the claim that there are any supererogatory actions. However, at the end of that discussion, I also suggest various ways in which DDT could instead accommodate supererogation, and one of them makes use of the idea of purely justificatory reasons. I am grateful to Tim Bayne for encouraging me to clarify these issues.
30. See in particular Raz (1999, pp. 102–104). Incommensurability is used by Raz to explain what he calls the 'basic belief,' namely that 'most of the time people have a variety of options such that it would accord with reason for them to choose any one of them and it would not be against reason to avoid any of them' (p. 100). The previous proposal that there are purely justificatory reasons also attempts to explain the same belief.
31. See Raz (1975). His official characterization is that an exclusionary permission may be established if

> [a] person may be permitted to φ, despite the existence of an overriding reason for not φ-ing, if there are reasons which entitle him to disregard the reasons for not φ-ing, or at least to disregard some of them so that those not excluded do not outweigh the reasons for φ-ing. (p. 163)

32. For a related discussion of ties between reasons, see Raz (1986, chapter thirteen) and Bratman (2003). An alternative way in which God might handle ties between reasons is by forming a desire that S *either* freely A or freely B in the circumstances. See also the related discussion in Wierenga (1983, pp. 390–391) and Sullivan (1994, p. 80, fn. 29).
33. In addition to the views cited above, see also the discussion in Bratman (1987, p. 59), Dancy (1988), and Scanlon (1998, p. 32).
34. According to what we might call divine judgment theory, God's consideration of the relevant reasons for action results in the formation of a cognitive judgment in favor of the agent's performing a particular action in the circumstance. So instead of a desire based on reasons, what would ground the agent's obligation to act in this way would instead be God's belief based on reasons. This theory also strikes me as plausible, and indeed more plausible than the leading views in the literature. Those who find it more attractive than DDT can still also accept most of the arguments in this paper, but unfortunately a comparative assessment of the two views will have to wait for another occasion.
35. For another response worth considering once it is modified to apply to DDT, see Sullivan (1993) and the discussion in Wainwright (2005, pp. 90–91).
36. Robert Adams has developed this objection against a view very similar to DDT. See his (1999, pp. 260–261).

37. 'If you really keep the royal law found in Scripture, "Love your neighbor as yourself," you are doing right' (James 2:8). For an extensive discussion of love as a Christian obligation, see Quinn (1996, 2000, pp. 57–59).
38. For a discussion of secular versions of this argument, see Raz (1975, 164) and Dancy (1988, 176). Note that the same line of reasoning applies equally well to God's intentions and commands too.
39. See, for example, Gibbard (1990, p. 45), Gert (1998, p. 16), Adams (1999, pp. 238–241), Zagzebski (2004, p. 151), and Sinnott-Armstrong (2005).
40. This proposal can be developed in two different directions. One would be to say that God's desire still grounds an obligatory action (so that supererogatory acts are also obligatory), but one whose non-performance does not merit feelings of guilt. (OG) would then need further modification to apply only to non-supererogatory obligatory actions. Another direction would be to say that God's desire does not make the action obligatory. For the distinction here between what is sometimes called strong versus weak supererogationism, see Dancy (1988, p. 175).
41. For the relationship between justificatory reasons and supererogation, see Gert (2004, pp. 106–109).
42. For exclusionary permissions and supererogation, see Raz (1975) and Gert (2004, pp. 106–109).
43. This paper was written during a research leave provided by Wake Forest University, for which I am very grateful. Much thanks as well to the editors for inviting me to contribute to this volume, and to Tim Bayne for very helpful written comments.

References

Adams, Robert. (1979). 'Divine Command Metaethics Modified Again.' *Journal of Religious Ethics* 7: 66–79.
——. (1999). *Finite and Infinite Goods: A Framework for Ethics*. New York: Oxford University Press.
——. (2002). 'Responses.' *Philosophy and Phenomenological Research* 64: 475–490.
Almeida, Michael. (2004). 'Supervenience and Property-Identical Divine Command Theory.' *Religious Studies* 40: 323–333.
Bratman, Michael. (1987/1999). *Intention, Plans, and Practical Reason*. Reprint Edition. Stanford: CSLI Publications.
——. (2003). 'A Desire of One's Own.' *The Journal of Philosophy* 100: 221–242.
Brody, Baruch. (1981). 'Morality and Religion Reconsidered,' in *Divine Commands and Morality*. Ed. P. Helm. Oxford: Oxford University Press.
Dancy, Jonathan. (1988). 'Supererogation and Moral Realism,' in *Human Agency: Language, Duty, and Value*. Ed. J. Dancy, J. Moravcsik, and C. Taylor. Stanford: Stanford University Press, 170–188.
——. (2000). *Practical Reality*. Oxford: Oxford University Press.
Davis, Wayne. (2005). 'Reasons and Psychological Causes.' *Philosophical Studies* 122: 51–101.
Gert, Bernard. (1998). *Morality*. New York: Oxford University Press.
Gert, Joshua. (2004). *Brute Rationality: Normativity and Human Action*. Cambridge: Cambridge University Press.
Gibbard, Allan. (1990). *Wise Choices, Apt Feelings*. Cambridge: Harvard University Press.
Miller, Christian. (2008a). 'Divine Motivation Theory and Thick Evaluative Properties.' Manuscript.

——. (2008b). 'Motivation in Agents.' *Noûs* 42: 222–266.

——. (2008c). 'Divine Will Theory: Desires or Intentions?' *Oxford Studies in Philosphy of Religion*, forthcoming.

Murphy, Mark. (1998). 'Divine Command, Divine Will, and Moral Obligation.' *Faith and Philosophy* 15: 3–27.

——. (2002a). 'A Trilemma for Divine Command Theory.' *Faith and Philosophy* 19: 22–31.

——. (2002b). *An Essay on Divine Authority*. Ithaca: Cornell University Press.

——. (2004). 'Reply to Almeida.' *Religious Studies* 40: 335–339.

Quinn, Philip. (1978). *Divine Commands and Moral Requirements*. Oxford: Clarendon Press.

——. (1990). 'An Argument for Divine Command Ethics,' in *Christian Theism and the Problems of Philosophy*. Ed. M. Beaty. Notre Dame: University of Notre Dame Press.

——. (1996). 'The Divine Command Ethics in Kierkegaard's *Works of Love*,' in *Faith, Freedom, and Rationality*. Ed. J. Jordan and D. Howard-Snyder. Lanham: Rowman & Littlefield, 29–44.

——. (2000). 'Divine Command Theory,' in *The Blackwell Guide to Ethical Theory*. Ed. H. LaFollette. Malden: Blackwell, 53–73.

——. (2002). 'Obligation, Divine Commands and Abraham's Dilemma.' *Philosophy and Phenomenological Research* 64: 459–466.

Raz, Joseph. (1975). 'Permissions and Supererogation.' *American Philosophical Quarterly* 12: 161–168.

——. (1986). *The Morality of Freedom*. Oxford: Oxford University Press.

——. (1999). 'Explaining Normativity: Reason and the Will,' in *Engaging Reason: On the Theory of Value and Action*. Oxford: Oxford University Press, 90–117.

Scanlon, T. M. (1998). *What We Owe to Each Other*. Cambridge: Belknap Press of Harvard University Press.

Schueler, G. F. (1995). *Desire: Its Role in Practical Reason and the Explanation of Action*. Cambridge: MIT Press.

Searle, John R. (1983). *Intentionality: An Essay in the Philosophy of Mind*. Cambridge: Cambridge University Press.

——. (2001). *Rationality in Action*. Cambridge: MIT Press.

Setiya, Kieran. (2003). 'Explaining Action.' *The Philosophical Review* 112: 339–393.

Sinnott-Armstrong, Walter. (2005). 'You Ought to Be Ashamed of Yourself (When You Violate an Imperfect Moral Obligation).' *Philosophical Issues* 15: 193–208.

Smith, Michael. (1994). *The Moral Problem*. Oxford: Blackwell Publishers.

Sullivan, Stephen. (1993). 'Arbitrariness, Divine Commands, and Morality.' *International Journal for Philosophy of Religion* 33: 33–45.

——. (1994). 'Why Adams Needs to Modify His Divine Command Theory One More Time.' *Faith and Philosophy* 11: 72–82.

Timmons, Mark. (2002). *Moral Theory: An Introduction*. Lanham: Rowman & Littlefield.

Wainwright, William. (2005). *Religion and Morality*. Aldershot: Ashgate.

Wierenga, Edward. (1983). 'A Defensible Divine Command Theory.' *Nous* 17: 387–407.

Wiggins, David. (1978). 'Deliberation and Practical Reasoning,' in *Practical Reasoning*. Ed. J. Raz. Oxford: Oxford University Press, 144–152.

Zagzebski, Linda. (2004). *Divine Motivation Theory*. Cambridge: Cambridge University Press.

8
The Puzzle of Prayers of Thanksgiving and Praise

Daniel Howard-Snyder

Celebrant	The Lord be with you.
People	And also with you.
Celebrant	Lift up your hearts.
People	We lift them to the Lord.
Celebrant	Let us give thanks to the Lord our God.
People	It is right to give him thanks and praise.
Celebrant	It is right, and a good and joyful thing, always and everywhere to give thanks to you, Father Almighty, Creator of heaven and earth.[1]

Thank you God for me, my mom and dad, and William, and my friends, and for this food, and my toys, and for chess, and for … everything else. You are very nice and you do a great job. Amen.[2]

Accept, O Lord, our thanks and praise for all that you have done for us.[3]

One of the things we do when we pray is to thank and praise God for what he has done. By so doing, we demonstrate our gratitude to him for his gifts and we express our wonder and admiration for the great things he has done. It is right to give God thanks and praise. Chiefly it is right in that it is a fitting response on our part; if we have no tendency whatsoever to thank and praise God for what he has done, we are broken. Indeed, it has been suggested that if we but for a moment forget what God has done for us, if our whole comportment and whole activity have not their root in gratitude, we are out of kilter.[4] We might also think that it is right to thank and praise God in that it is wrong not to do so. This seems clearer in the case of thanks than praise. Just as children owe their parents a debt of gratitude for the benefits that they have bestowed on them, so we owe God a debt of gratitude for the benefits he has bestowed on us. It would be wrong not to demonstrate our gratitude. So then: it is right to give God thanks and praise for what he has done.

On occasion it is right to thank and praise others for what they have done even though they are not worthy of it.[5] I take it, however, that it is right to thank and praise God for what he has done because he is worthy of our thanks and praise. Indeed, other reasons for thanks and praise either do not apply to God (e.g., his feelings would be hurt if we did not thank and praise him) or, if they do apply to him, they apply at least in part because he is worthy of our thanks and praise (e.g., thanking and praising promotes and preserves our relationship with him). So, it is right to thank and praise God for what he has done because he is worthy of our thanks and praise.

Here a puzzle begins to emerge. For how is it possible for God – an essentially unsurpassably good person[6] – to be worthy of our thanks and praise for his good actions? After all, one might think at first blush that if God is essentially unsurpassably good, he is unable to do something worse in place of what he does, in which case he is not worthy of our thanks and praise for doing it. We have here a proposition – that it is impossible for God to be essentially unsurpassably good and yet worthy of thanks and praise for what he does, the *Incompatibility Claim*, let us call it – and we have a formally valid argument for it, the *Incompatibility Argument* (add the relevant modal operators here and throughout):

1. If God is essentially unsurpassably good, then he is unable to do something worse in place of what he does.
2. If God is unable to do something worse in place of what he does, then he is not worthy of thanks or praise for what he does.

Why should we think these premises are true?

Here is an argument for the contrapositive of premise 1:

A. If God is able to do something worse in place of what he does, then it is possible for there to be a person who is morally better than God.
B. If it is possible for there to be a person who is morally better than God, then God is not essentially unsurpassably good.

B is analytically true, but what about A? One might argue for it as follows:

A1. If God is able to do something worse in place of what he does, then it is possible for him to do something worse in place of what he does.
A2. If it is possible for God to do something worse in place of what he does, then it is possible for there to be a person whose degree of moral goodness is such that he is not prepared to settle for a state of affairs that God is prepared to settle for.
A3. If it is possible for there to be a person whose degree of moral goodness is such that he is not prepared to settle for a state of affairs that God is prepared to settle for, then it is possible for there to be a person who is morally better than God.[7]

As for premise 2 of the Incompatibility Argument, we have this argument for its contrapositive:

C. If God is worthy of thanks and praise for what he does, then it redounds to his credit that he does it.
D. If it redounds to God's credit that he does something, then he is able to do something worse in place of it.

C is analytically true, but why affirm D? Well, because if D is false, then one of two options is possible – but neither option is possible. Argument: Suppose D is false. Then either

(I) An act of God's redounds to his credit, he was unable to do something worse, but he was *able* to do something better instead,

or

(II) An act of God's redounds to his credit, he was unable to do something worse, and he was *unable* to do something better instead

are possible. But (I) is impossible. If God's act is such that he was unable to do something worse but he was able to do something better, then his act is the worst he was able to do and he knows he was able to do better. But if one does the worst one is able to do when one knows one was able to do better, it does not redound to one's credit that one did it. There is no credit to be had in maximal underachievement, at least not when there is something better to be done. Likewise, (II) is impossible. One might think this is so because, necessarily, for each act God performs, there is a better act that he was able to perform in its place. Alternatively, consider the following dilemma: either for each act God performs there was a better act that he was able to perform in its place, or there was not. If there was, (II) is impossible. If there was not, then, since on (II) God was unable to do worse, his act was either the best act he was able to perform or tied for best. If his act was the best, then it does not redound to his credit since he was never able to do anything about any of the factors that entailed his performing that act. If his act was tied for best, then it does not redound to his credit since he was never able to do anything about any of the factors that entailed that he would have to choose between equally good acts.

The foregoing arguments would benefit from clarification and development. In what follows, I will try to do that while responding to several objections. But first, some preliminary remarks are in order.

Note that I run God's being worthy of thanks and his being worthy of praise in the same harness. I do that because God's being *worthy* of praise for what he does and God's being *worthy* of thanks for what he does both lexically imply the same fact: that it *redounds to God's credit* that he does what he does. It is this fact that is in tension with the doctrine of God's essential unsurpassable goodness. Some people might disagree. They might say: although one might see some tension between God's being worthy of thanks for what he does and his essential unsurpassable goodness, there is not a whiff of tension between his being worthy of praise for what he does and his essential unsurpassable goodness. Or, they might say: although one might see some tension between God's being worthy of praise for what he does and his essential unsurpassable goodness, there is not a whiff of tension between his being worthy of thanks for what he does and his essential unsurpassable goodness.[8] I think these folks are mistaken, but I am willing to accommodate them. If you belong to one of these two groups, simply read the arguments above and the discussion to follow while running your favored horse. If, however, you think that God is both worthy of praise and thanks for what he does even though it does not redound to his credit that he does what he does, then I have no way to accommodate you.[9]

Note that the schema 'S is able to do A' and its syntactic variants appear above. I do not know of any definition in simpler words. Still, it might help to locate the concept I mean to express if I briefly distinguish it from other concepts that are expressed with the same words. For starters, I do not mean to express the concepts of moral or legal permissibility, nor those of logical, metaphysical, physical, or epistemic possibility. Nor do I mean to express the concept of power or strength, or the concept of a general skill. A comatose woman might well have the power (strength) and skill to climb Mount Shuksan even though she is unable to do so. Moreover, I do not mean to express the concepts of opportunity or practical know-how. A man who is pathologically averse to snakes might well have the strength to handle one, as well as the skill (he is a former snake handler) and the opportunity (he is at the Washington Serpentarium); and he might have practical knowledge of his situation – of his power, skill, and opportunity, and how they might come together for the performance of such an act. Still, he is unable to do it. Strength, skill, opportunity, and know-how are neither individually nor jointly sufficient for ability, even if each is necessary. This is the concept expressed in our puzzle and in what follows, the concept of what this man lacks when we say, correctly, 'He has the requisite power, skill, opportunity, and know-how; nevertheless, he is unable to handle a snake.'[10]

Determinism is the thesis that the past and the laws of nature together entail a unique future. *The ability thesis* is the thesis that we sometimes simultaneously have both of the following abilities: the ability to perform an act and the ability to refrain from performing that act. *The credit thesis* is the thesis that sometimes we perform an act and it redounds to our credit that we performed it. In what follows, I presuppose that determinism is *in*compatible with both the ability thesis and the credit thesis. I also presuppose that we are not able to alter the distant past and the laws of nature, nor ever did we have that ability nor ever will we have it.

The discussion to follow will in no small part be about whether God was able to do better or worse than he did. Note that I am speaking of God's actions, whether he was able to perform a better or worse act in place of the one that he in fact performed. Two points here. First, sometimes people conflate the goodness of God's acts with the goodness of the states of affairs that result from them or with the goodness of God himself. To be sure, there are important relations between these things. Even so, we must not conflate them or suppose, without argument, that a judgment about one entails the same judgment about the other. Second, to say that God was able to perform a better act in place of the one that he performed does not imply that the act he performed was morally impermissible. It is possible for one act to be better than another even though both are morally permissible.

I now turn to the objections.

1. The First Objection

Even if it is metaphysically impossible for God to do something worse in place of what he does, he was able to do so. That is, A1 is false, as are A and premise 1. To begin to see why, let us distinguish being morally incapable of performing a bad act from being unable to perform it.

Let us say that a person is *morally incapable*, or *incapable* for short, of performing a bad act just when doing such a thing would be contrary to a firmly entrenched character that she has, that the desire or inclination to perform that action is not within the range of her current desires and inclinations, or that a serious intention to engage in the action is prohibited by a stable moral stance characteristic of her. This is a very different matter from anything having to do with strength, skill, opportunity, or practical knowledge. Now consider Jones, a healthy middle-aged former Special Forces operative. Suppose that a young boy with a precociously obnoxious personality and a proclivity to mischief lives next door to Jones. He bothers Jones daily in extremely irritating ways. A neighbor who witnesses this regular harassment comments to a mutual friend, 'If I were Jones, I'd throttle the kid. Why doesn't he just catch him, wrap his hands around that loud, whiny windpipe, and give it a good long squeeze?' The friend might reply, 'It's not possible for Jones to do anything like that.' The friend need not be attributing to Jones any lack of power, skill, opportunity, or practical knowledge. In fact, he is probably not. It is just that he is incapable of doing it. Despite his strength, skill, opportunity, and know-how, Jones is a big softy, as gentle as a lamb, so much so that hurting the boy is prevented by his character. But that does not mean that he is *unable* to hurt him. Hardly!

Now, just as Jones has the ability to throttle the kid even though he is *incapable* of doing it, so God has the ability to do something worse than he does even though it is *impossible* that he do it. To be sure, incapacity is not impossibility. However, the difference between God and Jones on this score is merely a matter of degree. Jones's firmly entrenched character prevents him from harming the boy. There is no possible world in which he has *exactly* that character, entrenched in *exactly* that way, and he hurts the boy in these circumstances. Nevertheless, he is able to hurt him. But in that case, it does not matter for what he is able to do if those traits were not just contingently firmly entrenched but necessarily firmly entrenched. Thus, it does not matter in God's case. Even if God's essential unsurpassable goodness makes it is impossible for him to do something worse instead of what he does, he is able to do worse. Ability does not imply possibility.[11]

What should we make of this objection?

It seems to me to be confused. According to the analogy, Jones was able to strangle the kid even though his character ruled out the possibility of his doing so in the circumstances. But that is not correct. Consider a different case. Suppose Jones's character does not prevent him but steel cords do. In that case, is Jones able to strangle the boy? Of course not. While he is bound by steel cords, the ability is eradicated. But there is no relevant difference between cords of steel that bind Jones's body to render him unable to hurt the boy and cords of character that bind his will to the same end. Both render him unable. To suppose otherwise is to conflate the ability to perform an act and the strength needed to perform it.

What goes for Jones goes for God. Suppose, as the view in question maintains, that God's essential unsurpassable goodness makes it impossible that he does something worse in place of what he does. In that case, just as Jones's firmly entrenched gentleness renders him unable to harm the boy, so God's essential unsurpassable goodness renders him unable to do something worse in place of what he does. Moreover, in that case, just as Jones has the strength to harm the boy despite the fact that his firmly entrenched gentleness renders him unable to do so, so it is that God has the strength to do something worse in place of what he does despite the fact that his essential unsurpassable goodness renders him unable to do so.[12]

2. The Second Objection

The argument for premise 2 appeals to principle D which is defended with an argument according to which it is impossible that

(II) An act of God's redounds to his credit, he was unable to do something worse, and he was *unable* to do something better instead.

But (II) *is* possible. Indeed, even if the only act that God is able to perform is the uniquely best act he is able to perform, it redounds to his credit that he does it, despite the fact that he was unable to do something else in its place.

To see how this is possible, suppose that

1.   In circumstances C, A is the single best action for God to do.

Now, given God's nature, and contrary to Adams (1972), it follows that

2.   In C, God knows that A is the best action, wants (all things considered) to do A, and has the strength to do A.

But it is a necessary truth that

3.   If in C, God knows that A is the best action, wants (all things considered) to do A, and has the strength to do A, then God does A in C.

Thus, given (1), it follows that, in C, God does A; indeed, it follows that, in C, he *must* do A. His nature *entails* it. Therefore, in C, he is unable to do anything else in place of A. Nevertheless, his doing A redounds to his credit.

Perhaps you will agree with me. Perhaps you think I have in mind a case in which God was able to do something about whether he was in C, in which case you might think his doing A redounds to his credit even if his nature entails that he do A in C. If that is what you are thinking, then you do *not* have in mind the case I have in mind. I have in mind a case in which *God was never able to do anything about whether he was in C*. Even in that case, I say, his doing A redounds to his credit, despite the fact that he was unable to do something else in its place.

To begin to see how this is possible, we might lean on the insight of some of our compatibilist friends, namely those who hold that it is possible for an action to redound to one's credit even though antecedent causal conditions sufficient for its performance exist. Of course, not just any antecedent causal conditions are so compatible – they have to be the right ones, arising in the right way. The right ones, they tell us, are a person's beliefs and desires, and the right way is the customary way in which people come to have beliefs and desires, not through drugs or hypnosis or nefarious neurosurgeons manipulating their brains. They then defend the claim that an action caused by a person's beliefs and desires arising in the customary way redounds to that person's credit by emphasizing that the beliefs and desires are the person's *own*, that they are internal to him or her. Many of us are unpersuaded by this account. We note that a person's beliefs and desires have antecedent causes stretching back to before the person ever existed if determinism is true. The relevant causal conditions are thus not really internal to the person in the right way.

The insight, to repeat, of these compatibilists is that the right antecedent causal conditions, internal to a person in the right way, are compatible with it redounding to his or her credit to perform a certain action. They are mistaken, however, in thinking our beliefs and desires, formed in the customary fashion in a deterministic world, are internal in the right way.

What would the right antecedent causal conditions, internal to a person in the right way, be like? It would be exactly like the antecedent causal conditions present in God's case envisioned above. Even if in some circumstances C, God's knowing that A is the best action, his wanting to do A, and his having the strength to do A is a logically sufficient condition of his doing A in C, and even if he was never able to do anything about being in C, it is nevertheless in virtue of *his own nature* that he knows that A is the best action, wants to do A, and has the strength to do A. There is no long chain stretching back to things separate from him that give him this particular constellation of knowledge, desire, and strength; it is due to his *own* knowledge and goodness and strength. Thus, the causal story is this: God's nature causes him, in C, to have this particular constellation of knowledge, desire, and strength which, in turn, causes him to do A. The ultimate cause of God's doing A in C is God's nature. I see no reason not to say that, in that case, it redounds to God's credit when he does A in C – even though he was unable to do anything else in place of A and even though he was never able to do anything about being in C.[13]

What should we make of this line of thought?

Note that, according to it, what is wrong with our compatibilists' contention that it is possible for a human person's act to redound to her credit despite being causally determined by the distant past and the laws of nature is that the relevant antecedent causal conditions are not internal to her in the right way. But that is not what is wrong with their contention at all. What is wrong is that *she was never able to do anything about any of the factors that entailed her act*. That is why her act does not redound to her credit. The deterministic push and shove of the distant past and the causal laws merely provide the occasion for what robs her of credit: her never ever having been able to do anything about those factors that entailed her act.

Now recall the position before us: even though God's nature causes him to perform the uniquely best act A that he is able to perform in circumstances C, and even though he was never able to do anything about being in C, his performing A in C redounds to his credit because it is the causal upshot of his own nature, which is internal to him in the right way. But, in light of what is *really* wrong with our compatibilists' contention, we must ask: was there ever a time when God was able to do anything about any of the factors that entailed his doing A in C? Was there ever a time when God was able to alter his nature or do something about being in C? No, not on the view before us.[14] So the solution before us fails to account for why God's doing A redounds to his credit.

3. The Third Objection

Let us take a look at the issues from a slightly different angle. Suppose that, as in the second objection, God must do A in C, given his nature. Furthermore, suppose that, as in the second objection, God was never able to do anything about being in C. I say that, nevertheless, God's doing A redounds to his credit. The proponent of the Incompatibility Argument disagrees. According to her, an act redounds to a person's credit only if she was able to refrain from what she did in C or she was able to do something about being in C. I disagree. A little reflection on the reasons for this condition will help us understand why God's failing to satisfy it is compatible with his good acts redounding to his credit.

There are three kinds of cases that primarily motivate it. They are: (a) the problem of past causally sufficient conditions for the action that pre-date the existence of the actor, (b) concerns about manipulation by other agents, and (c) worries about internal compulsions.

Regarding (a): If events that occured billions of years before I was born, together with the laws of nature that were in place then, set in motion a sequence of events that are causally sufficient for my performing a good act A, it seems far-fetched that, nevertheless, it redounds to my credit that I did A. Why? Because I did not exist when the matter of my doing A was causally settled. Notice, however, that there are no conditions or events spatially or temporally prior to God's existence which causally determine God's actions. Yes, God was unable to refrain from perform-ing A in C; yes, he was never able to do anything about being in C. But there is no past series of events and causal laws that is responsible for this.

Regarding (b): If my performing a good action is the result of my being manipulated by a nefarious neurosurgeon, devious hypnotist, or con-trolling creator, then the ultimate cause of my action is the intentional state of the agent who programmed me. My action does not redound to my credit because another agent is its ultimate source. Needless to say, this credit-compromising condition is not relevant to the volitions and actions of the omnipotent Source of Being.

Regarding (c): If my performing a good action is the result of a cogni-tive malfunction (e.g., a serendipitous brain lesion), then it is the result of non-rational internal forces. My action does not redound to my credit because it is a result of cognitive dysfunction, despite its fortunate out-come. Since God is perfectly rational and his volitions and actions are produced by his recognition of the best course of action and his desire to do the best, God's good actions are not the result of analogues of human cognitive malfunction brought on by serendipitous psychological disorder.

So the three primary motivations for insisting that an act of ours redounds to our credit only if we were able to refrain from what we did or we were able to do something about being in the circumstances we are in are simply out of place where God is concerned.

Let us go further. Let us say that one has effective choice over A if and only if one is able to do A *if one so wills* and able to refrain from doing A *if one wills*. While this is not sufficient for doing A to redound to one's credit, it is necessary (otherwise, doing A will not reflect one's volitions). Now, even if God's doing A in C is necessary given God's nature, and even if God never was able to do anything about being in C, God's doing A still satisfies these three conditions:

  (i) God has effective choice over doing A.

 (ii) Neither God's volition to A nor God's doing A itself is the result of an antecedent causal condition that predates God's existence.

(iii) God's doing A is not the result of the intentional state of another agent or a non-rational internal force.

But in that case, why should God's inability to refrain from A in C and his never having been able to do anything about being in C imply that his doing A does not redound to his credit? For what do these conditions come to here other than God's inability to act against what he has the best reason to do? Do we really want to say it would redound to God's credit in this context only if he were able to act against what he sees as the clearly best thing to do, the thing that he has every reason to do and no good reason not to do? That is, that an act of God redounds to his credit only if it is possible for him to be irrational?[15]
What should we make of these words?

The basic claim is that the three cases that motivate the condition in question do not apply to God. I agree that they do not apply to God. However – and this is crucial – we need to ask what it is about these cases in virtue of which our acts do not redound to our credit. Why is it that an act of mine does not redound to my credit if it is a result of antecedent causal conditions that predate my existence, or if another agent is its ultimate source, or if it is the result of a serendipitous psychological disorder? The reason is this: in each case, *I never was able to do anything about any of the factors that entailed my act.* I never was able to do anything about events that occurred billions of years before I was born, or the laws of nature that are in place. I never was able to do anything about the neurosurgeon's implanting the device in my head or the serendipitous lesion growing in my brain. If we modify the cases so that I had hired a neurosurgeon or taken drugs, with the aim of producing conditions that would entail my act, and if I had been able to do something about the hiring and the taking, the conviction that my good acts do not redound to my credit evaporates.

So there is a common explanation for why our acts do not redound to our credit in the three cases: we were never able to do anything about any of the factors that entailed those acts.

This explanation permits cases that motivate the condition in question but which, unlike the three cases above, are *not* out of place where God is concerned. Consider a person very much like a human being except for three things: (i) she comes into existence purely by chance and without any cause whatever; (ii) her nature entails that she will perform whatever act she sees to be uniquely best; and (iii) she is in circumstances C where she sees that act A is uniquely best and she never was able to do anything about being in C. She performs A. Let us call her *Bonnie Chance*, or *Bonnie* for short. In Bonnie's case, no past series of events and causal laws entails that she does A in C, no other agent is the ultimate source of her doing it, and her doing it is not the result of malfunction. Nevertheless, her doing A in C does *not* redound to her credit. Why? For the same reason that *our* acts do not redound to our credit in the three cases above: she was never able to do anything about any of the factors that entailed her doing A in C.[16]

However, even if we reject Bonnie, the main point remains: the common explanation for the three cases applies directly to God. If, as the third objection has it, God's doing A redounds to his credit despite the fact that, due to his nature he is unable to refrain from doing A in C, and he was never able to do anything about being in C, then he was never able to do anything about any of the factors that entail his doing A. Thus, that in virtue of which the three cases motivate the condition in question applies to God after all, contrary to the objection.

But what about the claim at the end of the objection, namely that if it redounds to God's credit that he does A in C only if he was able to refrain from doing A in C or he was able to do something about being in C, then it is possible for God to perform an act that redounds to his credit only if it is possible for him to act irrationally? This implication seems implausible in the extreme, one might think.

Here we need to note two things. First, the claim in question – that is, the complex conditional in the last paragraph – is false. What follows from the fact that it redounds to God's credit that he does A in C only if he was able to refrain from doing A in C or he was able to do something about being in C, is that it is possible for God to perform an act that redounds to his credit only if it is possible for him to act irrationally *or his unsurpassable goodness is contingent*. Second, suppose we stipulate that God, come what may, is essentially unsurpassably good. In that case, the claim in question is true. But, in that case, what is the objection? Something has to give in God's nature in order to provide him with the ability to refrain from doing A in C or the past ability to have done something about being in C in the first place. Otherwise his good acts will not redound to his credit. Thus, if we stipulate that it is not his essential unsurpassable goodness that takes the hit, then what is there left but his essential unsurpassable cognitive excellence? If, by stipulation, that is all that were left with, it does not seem implausible at all that it is possible for God to perform an act that redounds to his credit only if it is possible for him to act irrationally. What is the alternative? Saying that his good acts redound to his credit even though he was never able to do anything about any of the factors that entailed those acts? That way lies *madness* (read: compatibilism).

4. The Fourth Objection

Imagine someone putting forward the second objection with this twist at the end:...Thus, the causal story is this: God's nature causes him, in C, to have this particular constellation of knowledge, desire, and strength...[and now comes the twist]...but neither his nature nor that constellation cause him to do A in C. The cause of God's doing A is *God*, the agent. God is the *agent-cause* of A, or a volition to A, or some other more suitable effect of an agent-cause. But whatever the effect, God agent-causes it and there is no possible world in which he does not agent-cause it in C. I see no reason not to say that, in that case, it redounds to God's credit when he agent-causes A – even though he was unable to agent-cause anything else in its place and even though he was never able to do anything about being in C.

To develop this objection, consider the following account of agent-causation:

AC.   X is the agent-cause of event E if and only if each of the following three conditions is satisfied: (1) x is a substance that had the power (strength) to bring about E, (2) x exerted its power to bring about E, (3) nothing distinct from x (not even x's nature or beliefs or desires or any other psychological state or activity) caused x to exert its power to bring about E.

Notice that, unlike standard libertarian agency theories, AC does not rule out the possibility that x is the agent-cause of E even if x is unable to do otherwise than agent-cause E.[17] Moreover, notice that AC does not rule out the possibility that x is the agent-cause of E even though x's character or nature *entails* E. Furthermore, AC sheds light on why it redounds to God's credit that he does A when his nature entails that he do it. It is because his nature entails his doing A without causing him to do A; he agent-causes his doing A, and *nothing distinct from him causes him to agent-cause it*, not even his own nature. The causal buck stops with God, the agent. Thus, provided that God agent-causes his doing A for the right reasons, it redounds to his credit that he did it, and he is thus worthy of thanks and praise – never mind that he lacked the ability to do anything else instead.

Once it is granted that God agent-causes an act, without being forced to do so by something other than himself, it is difficult to see why one would resist the suggestion that it redounds to his credit that he did it. So he does as much at every possible world: why should that matter? Suppose God was unable to do anything else than raise this woman's child from the dead. And suppose *this good action flows from God himself* – God agent-caused it, nothing distinct from him caused him to perform it. And suppose God performed it for good reasons. (It is possible for agent-caused acts to be performed for reasons without being caused by those reasons. In such a case, the act is performed in light of reasons that incline the person to perform the act without causing the person to perform it.) If the mother recognized these facts, could not she tell God, without betraying confusion, that (i) she acknowledges this as indeed a good act, (ii) she realizes that he is its agent-cause, (iii) she is glad and greatly relieved that he performed it, and (iv) she considers herself to be in his debt (not someone else's or no-one's) since he and nothing else agent-caused her son to be raised from the dead? It seems so. But then there is no incoherence in saying that it redounds to God's credit that he raised her son from the dead, and hence there is no incoherence in saying that he is worthy of her gratitude and the praise of all for doing so – despite the fact that he was unable to do anything else instead.[18]

What should we make of the position put forward here?

Well, it exhibits the usual obscurity that attends agent-causal stories, but let that pass.[19] My main objection is that it sheds no light at all on how it redounds to God's credit that he did A in C when he was unable to do anything but A in C and he was never able to do anything about being in C in the first place. It would do that only if there was a time when God was able to do something about whether he agent-caused A in C. But there was no such time. His nature entailed that he agent-cause A in C, and he never was able to do anything about whether he would have that nature or whether he would be in C. So the causal buck stops with God, alright: but why should *that* matter? There is no honor in being the cause of something if one was never able to do anything about any of the factors that entailed one's causing it.

But what about the case of the mother whose son God raised from the dead? Is it not *just obvious* that since this good action flows from God himself, it redounds to his credit that he did it? The case is moving, of course. After all, if *I* were the mother, I would be glad and greatly relieved and thank God. But our question is not whether the mother would be glad and greatly relieved and thank God. Rather, our question is whether there would be any confusion on her part if she were to consider herself in God's debt – say, regard herself as owing God a debt of gratitude – given that he and nothing else agent-caused her son to be raised from the dead. I think the answer is 'yes.' Her confusion would consist in her failure to recognize four facts. First, she owes God a debt of gratitude for his agent-causing her son's rising from the dead only if God is worthy of such gratitude. Second, God is worthy of gratitude for agent-causing her son's rising from the dead only if it redounds to God's credit that he agent-caused it. Third, it redounds to God's credit that he agent-caused her son's rising from the dead only if there was a time when he was able to do something about some of the factors that entailed his agent-causing it. Fourth, God was never able to do anything about any of the factors that entailed his agent-causing it.[20]

We began with a puzzle: how is it possible for God to be essentially unsurpassably good and yet worthy of thanks and praise for his good acts? Although our solutions disagree over how, exactly, this is possible, they each imply that God's good acts would redound to his credit and that he would be worthy of thanks and praise for performing them even if it is metaphysically impossible for God to do anything in their stead. This implication has a repugnant consequence.

Let us say that *Spinozism* is the thesis that every truth is a necessary truth. In the vernacular of possible worlds, there is exactly one possible world. Notice that, on each of our solutions, it would redound to God's credit that he did A even if Spinozism were true. According to the first solution, although there is no possible world in which God refrains from doing A, he was able to refrain from doing A. Thus, there need be no possible world in which God refrains from doing A in order for him to be able to refrain. Thus, God would be able to refrain from doing A even if there were exactly one possible world. Since no other condition laid down by the first solution entails that if God's doing A redounds to his credit, then there is more than one possible world, it follows on the first solution that it would redound to God's credit that he did A even if Spinozism were true. According to the second solution, God was unable to refrain from doing A but, since the cause of his doing A, that is his nature, is internal to him in the right way, it redounds to his credit that he did it. Since God's nature would be internal to him in the right way even if there were exactly one possible world, it follows from the second solution that it would redound to God's credit that he did A even if Spinozism were true. According to the third solution, God was unable to refrain from doing A but, since he has effective choice over doing A, and his doing A is not the result of antecedent causal conditions that predate his existence, the intentional state of another agent, or a nonrational internal force, it redounds to his credit that he did it. Since these conditions would be satisfied even if there were exactly one possible world, it follows that, given the third solution, it would redound to God's credit that he did A even if Spinozism were true. According to the fourth solution, God was unable to refrain from doing A but, since the cause of his doing A was God himself, not his own nature or his reasons for doing A, it redounds to his credit that he did it. Since God would be the agent-cause of A even if there were exactly one possible world, it follows from the fourth solution that it would redound to God's credit that he did A even if Spinozism were true.

Therefore, on each of our solutions, God's good acts would redound to his credit and he would be worthy of thanks and praise for performing them, even if there were exactly one possible world. I do not know what to say to an *in*compatibilist who affirms a view that has this consequence. I do not know what to say to a compatibilist either, but at least such things are not unexpected from her. So, given my incompatibilist presuppositions, I have nothing more to say – except that *modus tollens* is a valid argument form.[21]

5. The Fifth Objection

> Suppose that for some good act A that God performs, he is not able to do better or worse in its place but he is able to do something equally good, in the circumstances C he is in. There are ties for the best act he is able to perform. Since God aims to perform one of the best acts available to him, and since there is no morally relevant reason for him to prefer one from among the others, he randomly selects A and performs it. That is not to say the he does not perform it for the right reason. On the contrary, he performs A for *exactly* the right reason, given C: A is one of the best acts available to him. (If you like, you may add that he agent-causes A, or the volition to A, or whatever.) I say that, in that case, it redounds to his credit that he performs A, in C, never mind that he was unable to do worse than A and he never was able to do anything about being in C.

Does this objection succeed where the others have failed?

I do not think so. For consider what it is about an act that redounds to our credit even if it was randomly selected from among equally good acts and we were never able to do anything about what good acts would be available to us. Suppose that, in my present circumstances, I am incapable (as defined earlier) of doing anything but one of these three equally good acts next Saturday morning: stack furniture at the Lighthouse Mission, sort second-hand clothes at Hope House, and wash dishes at Interfaith Kitchen. I am able to perform each of these acts but I am unable to perform any other, even refrain. Since there is no reason to favor one over the others, suppose I randomly select the second and perform it (or, if it helps, suppose I non-randomly select the second for a non-moral reason – say, I am especially fond of the smell of used clothes). Does it redound to my credit that I sort clothes at Hope House, in that case? Of course, if there was a time when I was able to do something about whether I would be presented with just these three alternatives, it would be relevant. But we are supposing that there never was such a time. Thus, whether it redounds to my credit when I sort clothes hangs on why I am unable to do anything but one of these three good acts, in the circumstances.

Suppose that I am unable for the following reason. There was a time when I was both able to do various things and able to refrain from doing those things; by doing them, repeatedly, over many years, I developed and confirmed a firmly entrenched character trait that rendered me unable to do anything but one of these three good acts, in the circumstances. In that case, it redounds to my credit that I sort clothes, even though I am unable to do anything worse and I was never able to do anything about being in the circumstances I am in. For by developing and confirming a firmly entrenched character trait that rendered me unable to do anything but one of these three good acts in the circumstances, I did something about some of the factors that entailed that I would perform one of the equally good acts available to me in my present circumstances, and I was able not to do it. Absent this fact, it does not redound to my credit when I perform one of those acts.

Of course, this explanation does not apply to God. It is impossible for an essentially unsurpassably good being to engage in the sort of soul-making I just described. So this explanation does not apply to God. Perhaps there is some other story to be told in God's case. Unfortunately, the ones I am familiar with run afoul of the same fact: on those stories, God was never able to do anything about any of the factors that entailed his performance of his good acts.

6. The Sixth Objection

There is considerable pressure to endorse the Incompatibility Argument. At any rate, incompatibilists who think that no act of ours redounds to our credit in a deterministic world because we would never be able to do anything about the factors that entail our actions will feel the pressure. For that thought applies directly to God if he is essentially unsurpassably good – even if nothing independent of him or his nature is the ultimate cause of his good acts. If God is essentially unsurpassably good, his nature entails that he must perform the best act or one of the best acts he is able to perform in the circumstances; thus, he was never able to do anything about any of the factors that entail his actions, for he was never able to do anything about his nature or the circumstances he is in.

But what if there is no such thing as the best act or one of the best acts God is able to perform in the circumstances he is in? Indeed, what if there is no such thing as the worst?[22] In that case, God's good acts redound to his credit, and he is worthy of thanks and praise for them. For in that case, no matter what good act God performs, he will be able to perform a worse act in its place. The way is then clear for his good acts to redound to his credit and for him to be worthy of thanks and praise for performing them.

We might develop this line of thought as follows. Imagine a morally good person who is essentially unsurpassable in power and cognitive excellence named *Jove*, and who, out of his goodness, aims on some occasion to perform the best act that he has the strength to perform. Unfortunately, as he holds the acts he has the strength to perform before his mind, he sees that for each there is a better; indeed, for each there is a worse. So Jove is unable to achieve his aim. Faced with this predicament, Jove sets about the task of deciding which act to perform. He decides to write up two lists, one of acceptable acts and the other of unacceptable acts. To do this, he uses certain criteria to sort the acts he has the strength to perform into those whose degree of goodness renders them acceptable and those whose degree of goodness renders them unacceptable. For example, acts that are impermissible go onto the unacceptable list, as do acts that are permissible but unloving. (I encourage the reader to use her own criteria.) Then he orders the infinitely many acceptable acts that remain according to their degree of goodness, randomly assigns '0' to one of them, '1' to its better neighbor, '2' to its better neighbor's neighbor, and so on, and '–1' to its worse neighbor, '–2' to its worse neighbor's neighbor, and so on. Finally, he randomly selects one and performs it, say act no. 777.

This story seems possible.[23] But now consider the proposition that Jove is not only good but essentially unsurpassably good. Suppose we add it to our story. Does some glaring *im*possibility reveal itself? I do not see one. If there is not one, then it is possible that an essentially unsurpassably good person who is essentially unsurpassable in power and cognitive excellence is able to do something worse in place of what he does.

One might beg to differ: Jove *is* morally surpassable, contrary to what I say. To see who is right, let us consider various ways in which a person who is relevantly like Jove might behave differently. (By 'a person who is relevantly like Jove' I mean a morally good person who is essentially unsurpassable in power and cognitive excellence and who is faced with Jove's predicament.)

Consider Juno. Juno sorts the acts in exactly the same way Jove does and uses exactly the same random selection procedure that Jove does, but she performs a different act, say no. 999, since it is randomly selected. In that case, Juno performs a better act than Jove. But it does not follow that, all else being equal, Juno is morally better than Jove. For given their resolve to perform whatever act is randomly selected, they are not able to perform any act but the one they perform. Thus, even though a better act results from Juno's selection procedure, it does not imply that she is morally better than Jove. Indeed, all else being equal, they are morally equivalent.

Now consider Thor. Suppose Thor is relevantly like Jove but he does not use Jove's sorting criteria and he does not use a random selection procedure. Instead, Jove non-randomly selects act no. 888 from Jove's list of acceptable acts because he sees that *it* is better than any lesser act and prefers performing *it* to performing any lesser act.[24] In that case, Thor performs a better act than Jove. But does it follow that Thor is morally better than Jove?

Well, if Thor is morally better than Jove, it is not simply because Thor performed a better act than him. For Jove and Juno are moral equals. Thus, if Thor is better than Jove, then he is better than Juno; but the act Thor performs is worse than the act Juno performs. So if Thor is better than Jove, it is in virtue of some other difference, presumably a difference in attitude.

And here there is a difference. Thor selects no. 888 *because he sees that it is better than any lesser act and prefers performing it to performing any lesser act.* Jove lacks the analogous preference. Perhaps this is the difference that makes Thor morally better than Jove.

If so, it is not simply because Thor preferred a better act than Jove. Thor's preference for act no. 888 must not be morally defective or wholly frivolous. For example, if he prefers it because he is vain or fond of that number, then the fact that he prefers it does not imply that he is better than Jove. Moreover, Thor's preference must be rational, as befits his unsurpassable cognitive excellence, in which case he must have a reason to prefer it and that reason must be a reason for him to select no. 888 non-randomly (since he non-randomly selected no. 888 on the basis of that reason).

Unfortunately, Thor's reason is not a reason for him to select no. 888 non-randomly. For recall that the reason Thor has to prefer act no. 888 is that it is better than any lesser act. This means that Thor's reason to prefer act no. 888 is that it has the property of *being better than any lesser act than no. 888.* But every act that is *better* than no. 888 has that property. Thus, as Thor begins to perform act no. 888, he will pull up short, for he will notice act no. 889 out of the corner of his eye and reason as follows: 'Like act no. 888, act no. 889 is better than any lesser act too; indeed, act no. 890 is better than any lesser act than no. 888 as well; and act no. 891 . . . Hold on! If I keep up this line of reasoning, I won't do *anything*. I had better randomly select . . . ' The upshot is that Thor's reason is not a reason to select no. 888 *non-randomly*; it is a reason to select randomly from no. 888 and above. Thus, the case of Thor is incoherent.

Now consider Minerva. Minerva, who is relevantly like Jove, does not use Jove's sorting criteria. Rather, she uses the following two principles to separate acceptable from unacceptable acts:

P1. Do not perform any act that is not a good act.
P2. Do not perform any good act whose degree of goodness is less than what one judges as acceptable, given that one is able to perform a better act.[25]

As a result, no. 888 from Jove's list of acceptable acts is the worst act she is prepared to perform. Next, she uses the same random selection procedure that Jove used, and performs no. 888 since it was randomly selected. Note that Jove is prepared to settle for acts Minerva is not prepared to settle for.[26] Perhaps this difference makes Minerva better than Jove.

If so, it is not simply because Minerva is not prepared to settle for acts that Jove is prepared to settle for. Her not being prepared to settle for any act worse than no. 888 must not be grounded in moral defect or frivolousness, and it must be rational, as required by her cognitive excellence, in which case she must have a reason to draw the line at no. 888 and it must be rational for her to act on that reason as she separates the acceptable from the unacceptable.

Unfortunately, it is not rational for Minerva to draw the line at act no. 888 on the basis of P1 and P2. Imagine her mulling over good act A. Is it good enough to be placed on the list of acceptable acts? P2 offers Minerva this advice to decide the matter: do not perform A if its degree of goodness is less than what you judge to be acceptable. But she has yet to judge whether A's degree of goodness is less than acceptable. That is what she is trying to judge. Principle P2 presupposes that she has already made that judgment when she has not. Thus, it is not possible for Minerva to *act on* P2 as she separates the acceptable good acts from the unacceptable good acts. Thus, her drawing the line at act no. 888 is not rational. Like the case of Thor, the case of Minerva is incoherent.

Much more might be said about the line of thought here. For example, there are other ways in which a person relevantly like Jove might behave in Jove's predicament.[27] But, if we apply a little ingenuity to the points above, we will see, I think, that they too are incoherent. So then: Jove is unsurpassably good, even though he is able to do something worse in place of what he does. And this fact about Jove is unaffected even if he is essentially unsurpassably good. The way is clear, then, to view God's good acts as redounding to his credit, and to view him as worthy of thanks and praise for performing them, even if he is essentially unsurpassably good.[28]

What should we make of this line of reasoning?

I suspect that, if any philosophical story exhibits a possibility, the story of Jove exhibits how it is possible for a person who is essentially unsurpassable in power, cognitive excellence, and moral goodness to perform a good act even though he is able to do something worse in place of what he does – in which case premise 1 of the Incompatibility Argument is false, as are A and A3. Unfortunately, it does not exhibit how it is possible for the good acts of such a person to redound to his credit and for him to be worthy of thanks and praise for performing them. Indeed, it does quite the opposite. Let me explain.

Jove randomly selected the good act he performed from a set of acts he judged to be acceptable, and he selected the members of that set on the basis of certain criteria. Now, *if* Jove was *essentially* unsurpassably good, then his nature entailed that he use those criteria and that he judge those acts to be acceptable. Thus, since he was never able to do anything about his nature, he was never able to do anything but select those acts on the basis of those criteria. Furthermore, since Jove is, by hypothesis, *essentially* unsurpassable in cognitive excellence and power, given the predicament he was in, he was never able to do anything but resolve to randomly select from the set of acceptable acts, in which case he was unable to do anything but perform whatever act that was randomly selected from among the acceptable acts. In sum, he was never able to do anything about those factors that entailed his performance of whatever act was randomly selected, and so it did not redound to his credit that he performed act no. 777. Thus, he is not worthy of thanks or praise for performing it.

The application to God is clear. We have, then, a new argument for the Incompatibility Claim, one that is not subject to the sixth objection:

1. If God is essentially unsurpassably good, then *either* (a) he is unable to do anything worse in place of the actions he performs *or* (b) he was never able to do anything about those factors that entailed his performance of whatever actions he randomly selected.
2. If God is unable to do anything worse in place of the actions he performs, he is not worthy of thanks or praise for performing them.
3. If God was never able to do anything about those factors that entailed his performance of whatever actions he randomly selected, then he is not worthy of thanks and praise for performing them.
4. So, it is impossible for God to be essentially unsurpassably good and yet worthy of thanks and praise for what he does.

One might try to blunt the force of the preceding lines of thought as follows:

Even if the Incompatibility Argument is sound, it hardly follows that God is not worthy of praise for something other than his actions. Indeed, it is something else for which God is worthy of praise that is paramount in the theist tradition. When theists claim that God is to be praised, they mean that God is to be praised for *who God is*, not for *what God does*. Now what makes God praiseworthy includes his awesome power – the fact that not only is there no being as powerful as God but that it is not possible since God is the source of all power. But while sheer power might make a being literally awesome, it wouldn't make it praiseworthy. What makes God praiseworthy is his power together with his nature as fair, merciful, and loving – his embodying all that is valuable. God's nature as both the source of all that is and as a benevolent Creator is what makes him worthy of our praise. Even if God's good acts do not redound to his credit, and even if he is not worthy of praise for those good acts, God *himself* is nevertheless worthy of praise; for he is the ground of all being and power and yet treats such finite, flawed beings as ourselves with love, kindness, and mercy. I submit that when theists offer their praise to God in worship, they intend to praise God as the loving, benevolent source of all being and power. Offering praise to the paraplegic who climbs Mount

Everest, and offering praise to God for being the loving Creator of the Heavens and Earth is not to offer the same thing to different individuals. The paraplegic has done something for which she is worthy of praise; God is worthy of praise for being Who God is.[29]

What should we make of this effort to blunt the force of the Incompatibility Claim, or that part of it that involves God's being worthy of praise for what he does? (The part that involves God's being worthy of thanks will have to be dealt with in another fashion since it makes no sense whatsoever to suppose that God is worthy of thanks for who he is but not for what he does.)

I find it unconvincing for two reasons.

First, when theists claim that God is to be praised, they do *not* mean that God is to be praised for who he is *but not* for what he does. They mean that he is to be praised for *both*, as illustrated by the Song of Moses, the Song of Daniel, the first Song of Isaiah, Mary's Song, the Psalms of praise, the thunderous hallelujahs of John's vision, and scores of other liturgies and hymns. Theists are prone to say things that are not much different in content from 'Wow! Did you see *that*? Amazing! Way to go, God!,' where 'that' denotes something they think God *did*, like create the Heavens and the Earth, change a jerk into a gentleman, or cure your friend's cancer.[30]

Second, the basic line of thought given in the preceding sections for the conclusion that it is impossible that God is essentially unsurpassably good and yet worthy of praise for *what he does* applies with equal force to the claim that it is impossible that God is essentially unsurpassably good and yet worthy of praise for *who he is*. Roughly, if God is worthy of praise for who he is, he is worthy of praise for his goodness, in which case it redounds to his credit that he is good, which implies that there was a time when he was able to do something about whether he is good. But, if God is essentially unsurpassable in goodness, there never was such a time. Thus, if God is essentially unsurpassable in goodness, he is not worthy of praise for who he is.

I began with a puzzle, the puzzle of prayers of thanksgiving and praise. I also began with the intention of solving it. I now see no solution. To be sure, I have not assessed every attempt at a solution. Notably, I have not mentioned the role that the doctrines of divine simplicity or aseity might be called upon to play here.[31] For my own part, I find these doctrines either unintelligible (simplicity) or simply unhelpful (aseity) in providing a solution. Thus, by my lights, there are only three reasonable alternatives: give up the practice of thanking and praising God, give up the incompatibilist presuppositions that drive the puzzle, or give up the doctrine of God's essential unsurpassable goodness. Speaking only for myself, as Jerry Fodor once said in a different connection, if compatibilism is literally true, everything I believe about virtually anything is false and it is the end of the world. Therefore I must concede that the practice of thanking and praising God, the practice in which I have raised my children and live and move and have my being, is irrational – unless I reject the doctrine of God's essential unsurpassable goodness.

Perhaps I might find succor in the fact that the Incompatibility Argument leaves untouched great swaths of what goes under the rubric of prayer, for example petition, intercession, adoration, contrition, oblation, and contemplation. Still, I find the results of my investigation disturbing and saddening, for it is praise and, especially, thanksgiving that resonates most deeply with me in my participation in the practice of prayer. I might find a way out of my dilemma if there were little cost to jettisoning the doctrine of God's *essential* unsurpassable goodness. Is there? To my mind, that is the question to which my reflections in this chapter naturally lead.[32]

Notes

1. *The Book of Common Prayer*, The Holy Eucharist, Rite Two, Eucharistic Prayer A.
2. Peter Edward Howard-Snyder, age 6, prayer before dinner, October 26, 2006.
3. *The Book of Common Prayer*, General Thanksgivings.
4. Baillie (1962, p. 237).
5. In Fitzgerald (1998), we find six reasons to express gratitude to our benefactors, only one of which is that they are worthy of it. The other five are: if we don't express gratitude they will be hurt; if we express gratitude they will be pleased; and expressing gratitude promotes communal bonds, personal virtue, and friendship.
6. To say that an individual is *essentially* F, for some property F, is just to say that it is not metaphysically possible for that individual to exist without having F. To say that an individual is *contingently* F, for some property F, is just to say that it is metaphysically possible for that individual to exist without having F. In what follows, the traditional theistic God is my focus, whose other essential properties include unsurpassable power and cognitive excellence.
7. William Rowe, in his defense of the principle that if an omniscient person creates a world when it could have created a better world, then it is possible for there to be a person morally better than it, writes:

    > [I]f an omniscient being creates a world when it could have created a better world, then that being has done something less good than it could do (create a better world). But any being that knowingly does something (all things considered) less good than it could do falls short of being the best possible being. (Rowe, 2004, p. 89; cp. 100)

    More frequently, Rowe argues in a way indistinguishable from this: If an omniscient person creates a world when it could have created a better world, then it is possible for there to be another person who creates a world but whose degree of moral goodness was such that it judged as unacceptable for creation what the first judged as acceptable. The second person was not prepared to settle for a world that the first was prepared to settle for. In that case, the second person's degree of moral goodness is greater than the first person's degree of moral goodness. But then it is possible for there to be a person morally better than the first. See Rowe (1993, 1994, 2002, and 2004, pp. 92–98, and repeatedly thereafter); cp. Quinn (1982) and Grover (1988).

8. See Bergmann and Cover (2006, p. 404, n1) for an instance of the first type. Frances Howard-Snyder reports that she is an instance of the second type.
9. Neal Tognazzini notes another reason to think they hang together: praise and blame are often connected with P.F. Strawson's 'reactive attitudes', and the second-personal positive reactive attitude is often taken to be *gratitude*. So, on this view, one way to be worthy of praise is to be worthy of gratitude.
10. If you think this is too brief, see van Inwagen (1983, pp. 8–13) and Morris (1991, pp. 69–73). I do not commend everything said on those pages, however. Note that 'can,' 'control,' and their cognates do not appear in the paper. I try to do everything with 'able,' following van Inwagen's advice. See van Inwagen forthcoming.
11. The first objection is inspired by Morris (1991, pp. 71–72); in fact, it contains several sentences quoted verbatim but for minor tweaking. I do not attribute it to him, however; nor should anyone else.
12. In thinking about the first objection, I was helped by Senor (2006, pp. 428–29). Cp. The first objection with Talbott (1988, p. 22): '[God] has the power to perform malicious and cruel acts.... He has this power even though it is logically impossible that he would want to exercise it'. By 'power' here Talbott means what I mean by 'ability,' I think. Note that his example of the man who loves his wife so dearly that it is psychologically impossible for him to torture her, even though he is (allegedly) able to do so (pp. 17–18), is just our Special Forces operative in the relevant respect. Note also how Talbott flip-flops between power or strength, on the one hand, and ability, on the other hand, in his discussion of the three cases on pp. 10–11.
13. The second objection here is inspired by several paragraphs of Wierenga (2002, pp. 433–34); in fact, it contains several sentences quoted verbatim but for minor tweaking. I do not attribute it to him, however; nor should anyone else.
14. Not even the theistic activist, according to whom God creates those properties in which his nature consists and eternally and necessarily causes himself to exemplify them, thinks that God was able to make himself have a different nature. See Morris (1987, pp. 170–71): causing something does not imply being able to alter or change it.
15. The third objection is inspired by several paragraphs in Senor (2007, pp. 182–84); in fact, it contains several sentences quoted verbatim but for minor tweaking. I do not attribute it to him, however; nor should anyone else.
16. This is Wes Morriston's case, altered for my purposes; Morriston (2006, 95ff). Even though Bonnie is impossible, it is non-trivially true that if she were to exist, it would not redound to her credit that she did A. I see no relevant intelligible dissimilarity between God and Bonnie.
17. In this respect, AC is like Markosian (1999).
18. The fourth objection is inspired by Bergmann and Cover (2006, pp. 392–93 and 399–400); in fact, it contains several sentences quoted verbatim but for minor tweaking. I do not attribute it to them, however; nor should anyone else.
19. Chapters 5 and 6 of Kane (2005) nicely display the obscurity of several agent-causal approaches. For a more general expression of bafflement, see van Inwagen (2000).
20. A similar diagnosis applies to Senor's beneficent aunt and self-serving uncle. See Senor (2007, p. 186).
21. Neal Tognazzini notes that if there is some necessary condition on one's being worthy of praise and thanks for doing something other than its redounding to

one's credit and satisfying it is incompatible with Spinozism, then the argument here fails. I agree. But if there is such a condition, it must not be *ad hoc*. Moreover, if it is to have any bearing on my argument, it must be at home with the incompatibilist presuppositions I have made explicit.

22. Thanks to Peter van Inwagen for making this suggestion to me in 1992. Cp. Wierenga (2002, p. 432).

23. Of course, I have represented Jove as being spatially located and as being both unsurpassable in cognitive excellence and coming to learn things. Moreover, I have assumed that all of the acts that Jove has the strength to perform are feasible for him to perform. Furthermore, I have assumed that the ranking Jove gives to the items on the list of acceptable acts do not admit of ties and that there wouldn't be so many acts on the list that it is impossible for them to be mapped one-to-one to the positive and negative natural numbers. And I haven't said anything about the workings of the random selection procedure. I invite the fastidious reader to retell the story so as to avoid these and other mundane infelicities.

24. Cp Rowe (1994, p. 270): 'Thor doesn't use a randomizing machine but selects world no. 888 over Jove's world no. 777 *because he sees that it is better and prefers creating no. 888 to creating any lesser world*' (emphasis added); quoted in Rowe (2004, p. 93).

25. Cp. Rowe (2002, p. 414, and 2004, p. 95). Note: *my* Jove does *not* act *on* P2, even if he acts *in accordance* with P2. Failure to tend carefully to the difference between acting on a principle and acting in accordance with a principle has led some people in this debate into error.

26. Provided she is able to perform a better act. Keep this proviso in mind here and throughout.

27. See, for example, Kraay (2005, 2006), Steinberg (2005), and Grover (2003).

28. The sixth objection is inspired by Howard-Snyders (1994); in fact, it contains several sentences quoted verbatim but for minor tweaking. I do not attribute it to them, however; nor should anyone else.

29. This speech is inspired by Senor (2007, pp. 185–86); in fact, it contains several sentences quoted verbatim but for minor tweaking. I do not attribute it to him, however; nor should anyone else.

30. And let us not have any silliness like this: 'What's *really* going on in these cases is that we are praising God for who he is, not for what he does, since, after all, we are offering praise to God for *being* the Creator of the Heavens and Earth, *being* the changer of a jerk into a gentleman, or *being* the curer of a friend's cancer.'

31. On the relevance of simplicity, see Morriston (2006, p. 98). On the relevance of aseity, the suggestion is that, unlike us, God does not depend for his nature, existence, and actions on anything else and so, unlike us, there is no need for him to be able to do something in place of what he does in order for his good acts to be his own and for them thus to redound to his credit. Thanks to Tom Senor and Michael Murray for calling my attention to this line of thought.

32. For comments on previous drafts of this chapter, I thank Nick Beckstead, Timothy Campbell, Frances Howard-Snyder, Hud Hudson, Casey Knight, Christian Lee, Elizabeth Miller, Michael Murray, William Rowe, Tom Senor, Meghan Sullivan, Neal Tognazzini, Jennifer Wang, and Dean Zimmerman. Thanks to Edward Wierenga for shaking me up. Thanks to the Office of Research and Sponsored Programs at Western Washington University for the Financial Support provided by a Summer Faculty Research Grant.

References

Robert Adams, 1972. 'Must God Create the Best?' *Philosophical Review* 81, 317–332.

James Baillie, 1962. *The Sense of the Presence of God.* New York: Charles Scribner's Sons.

Michael Bergmann and Jan Cover, 2006. 'Divine Responsibility without Divine Freedom,' *Faith and Philosophy* 24, 381–408.

Patrick Fitzgerald, 1998. 'Gratitude and Justice,' *Ethics* 109, 119–153.

Stephen Grover, 1988. 'Why Only the Best is Good Enough,' *Analysis* 48, 224.

Stephen Grover, 2003. 'This World, "Adams Worlds", and the Best of All Possible Worlds,' *Religious Studies* 39, 145–163.

Daniel Howard-Snyder and Frances Howard-Snyder, 1994. 'How an Unsurpassable Being Can Create a Surpassable World,' *Faith and Philosophy* 11, 260–268.

Robert Kane, 2005. *A Contemporary Introduction to Free Will.* New York: Oxford University Press.

Klaas Kraay, 2005. 'William Rowe's A Priori Argument for Atheism,' *Faith and Philosophy* 22, 221–234.

Klaas Kraay, 2006. 'God and the Hypothesis of No Prime Worlds,' *International Journal for Philosophy of Religion* 59, 49–68.

Ned Markosian, 1999. 'A Compatibilist Version of the Theory of Agent Causation,' *Pacific Philosophical Quarterly* 80, 257–277.

Thomas Morris, 1987. *Anselmian Explorations.* Notre Dame, Indiana: University of Notre Dame Press.

Thomas Morris, 1991. *Our Idea of God: An Introduction to Philosophical Theology.* Downer's Grove, Illinois: InterVarsity Press.

Wesley Morriston, 2006. 'Is God Free?: Reply to Wierenga,' *Faith and Philosophy* 23, 93–98.

Philip Quinn, 1982. 'God, Moral Perfection, and Possible Worlds,' in Frederick Sontag and M. Darrol Bryant eds, *God: The Contemporary Discussion.* New York: The Rose of Sharon Press, 197–215.

William Rowe, 1993. 'The Problem of Divine Perfection and Freedom,' in Eleonore Stump ed., *Reasoned Faith.* Ithaca, New York: Cornell University Press, 223–233.

William Rowe, 1994. 'The Problem of No Best World,' *Faith and Philosophy* 11, 269–271.

William Rowe, 2002. 'Can God be Free?' *Faith and Philosophy* 19, 405–424.

William Rowe, 2004. *Can God Be Free?* New York: Oxford University Press.

Thomas D. Senor, 2006. 'God's Goodness Needs No Privilege: A Reply to Funkhouser,' *Faith and Philosophy* 23, 423–431.

Thomas D. Senor, 2007. 'Defending Divine Freedom,' *Oxford Studies in the Philosophy of Religion* 1, 168–195.

Jesse Steinberg, 2005. 'Why an Unsurpassable Being Cannot Create a Surpassable World,' *Religious Studies* 41, 323–333.

Thomas Talbott, 1988. 'On the Divine Nature and the Nature of Divine Freedom,' *Faith and Philosophy* 5, 3–24.

Peter van Inwagen, 1983. *An Essay on Free Will.* Oxford: Oxford University Press.

Peter van Inwagen, 2000. 'Free Will Remains a Mystery,' *Philosophical Perspectives* 14, 1–19.

Peter van Inwagen, forthcoming. 'How to Think About the Problem of Free Will,' *Journal of Ethics.*

Edward Wierenga, 2002. 'The Freedom of God,' *Faith and Philosophy* 19, 425–436.

9
A Participatory Model of the Atonement

Tim Bayne and Greg Restall

> What? Humanity sins but it's God's Son who pays the price? I tried to imagine Father saying to me, 'Piscine, a lion slipped into the llama pen today and killed two llamas. Yesterday another one killed a black buck. Last week two of them ate the camel. The week before it was painted storks and grey herons. And who's to say for sure who snacked on our golden agouti? The situation has become intolerable. Something must be done. I have decided that the only way the lions can atone for their sins is if I feed you to them.'
>
> 'Yes, Father, that would be the right and logical thing to do. Give me a moment to wash up.'
>
> … What a downright weird story. What peculiar psychology.
>
> — *Life of Pi*, Yann Martel

Although the atonement is at the heart of Christian theology, it has not been at the heart of Twentieth Century Christian philosophy of religion: at least, you would not get the impression that it was from the volume of literature on the topic. Nonetheless, in recent years there has been a noticeable change in the intellectual climate, with a renewed interest in the atonement within philosophy of religion. Although much of this work contains valuable insights, it also suffers from a notable lack of engagement with work in theology and New Testament scholarship. Contributors to the philosophical discussion of the atonement have been almost exclusively concerned with what we might call Abelard's constraint: their goal has been to develop a model of the atonement that is 'neither unintelligible, arbitrary, illogical nor immoral'. While there is much to be said in favour of Abelard's constraint—who would not prefer a theory which was intelligible, non-arbitrary, consistent and morally acceptable over one which was not?—accounts of the atonement should also be informed and constrained by the New Testament and later church history.[1] Any account that is not so informed either by Scripture or by tradition forfeits its right to be thought of as a Christian account of the atonement. Our central brief in this chapter is that philosophical accounts of the atonement have much to learn from recent work in New Testament scholarship, in particular, Pauline scholarship.

This chapter has two parts: a negative part and a positive part. We begin in part 1 by criticizing certain accounts of the atonement that dominate the contemporary philosophical landscape. Painting with a broad brush, we suggest that many of these accounts suffer from a commitment to a naïve (and, we daresay, unscriptural) conception of sin. We also argue that these accounts fail to draw an intelligible connection between the atonement and the incarnation. In part 2 we turn to the task of developing a Pauline model of atonement. We develop a Pauline model of the atonement that accords a central role to participation in the death and resurrection of Christ.

1 Current models of the atonement

1.1 Conceptions of sin

A number of models of the atonement jostle for space in current philosophy of religion. Some theorists follow Anselm in endorsing a satisfaction account of the atonement (Aspenson, 1990). According to Anselm's *Cur Deus Homo*, atonement involves the payment of a moral debt. The debt is paid when Christ, by dying, gives God the honour that the human race owes him. According to the penal model, the debt of sin is not paid but satisfaction for it is achieved by way of punishment: Christ is punished in place of our non-payment of the debt (Morris, 1966; Packer, 1974; Porter, 2002). According to Swinburne's self-described 'sacrificial model', Christ's death constitutes reparation and penance for non-payment of the debt (Swinburne's, 1988, 1989). According to the merit account, Christ's life and death is a meritorious act that persuades God to forgive the debt of sin that we owe him (Purtill, 1991; Quinn, 1994; Cross, 2001).

A number of specific objections can be levelled against these models (see below), but our central concern is with a feature that they share. These models are all committed to a deontic conception of the problem to which the atonement is the solution—*viz.* sin. These models construe sin as purely a failure on our part to fulfil our moral obligations. This failure leads to a breach in the relationship between God and humanity, a breach which God repairs by means of the atonement. This repair job—so the story goes—involves dealing with this moral debt in some way: the restoration (and continued health) of the relationship is conditional on and grounded in the good standing of humanity vis-à-vis our moral obligations to God. Since we are unable to secure that good standing by our own merits alone, God must take the appropriate actions to secure it for us (or with our help). As we have seen, models of the atonement differ on exactly how this good standing is achieved (and maintained)—some give a role to restitution, others to punishment, others to forgiveness—but there is a broad consensus that reconciliation between humanity and God is conditional on a solution to a deontological problem, a breach of obligations and duties. Quinn gives expression to this conception of sin when he writes, 'The concept of sin is the concept of a human fault that offends a morally perfect God and brings with it guilt' (2000, p. 541).[2]

We beg to differ. Although the notion of sin certainly has a deontic component, it is not a solely deontic matter—indeed, we think it not even *primarily* a deontic matter. And if sin is not primarily a deontic matter, then accounts of the atonement that construe sin in purely deontic terms will be in trouble. We begin with some comments on the deontic conception of sin itself before turning our attention to other components of the notion of sin.

Although analytical philosophers of religion typically construe sin as a matter of moral debt, they have not said much about what exactly this moral debt involves. To whom are the obligations in question owed? What is their content? And what is their ground?

There is general agreement amongst those who hold the deontic picture that the obligations in question are owed to God. Some (or even most) sin might involve flouting one's obligation to oneself, or to other human beings, but on this picture sin is first and foremost an offence against God. Sin is a matter of failing to honour God. We find this Anselmian claim problematic. If the obligation to honour God is the ground of our obligations, then God's relation to us is akin to that of a petty bureaucrat, whose relations with his inferiors are controlled by whether or not those inferiors show him the appropriate amount of respect. This is not to deny that respect may be appropriate in a right relationship, but to analyse the rightness of the relationship in terms of respect is to conceive of God's desires for his creatures in terms of their compliance and deference. This does grave injustice to the Gospel imperatives for the believer to love God and love neighbour.

Swinburne suggests that sin involves a failure to meet the obligation to live a good life. We sin when we live second-rate lives, despite having been given the opportunities by our creator to do otherwise (Swinburne, 1989, p. 157). This too we find problematic. Perhaps we have obligations to live good lives, but do we have such obligations *to God*? Swinburne seems to think that we have this obligation to God because God created us, but this justification seems inadequate to us. Does Frankenstein's automaton have obligations to Frankenstein on the grounds of its origin? That seems implausible. Of course, Christians believe that we owe our being to God in a more thorough-going way than the automaton owes its being to Frankenstein; even so, ontological dependence alone is a tenuous basis on which to ground a deontological conception of sin. In the presence of other considerations, our ontological dependence upon God may well form a part of the ground of our obligations, but any link between our dependence on God and our obligations to God cannot be the only explanation.

Swinburne's conception of sin also sits uneasily with the biblical claim that all are subject to sin. Do we all live second-rate lives? That is doubtful.

All lives have some degree of ordinariness to them, but surely some lives are very virtuous—yet all have sinned. Of course, we *could* regard all lives as 'second-rate', but this is to evacuate the term of descriptive power. We then understand being second-rate in terms of sin rather than vice versa, which was the aim. We might also point out that if we have an obligation to God to live first-rate lives, then (surely!) God has an obligation to us to give us the opportunity to live first-rate lives. Given the prevalence of evil and suffering, one might think that God has failed in this respect. Someone brought up in a violent and abusive household has little opportunity to live a first-rate life. At the very least, we do not think that Swinburne's conception of sin is particularly helpful; it cannot be the point from which we explain the atonement.

Might we ground the obligation to honour God in the obligation that we have to love God and our neighbour?[3] There is much to be said in favour of this notion, of course, and any properly Christian account of the imperatives of the Christian life will focus on the these commandments. But to think of love for God and love for neighbour as the grounds of an obligation is to undercut the explanatory force of the deontological vocabulary. To conceive of sin in these terms rather than in terms of compliance to a code is to recast the discussion in relational terms (about which more below).

None of these criticisms is conclusive, but they do call into question the assumption that deontic notions should be at the heart of our conception of sin. We do not deny that deontic notions capture *a* component of the New Testament conception of sin, but they clearly do not exhaust the New Testament conception of sin, and we very much doubt that they form the heart of the New Testament conception of sin. (They are certainly not at the heart of *Paul's* conception of sin, as we discuss in more detail below.) Sin, as the New Testament conceives of it, is both relational and ontological: it is a matter of alienated relationships, and it is a feature—a deep feature—of our nature as members of fallen humanity. Those accounts of the atonement that treat the atonement as first and foremost a solution to the problem of moral guilt leave the relational and ontological facets of sin unaddressed.[4] Indeed, matters are actually worse than this, for there is considerable *tension* between deontological language on the one hand and relational and ontological language on the other. Let us explain.

Even where is it justified, the language of rights and duties is ill-suited to the most intimate of human relationships.[5] The surest sign that a marriage or friendship is in trouble is when the participants start invoking their rights, or calling attention to their partner's obligations. Friends do indeed have obligations to each other, but it is not in the nature of friendship to call attention to such obligations. Outsiders seeking to understand the relationship would not be advised to conceive of the relationship in terms of obligations, and it is unlikely that deontic language will play a central role in the restoration of the relationship when it breaks down. We grant that the repair of a relationship may require the meeting of obligations that have been broken, but deontic features rarely provide us with the best way to understand either the break of the relationship or its rehabilitation.

Consider also another intimate relationship, that between children and parents. Although there may be some room for a deontological approach to the parent–child relationship, this is surely not how this relationship ought to be understood in the first instance. Children may have an obligation to care for their parents in old age simply because they are their parents, but their primary motivation and ground for such activity ought surely to be that of love. Similarly, parents may have obligations to care for their children simply because they are their children, but their primary motivation to care for them ought to be grounded in love rather than duty. At the very least, there is something deeply wrong with the relationship if obligation has to play an important motivational role in parental concern. Invoking deontological language in a last-ditch effort to fix what is broken is unlikely to mend an intimate relationship, and may well sour it further. So too, it seems to us, to conceive of restoring a broken relationship between a person and God in terms of compliance with obligations is to do grave injustice to scripture and to Christian tradition. According to the prophets, God desires mercy, not compliance with ritual commands. Compliance with obligations is a consequence of atonement rather than its ground (Isaiah 1:11ff, Hosea 6:6, Matthew 9:13, Romans 3:20, Galatians 2:16).

Although this point has been extensively discussed in recent theological literature, it has been only dimly appreciated in the literature in the philosophy of religion. Swinburne rejects penal models of the Atonement on the grounds that 'talk of law courts and punishment makes the whole process too "mechanical" for a means of reconciliation that ought to be intimate and personal' (1989, p. 152). This is surely true, but Swinburne himself describes sin as a debt that we have incurred as a result of failing to fulfil our obligations to God (1989, p. 149; see also Swinburne, 1988). Porter's (2002) version of the penal model suffers from precisely the same shortcoming. Porter claims that 'fundamental to sin is a prideful usurpation of God's rightful place in one's life and thereby a rejection of God's offer of intimate friendship. Hence, sin is a form of rebellion that cannot be repaired by positive efforts, and thus, reparation and penance can be better captured by punishment' (Porter, 2002, p. 603). Is punishment really an appropriate response to a rejection of intimate friendship? One would not have thought so, especially if the parties involved were attempting to restore the relationship![6]

We turn now to sin as an ontological notion, that is, to the notion that sin is something under which we (together with the rest of creation) labour. A central Biblical conception of sin is as a sickness and pollutant – something that corrupts (see, e.g., Gunton, 1988, Chapter 5). This conception of sin – markedly absent from discussions of the atonement within philosophy of religion – is clearly in tension with the deontic conception of sin. The sick need a doctor not a judge or jailor. Even if deontic models of the atonement are able to deal with sin as a deontological problem, they fail to deal with it as a problem of human nature: they leave the sinner right where he or she was.[7] None of this is to say that talk of obligations and duties has no role to play within a conception of sin as a feature of the human condition, but it is to say that such talk does not get to the heart of the problem. In the case of sin as diagnosed in the New Testament, our failures of duties and obligations are at most a sign and symptom of the illness and not the disease itself. Curing the disease by merely correcting the symptoms is no more likely to be successful in treating the problem in this case than it is in everyday medical practice.

1.2   Atonement and the role of the incarnation

A satisfactory model of the atonement should draw an internal connection between the atonement and Christ's incarnation, death and resurrection; ideally, it should tell us why the atonement requires the incarnation. Arguably, an account of the atonement need not show that the incarnation was the only way that the atonement could be brought about, if only because we tread on difficult ground and judgements of necessity and what is possible for God to achieve in atonement are, at best, extremely difficult to justify. Nonetheless, an account of the atonement should at the very least draw a meaningful connection between the atonement and the incarnation.

Few of the conceptions of the atonement in the current literature are able to meet this criterion. Consider, for example, Quinn's modified version of the substitution model:

> Christ's life and death persuade God to be lenient rather than severe in his treatment of human sinners. Just because the supererogatory goodness in Christ's life and his voluntary submission to suffering and death are a sacrifice that is enormously pleasing to God, their effect is to forestall the severe but just demand for reparation and not to make the reparation that would be demanded in their absence. They function not to remove a debt of punishment that human sinners owe by paying it, but to persuade God to remit or cancel the debt.
>
> (1994, p. 298)

Quinn fails to explain here how Christ's life and death persuades God to be lenient. Why was the sacrifice that Christ paid to God enormously pleasing to him? If it were sacrifice alone that God desired, why must God incarnate make that sacrifice? Why could not someone else make the sacrifice? Quinn fails to address any of these questions.

Brümmer's accounts of the atonement raises similar questions. Brümmer summarizes his model as follows: 'through sincere penitence and divine forgiveness I can be restored to loving fellowship. Such fellowship bestows ultimate meaning on my very existence and enables me to "live with myself"' (1992, p. 451). Why does divine forgiveness require the incarnation, the cross, and the resurrection? Brümmer's answer is this:

> the person who forgives us is the person who has to pay the price for reconciliation. Since in restoring our fellowship with God it is God who forgives, it is also God who has to pay the price and has to absorb into his own suffering the consequences of the wrong that we have done to him. On Calvary God reveals to us the cost of his forgiveness.
>
> (1992, p. 452)

We find this unsatisfactory. What does God's forgiveness cost God? Does God have to struggle to overcome feelings of anger and resentment towards us? That does not sound like the God of the New Testament – a God whose very essence is love and whose nature it is to always show mercy. Why cannot God simply decide to forgive us? (After all, are we not commanded to forgive those who sin against us?) What exactly is the price that God must pay, and to whom must it be paid? What are the consequences of the wrong that we have done to God, and how does Christ's death and resurrection reveal them? To leave these questions unanswered is to indicate points at which an account is radically incomplete.

Perhaps the best that can be made of Brümmer's line is this. The death of Christ is not in any way a mechanism or a means of forgiveness, but a manifestation of God's attitude towards us. In order for the relationship to be restored we need to know *that* God has forgiven us, and this is how God shows us. But now one wonders why God would choose to reveal the fact that we are forgiven in this peculiar and costly way, unless that action was more than simply a revelation of God's love.

The most sustained attempt to answer these questions that we know of is Purtill's. Purtill suggests that

> in suffering and dying, Christ was giving God a *good reason* to punish us less and reward us more than we deserve on our own merits. His suffering and death for our sake give us a *claim* on God's mercy and generosity. God became a man; as a man he offered his suffering and death for our sake. God now has *good reason* to show us justice and mercy.
>
> (Purtill, 1991, p. 44; original emphasis)

What is the 'good reason' that Christ's death provides? Purtill suggests that God could have forgiven us without Christ's suffering, but to do so would have removed our motivation for gratitude and repentance, for 'we do not value what seems easy' (1991, p. 44). On Purtill's account Christ's death is only externally related to the atonement: dealing with sin is costly, but only because it is necessary that it *appear* to be costly. Our salvation must appear to cost God much, for otherwise we will take it for granted. Since God cannot (or will not) deceive, God must obtain our salvation in a costly manner.

Purtill's suggestion is ingenious, but there is something unsavoury about it. Consider the following analogy. An eight-year-old wants a bicycle. Her parents can easily afford it, but they worry that if their daughter realizes this then she will not value it. So they pretend that they can barely afford to purchase the bike for her. There may be something honourable about the motives of such parents, but there is something dishonourable about their means. Similarly, one ought to wonder about God who makes a process that is not intrinsically costly appear to be so.

There is a further problem with Purtill's account. The costliness of an action can be a motive for gratitude, but only if its costliness is seen to be internally related to the offence. Should the eight-year-old discover that her parents could easily afford the bike, she would be angry, and justifiably so. Her parents take a risk in pretending that their daughter's present cost them more than it did, and their actions might well alienate her from them. Similarly, on Purtill's account, God takes a risk when he makes our atonement appear costly. The motivational force of the atonement is dependent on our failure to realize that the atonement does not intrinsically cost God anything.

Not only do these accounts of the atonement fail to draw an intelligible connection between the atonement and the incarnation, they also run the risk of positing problematic intra-Trinitarian relations. Consider the penal model. The idea that God might punish God for a debt owed to God seems to posit a kind of disunity in the being of God that is foreign to Christian thought. Is God punishing Godself? That seems pathological. Is God the Father punishing God the Son? That seems sadistic. Something similar can be said about the merit model, according to which Christ's life and death persuades God the Father to forgive the debt of sin. In his letter to the Romans St. Paul claims that the Father sent the Son for our salvation (Rom. 8:3), and indeed the entire thrust of Paul's thought represents the atonement as the unified work of the Father, the Son and the Spirit. It is difficult to reconcile this with the thought that Christ's death persuades God the Father to cancel the debt of sin. Similar problems trouble the Anselmian line, according to which Christ pays God the honour that we owe him. There are two ways to understand this position. On one view, Christ honours God the Father and not God as such. If this is Anselm's view it is a strange one, for surely God as such ought to be honoured, and not solely God the Father. So perhaps Christ honours God. This view too is strange, for Christ as a member of the Trinity *is* God. Is Christ honouring himself? Is that what the atonement is all about? That too seems hard to square with Christian tradition.

We end our discussion of current models of the atonement with some brief words on the exemplary approach, according to which Christ's death was nothing but an inspiring example of love and obedience. The exemplary approach dates back to Abelard, and has been recently defended by McNaughton (1992) and Quinn (1993).

There is much that is attractive about this model of the atonement. Unlike many models, it offends against neither moral nor metaphysical scruples. There are no dubious moral transactions at work when we take Christ's death as an example to follow, for we all understand how it is that someone's life can be inspirational. And most crucially, we applaud the fact that it sees the atonement as dealing with a feature of human nature. But for all that the exemplary model has fatal weaknesses.

One problem concerns what exactly it is that we are meant to emulate. For the emulation to have any purpose, we need to be able to characterize Christ's death as having an objective, intrinsic point. Campbell captures the problem here well:

> A meaningless or trivial death cannot reveal love: it reveals nothing – except perhaps foolishness. If I drive my car at high speed into a brick wall, loudly proclaiming my love for all humanity, my surviving family would probably wonder how I had left my senses, not how extraordinarily loving my gesture was.
>
> (Campbell, 1994, p. 239)

The problem, in a nutshell, is that the exemplary model needs to be able to characterize Christ's death as accomplishing something in and of itself, apart from its inspirational value.

Proponents of the exemplary model are not blind to this problem. McNaughton suggests that 'Christ's death can be seen as showing the believer, in the most vivid way imaginable, the costs of human sin' (McNaughton, 1992, p. 144). But how does Christ's death show the costs of human sin? McNaughton does not say. We need an account of how Christ's death is a response to (or a cost of) sin, and this is precisely what exemplary accounts fail to provide. Unless one has some understanding of how Christ's death functions as a response to human sin it is hard to see how it could be taken to show the costs of human sin, far less show them 'in the most vivid way imaginable'. Perhaps McNaughton means only to suggest that the atoning value of Christ's death derives from the fact that Christ's death, as the death of an innocent and just man, was a very vivid example of sin, but surely we are not lacking for vivid examples of undeserved suffering.

A further problem with the exemplary model is that it does not really deal with sin as a problem of human nature. Although the New Testament certainly does present Christ as a model of self-sacrificial love, it does not suggest that our primary problem is a lack of such models, nor does it suggest that we are ignorant of the costs of sin. Instead, it suggests that our sinful nature puts us at odds with each other and with God. Why think that another example of self-sacrificial love will enable us to repair the gulf of alienation between God and humanity when other examples have failed?

2   The participatory model

In the light of the above considerations we would seem to have ample justification for exploring new conceptions of the atonement. In what follows we will do just that, not by introducing a new model but by rehabilitating an old model that has been undeservedly neglected: the participatory model. There are hints of the participatory model in the recent philosophical discussion of the atonement, but the model has not received the detailed attention that it deserves.[8]

2.1   St. Paul and the language of participation

The participatory model of the atonement goes back not to Calvin, Luther, Abelard, Aquinas or Anselm, but to Paul. Consider the following excerpt from a summary of Paul's thought by the eminent New Testament scholar Morna Hooker:

> The sin of Adam was reversed and the possibility of restoration opened up when Christ lived and died in obedience and was raised from life to death. Those who are 'baptized' into him are able to share his death to sin (Rom. 6:4–11) and his status of righteousness before God (2 Cor. 5:21). Since Adam's sin brought corruption to the world, restoration involved the whole universe (Rom. 8:19–22; Col. 1:15–20)... [Christ] shared our humanity, and all that means in terms of weakness... in order that we might share in his sonship and righteousness. To do this, however, Christians must share in his death and resurrection, dying to the realm of flesh and rising to life in the Spirit. Thus Paul speaks of being crucified with Christ in order that Christ may live in him (Gal. 2:19–20). The process of death and resurrection is symbolized by baptism (Rom. 6:3–4). By baptism 'into Christ', believers are united 'with him', so that they now live 'in him'. These phrases (in particular 'in Christ') express the close relationship between Christ and believers that is so important for Paul.
>
> (Hooker, 2000, p. 522; see also Hooker 1994 and Campbell 1994)

This is a remarkable passage from the perspective of philosophical discussions of the atonement. It contains no trace of deontic or exemplary language. Christ's death is not presented as persuading God to forgive us, as constituting restitution for our debts, as punishment for our misdeeds or as something we must emulate. Instead, the passage portrays Paul as focused on ontological and relational matters. This focus is encapsulated in Paul's frequent references to Christ as 'the Second Adam', a phrase that is code for Paul's conception of Christ's death as inaugurating a new human nature (Rom. 8:19–22; Col. 1:15–20). In Paul's eyes, there is a deep sense in which we really are new creatures (Gal. 2:20).[9] This new identity, grounded in the Christian's participation in the death and resurrection of Christ is symbolized—and perhaps even constituted—by the rites of Baptism and the Eucharist. Baptism symbolizes death to the old self and rebirth, participating in new life 'in Christ'; the Eucharist involves partaking in the blood and body of Christ. These rites are thoroughly participatory. Participatory language also infuses Paul's conception of the Church, which he describes as the body of Christ. Paul describes the Spirit as marrying the Christian to Christ so that 'the two become one flesh' (Rom. 7:1–4; I Cor. 6:15–18).

How does participation deal with sin? According to Paul, our change of identity liberates us from sin: since we are no longer bound by (or under the sway of) sin, we are free to participate in a restored relationship with God. In fact, Paul seems to think that in some way we participate in Christ's relationship with God (cf. Romans 6:8–11: the Christian is 'alive to God in Christ Jesus'). Paul's conception of sin is not, primarily, deontic. He does not see Christ's death and resurrection as the salve for a troubled conscience—indeed, Paul is adamant that his conscience was clear. 'I was blameless as to righteousness—of the Law, that is' (Philippians 3:6; see also Acts 23:1, 2 Cor. 1:12). As Stendahl (1963) noted in his rightly influential 'The Apostle Paul and the Introspective Conscience of the West', Paul never presents Christ as the salve for a guilty conscience. Instead, he sees Christ's death as dealing with sin as part of the human (indeed: cosmic) condition. The participatory strand in Paul's theology takes sin to be a problem of our identity—the atonement is not a matter of balancing the moral ledger but involves the inauguration of a new form of humanity.

But is there not some sense in which sin is a deontic problem? And if so, how does the participatory model deal with it as such? We have granted that there is some sense in which sin is a deontic problem, and the participatory model can do justice to the deontic component of sin. If the sinner is the 'old person', and the old person died with Christ on the cross, then there is no one who ought to be regarded as guilty for their sin; indeed, there is no longer anyone who ought to feel guilty for their sin.[10] The moral debt we owe to God is not punished or forgiven, nor is satisfaction or reparation made for it. Instead, it is dealt with by changing the identity of the sinner: in the sense which matters, the person who is in the wrong before God no longer exists. We think that this is an advantage of the model. God's forgiveness cannot be coerced or merited, even by Godself.

That, in outline, is the participatory model. Its Biblical credentials are clear, as are its theological credentials. It does not involve any problematic intra-Trinitarian transactions; it does justice to a relational and ontological conception of sin; and—unlike other models of the atonement—it forges a deep connection between the atonement and the death and resurrection of Christ. On this model, the death and resurrection of Christ are essential to atonement insofar as atonement involves dying with (or 'in') Christ and then being resurrected with (or 'in') him. It is only insofar as Christ's resurrection brings about the new Adam that the problem of sin is dealt with.

2.2 Objections and replies

If the participatory model is so powerful why has it been neglected? Why does one struggle to find references to it within contemporary philosophy of religion?

One reason for the neglect of the participatory model is that Paul's thought has all-too-often been understood in deontic terms: specifically satisfaction and penal terms. Within the Western tradition Paul has often been presented as concerned with the question of how guilty man can be justified—that is, declared morally pure—before God. As we pointed out above, recent Pauline scholarship has undermined this conception of Paul's thought, and replaced it with a view on which participatory notions lie at the heart of Paul's understanding of the atonement (see Hooker, 1994; Campbell, 1994, 2001; Sanders, 1977; Ziesler, 1990; Torrance, 2000). Paul is concerned with the justification of the individual, but his account locates that justification within a participatory (and cosmic) context.

But what are we to make of those passages in which Paul does seem to endorse a deontological conception of sin, such as Rom. 1:16–4:25, and Gal. 2:15–4:7? There are a number of options here. One option is to adopt a two-crater view, on which Paul endorsed (perhaps at different times) two models of salvation (see Sanders, 1977). Another option, which we prefer, is an argumentative reading of these passages according to which Paul's use of deontic language is largely a dialectical device, forced on him by the rhetorical framework of the theological battles he is waging (see Campbell, 2001). Although we find this position attractive, we need not presuppose it here. For our purposes we need claim only that participatory notions play a vital and centrally explanatory role in Paul's conception of the atonement.

We suspect that the central objection to the participatory model is that it is metaphorical at best and unintelligible at worst. The objection can be phrased as follows:

> The Christian doesn't literally die on the cross with Christ, and she isn't literally reborn with Christ in his resurrection. What sense can we really make of participating in the death and life of Christ? There is really no such thing as a participatory model of the atonement; instead, all we have are a motley and confusing assortment of metaphors. The participatory model might not be immoral or arbitrary, but it is either illogical or unintelligible (or both). In short, it flouts Abelard's constraint.

This is a serious objection, and it deserves a detailed response. We can begin by noting that any theorist who is committed to a Trinitarian and Incarnational view of the divine has reason to wield Abelard's constraint with caution. It would be puzzling, to say the least, to endorse (say) a realist conception of the incarnation or the Trinity only to dismiss the participatory model of the atonement on the grounds that it is difficult to conceive of how we might really—that is, non-metaphorically—participate in the death and resurrection of Christ. Indeed, it is tempting to suspect that the conceptual difficulties involved in unpacking the participatory model are not unrelated to those involved in the Trinity and incarnation. But we regard this as a benefit of the current approach rather than a cost. Given that problematic conceptions of identity feature prominently in Christian philosophical theology it should be no surprise to find them at the heart of the Christian doctrine of the atonement. We grant that there are challenges making sense of the participatory model of the atonement in the abstract, so to speak, but in the context of Trinitarian theology such challenges are to be expected.

But perhaps these points evade the central question: is the participatory model really intelligible? There are really two questions here: (1) what can be said by way of explicating what it is to be 'in Christ', and (2) what can be said by way of explicating the relationship between the old person and the new person. (These two questions are, of course, not unrelated.) We do not have detailed answers to these questions, but we do offer the following tentative thoughts.

Consider the difference between what we might call numerical (or thin) personal identity and moral (or thick) personal identity. The standard accounts of personal identity are best understood as accounts of personal identity in the numerical (or thin) sense of the term.[11] The question these accounts attempt to answer is this: what, fundamentally, are we? What are our identity conditions? In addition to the question of numerical identity, one might also think that there is such a thing as moral identity, where 'moral' is to be understood in a broad sense of what one is committed to. One's moral identity is one's identity as a moral agent, as an entity that is answerable for its actions. The need to distinguish between numerical and moral identity is, we think, amply motivated. Think about actions performed while asleep, under the influence of a drug, or in a fugue state. Are such actions things one has done? Should one feel guilty for them? In some sense these are things that one has done and some feeling of responsibility for them might be appropriate. (Think, for instance, of a motorist who runs over and injures a young child who runs out in front of her. The motorist might not be morally responsible for the child's injuries, but she will—and arguably should—feel some sort of responsibility for her actions.) But at the same time we might want to distance ourselves from such actions, and such distancing seems defensible. Such actions are not a part of one's real self: they are not expressive of one's identity as a moral agent.

Moral identity is a matter of one's commitments, values and relationships. My identity qua moral agent is bound up with those projects and values with which I identify. I could survive the transition from one set of relations and commitments to another as one and the same person, but not as one and the same moral agent. The notion of moral identity gives us some handle on what it is to be in Christ. To be in Christ is for one's identity as a moral agent—as a moral self—to be centred on Christ.

What about the second problem: how are the old and new persons related? The first thing to note is that Paul regards the transition from the old to new as a work in progress. The process has been inaugurated, but it is not yet complete. We are, in some sense, caught between the new and old creation; the process of identification has begun and is continuing (Rom 5:5; 8:1ff). Here too the notion of moral identity is useful. Whether or not numerical identity is always determinate (and reductionists claim that it is not), moral identity is certainly not always determinate. One and the same person can be caught between two or more moral identities, as they endorse and affirm different sets of relations, values and commitments. Paul's lament of feeling torn between the old humanity and the new humanity is not unfamiliar to us (Romans 7).

3 Conclusion

We have argued that the participatory model should be taken seriously within the contemporary philosophical discussion of the atonement. It has strong Biblical credentials, and it avoids many of the objections that plague other models. But embracing the participatory model does not demand that one reject all other accounts of the atonement; indeed, the participatory model can illuminate a number of the other models of the atonement. The atonement does indeed involve sacrifice on the part of God, but it is not a sacrifice that God makes (to Godself) as restitution for our debt (Swinburne), or in order to convince God to forgive us of our debt to God (Quinn). Instead, the participatory account follows Paul in drawing on Old Testament conceptions of sacrifice and expiation, on which one's transgressions are transferred to the animal, so that they die with the animal (see, e.g., Childs, 1992). Although the participatory approach does not, as such, see participation as a mechanism for the transfer of sin, it does build on the idea of participation and identification that is inherent in the notion of the sacrificial animal. The participatory model can also make sense of exemplary language, although it will regard such language as highly impoverished in and of itself. The Christian is, of course, invited to emulate Christ's life and death, but this is not where the action is. The New Testament does not merely encourage the

Christian to do good works, but reminds them that since they are in Christ they must act in accordance with who they are. That is, they must live up to those commitments, values and relations that now constitute their identity. As the protagonist of *The Life of Pi* remarks, the atonement may indeed be 'downright weird', but perhaps it is not quite as weird as some philosophers would have us believe.[12]

Notes

1. We beg the readers' forgiveness for where we fail our own standards in this chapter. While we consider New Testament theologies of the atonement, we pay scant attention to Church History. For this we plead constraints of space, and of expertise.
2. This notion is particularly strong in Hare's writing on the atonement. Hare sees the need for atonement as deriving from the gap between what morality requires of us and what we can achieve. It is also strongly operative in much of Quinn's writing on the atonement. See in particular Quinn (1986).
3. We thank Christian Miller for pressing this point in comments on an earlier draft of this chapter.
4. Swinburne's comment is symptomatic: 'Before anyone can understand how Christianity provides salvation from the past, he needs to understand three crucial concepts – guilt, atonement, and forgiveness.' (Swinburne, 1988, p. 15).
5. Christian Miller points us to the literature on virtue ethics and the ethics of care. Michael Stocker's 'The Schizophrenia of Modern Ethical Theories' (1976) is particularly apposite.
6. One interesting objection we can only mention here is charted in the research of Timothy Gorringe (1996), who shows convincingly that penal understandings of the atonement not only influenced penal strategies in England in the 18th and 19th strategies, but also lent sanction to judicial violence. It stands to reason that a theory of the atonement which enshrines punishment and violence as effective in the realm of the sinner's relationship with God will also find a role for punishment and violence in the realm of the criminal's relationship with the state.
7. Fiddes makes this point powerfully (1989, p. 70).
8. There are hints of it in Quinn (2000), Hare (1996) and Purtill (1991). Fiddes (1989) makes frequent references to atonement as participation, but he seems to locate the participatory model in the context of the penal account rather than as an independent model in its own right (see especially p. 95). Of recent accounts Lucas (1994) is perhaps the closest to our own. Whilst readying this chapter for publication we discovered that there is a participatory component to Aquinas's account of the atonement (*Summa theologiae* III, q. 8, a. 1 and a. 5). See Stump (1988) for some discussion.
9. Of course, this conception of the new life of the believer is not just Pauline, but also Johannine (John 3:16).
10. There are echoes here of Kant's (1793/1960) account of the atonement. See Quinn (1986) for discussion.
11. The distinction between numerical and moral identity is complicated by the fact that Lockeans typically take the concept <person> to have moral content.

12. We are very grateful to Oliver Crisp, Jay Garfield, Andrew Howie, Christian Miller, Daniel Nolan, Christine Parker and Charles Taliaferro for helpful comments on this chapter. We owe a special debt of gratitude to Douglas Campbell, without whose impetus it would not have been written.

References

Aspenson, S. S. (1990) 'In Defence of Anselm', *History of Philosophy Quarterly*, 7/1:33–45.

Brümmer, V. (1992) 'Atonement and Reconciliation', *Religious Studies*, 28: 435–452.

Campbell, D. (1994) 'The Atonement in Paul', *Anvil*, 11/3: 237–250.

Campbell, D. (2001) 'Natural Theology in Paul? Reading Romans I.19–20', *International Journal of Systematic Theology*, 1/3: 231–252.

Childs, B. S. (1992) *Biblical Theology of the Old and New Testaments*. London: SCM.

Cross, R. (2001) 'Atonement without Satisfaction', *Religious Studies*, 37: 397–416.

Fiddes, P. (1989) *Past Event and Present Salvation: The Christian Idea of Atonement*. London: Darton, Longman and Todd.

Gorringe, T. (1996) *God's Just Vengeance: Crime, Violence and the Rhetoric of Salvation*. Cambridge: Cambridge University Press.

Gunton, C. (1998) *The Actuality of Atonement: A Study of Metaphor, Rationality and the Christian Tradition*. London: T&T Clark.

Hare, J. E. (1996) *The Moral Gap*. Oxford: Clarendon Press.

Hooker, M. (1994) *Not Ashamed of the Gospel: New Testament Interpretations of the Death of Christ*. Carlisle: Paternoster.

Hooker, M. (2000) 'Paul', In A. Hastings, A. Mason, and Hugh Piper (eds), *The Oxford Companion to Christian Thought*. Oxford: Oxford University Press.

Kant, I. (1793/1960) *Religion within the Limits of Reason Alone*. Trans. T. M. Greene and H. H. Hudson. Harper and Row: New York.

Lucas, J. R. (1994) 'Reflections on the Atonement', In A. G. Padgett (ed.), *Reason and the Christian Religion: Essays in Honour of Richard Swinburne*. Oxford: Clarendon Press.

McNaugton, D. (1992) 'Reparation and Atonement', *Religious Studies*, 28: 129–144.

Morris, L. (1966) *The Cross in the New Testament*. Exeter: Paternoster Press.

Packer, J. I. (1974) *What Did the Cross Achieve? The Logic of Penal Substitution*. Leicester: TSF Monograph.

Porter, S. (2002) 'Rethinking the Logic of Penal Substitution', In William Lane Craig (ed.), *Philosophy of Religion: A Reader and Guide*. Rutgers, NJ: Rutgers University Press, 596–608.

Purtill, R. (1991) 'Justice, Mercy, Supererogation, and Atonement', In T. P. Flint (ed.), *Christian Philosophy*. Notre Dame, IN: University of Notre Dame Press, 37–50.

Quinn, P. L. (1986) 'Christian Atonement and Kantian Justification', *Faith and Philosophy*, 3: 440–62.

Quinn, P. L. (1993) 'Abelard on Atonement: Nothing Unintelligible, Arbitrary, Illogical or Immoral About It', In E. Stump (ed.), *Reasoned Faith*. Ithaca, NY: Cornell University Press.

Quinn, P. L. (1994) 'Swinburne on Guilt, Atonement and Christian Redemption', In Alan G. Padgett (ed.), *Reason and the Christian Religion: Essays in Honour of Richard Swinburne*. Oxford: Clarendon Press.

Quinn, P. L. (2000) 'Sin and Original Sin'. In Philip L. Quinn and C. Taliaferro (eds), *A Companion to Philosophy of Religion*. Oxford: Blackwell.

Sanders, E. P. (1977) *Paul and Palestinian Judaism*. Philadelphia: Fortress Press.

Stendahl, K. (1963) 'The Apostle Paul and the Introspective Conscience of the West', *The Harvard Theological Review*, 56/3: 199–215.

Stocker, M. (1976) 'The Schizophrenia of Modern Ethical Theories', *Journal of Philosophy*, 73/14: 453–466.

Stump, E. (1988) 'Atonement According to Aquinas', In T.V. Morris (ed.), *Philosophy and the Christian Faith*. Notre Dame: University of Notre Dame Press.

Swinburne, R. (1988) 'The Christian Scheme of Salvation', In Thomas V. Morris (ed.), *Philosophy and the Christian Faith*. Notre Dame Press University Press, 1988.

Swinburne, R. (1989) *Responsibility and Atonement*, Oxford: Oxford University Press.

Torrance, A. (2000) 'Justification', In Adrian Hastings, Alistair Mason, and Hugh Piper (eds), *The Oxford Companion to Christian Thought*. Oxford: Oxford University Press.

Ziesler, J. A. (1990) *Pauline Christianity*. Oxford: Oxford University Press.

10
Basic Human Worth: Religious and Secular Perspectives

Christopher J. Eberle

1 Introduction

A theist who comes to deny that God exists may very well have initiated a morally ramifying event. It is hard to see how one can respond appropriately to God's existence, then conclude that God does not exist after all, and yet for nothing to change with respect to how one conceives of morality and the moral life. And of course, one would expect changes in how one conceives of the moral life to have some impact on how one lives it.

So, for example, belief in God can, and often does, play an important motivational role: love for God or respect for God's authority can, and often does, provide theists with powerful motivating reason to comply with the moral law. For a theist to deny that God exists is to deny that those reasons have normative weight and is therefore to alienate herself from a potentially powerful source of motivating reasons. That can have morally important results: given that she will sometimes have an aversion to fulfilling personally costly moral obligations, a person who no longer acts out of love or respect for God might not fulfill obligations she would otherwise have satisfied.[1]

Again, theists typically and reasonably believe that some of their moral obligations obtain only if God exists. So, plausibly, parents have a moral right to issue commands to their children and in so doing make it the case that their children have obligations that they would otherwise not have. However we account for that right, God cannot stand with respect to God's creatures in any less authoritative a position than parents stand with respect to their children. If so, then God's commands generate moral obligations. Moreover, if God commands us to act in ways we are not antecedently required to act, as theists typically believe, then some of our moral obligations obtain only if God exists.[2] And then, of course, for a theist to deny that God exists would provide her with reason not to comply with those command-generated obligations.[3]

The interesting question is not whether belief in God shapes the moral life but *how* it does and whether its influence is trivial, crucial, or somewhere in between. And we might think that the two respects I have just mentioned tend toward the trivial. After all, although our parents can make it the case that we have some obligations that we would otherwise lack, many of our most important moral obligations do not depend on our parents' commands. And if God's contribution to the moral life is roughly that of our parents, well, then we have all manner of obligations that do not depend on God's commands and so we can deny that God exists while retaining many of our deepest moral commitments. We might expect a more substantial moral impact from the maximally excellent Creator of all that is. Again, although theists are often powerfully motivated by respect or love for God to comply with their moral obligations, non-theists have no such motivation and it is surely possible for those who conclude that God does not exist to find some compensatory motivational source. Something changes, but perhaps not much.

Of course, various authors have argued that theism shapes the moral life in a far more thoroughgoing manner than either of the contributions I have mentioned. Perhaps the most ambitious claim in that regard is not merely that some of our obligations depend on God's existence, but that all of them do: they all depend on God's existence because, in one formulation, a moral obligation is identical to a divine command such that, if God does not exist, then we have no obligations. If God is dead, the cold and calculating Ivan Karamazov says, then anything is permissible – a sentiment also expressed, in a fit of despair, by his monkish step-brother Alyosha. To deny that God exists, on this view, would have the most profound moral implications.

Between these two extremes, there is much room for maneuver regarding the relation between theism and the moral life. I will remain entirely within that territory for the duration of this chapter. I will argue that theism provides crucial justificatory support for an important claim about human dignity, that is, that each human being has what I will call 'basic worth.' More precisely, I take theism to provide an adequate account of what makes it the case that each human being has basic worth, but I doubt that there is a similarly adequate secular account. In so doing, I present my own reasons for a position that has recently been advanced by Michael Perry,[4] Nicholas Wolterstorff,[5] Duncan Forrester[6] and, perhaps, Jeremy Waldron.[7] Of course, I expect to accomplish nothing definitive in this short space; this essay is exploratory and tentative. Moreover, there are objections to my theistic account of basic worth to which I am unsure how to respond. But if those objections can be met, and if my central thesis is correct, then theism shapes the moral life in at least one more than trivial respect.

2   Basic human worth

Few moral claims are more central to a liberal sensibility than that each human being has some very special moral status, a status construed variously as each human being's having great worth, basic equality, equal worth, dignity or sacredness. For reasons I hope will be clear, I prefer the language of basicality: each human being has basic worth. What does that claim amount to?

The normative status of each human being's having basic worth is a function of three distinct normative facts. (1) Each human being has *great* worth: excellence is a degreed property, some things are more excellent than others, and human beings have a degree of worth – a *greatness* of worth – that far exceeds that enjoyed by rocks, plants, cats and works of art. The worth involved here is intrinsic, not instrumental and it applies not to a human being's conditions (such as her feeling pleasure, an intrinsically good state of mind) but to a human being as such.[8] (2) Each human being has *equal* worth in the sense that the very feature that gives each human being great worth provides each with a degree of worth no lesser or greater than it provides to any other. (3) No human being has it within her power to make it the case that she, or any other, lacks great and equal worth.[9] Simply put, a human being's basic worth consists in her having a level of intrinsic worth that is high in magnitude and that neither she nor anyone else can do anything to reduce, much less eliminate.[10]

The claim that each human being has basic worth seems morally and politically important. After all, it is on the basis of some claim such as that 'all men are created equal' that liberals often affirm that each and every human being enjoys the familiar package of natural human rights – to freedom of religion, equality before the law, freedom from arbitrary arrest, torture, enslavement and the like. But the claim that human beings have basic worth might have morally interesting implications even if human beings lack natural human rights. After all, if each human being has basic worth, then we have powerful reason to care deeply about each's well-being.[11] It is not clear that we would have *no* reason to care about the well-being of others were they to lack any worth, or were they to have less than they actually have, but we would in either of those cases have far less weighty reason. Moreover, it seems plausible to suppose that the degree of worth something enjoys augments or diminishes the weight of other normatively relevant factors. So, for example, if I am forced to choose between causing a greater quantity of chimp pain and a lesser quantity of human pain, I might have good reason to cause greater chimp pain precisely because the normative weight of the lesser human pain is augmented by the far greater worth of human beings.[12] So it seems that basic human worth has morally interesting implications whether or not it grounds natural human rights and merits analysis independently of its relation to natural human rights.

Fair enough. There is a widely affirmed claim that human beings have some special normative status and that claim has some interesting moral implications. But it might also seem puzzling – a puzzle the skeptical might be inclined to parlay into an objection. The puzzle is this. If each human being has basic worth, then it might seem that no human being has it within her power to *degrade* any human being (herself or others): if each human being has some feature that *guarantees* great worth, well, then no-one can do anything about that, however much they might desire. But this seems to deny that the actual is possible. It is all too common for some human beings to make it the case by action or inaction that some are less excellent than they once were. So, for example, prisoners of war forced to labor under the most grueling conditions, beaten within an inch of their life for the most trifling act of independence, subjected to solitary confinement in cramped quarters for soul-crushing periods of time, and required to grovel for nutritionally inadequate scraps of food – these human beings are genuinely damaged by their treatment and as a consequence can become far less excellent instances of the human species than they once were. Again, we seem to have it within our power to degrade ourselves: by embracing corruption as a good in our life, by bending the full efforts of our will to achieve some despicable end, we can make it the case that we no longer have a worth we once had. Does the claim that each human being has basic worth imply that such degradation cannot happen or that it cannot affect our worth?

No. The claim that each human being has basic worth is a claim about a guaranteed minimum and is consistent with normatively important variations above that threshold. If that is the case, then we can distinguish between basic human worth and (something like) total individual worth: the guaranteed minimum that each and every human being indelibly possesses as distinct from the amount of worth each human being has when we 'add up' each increment of excellence she acquires from all of her worth-engendering properties. If the notion of a human being's total worth is intelligible[13] – (I feel your pain here), then, whereas basic worth will be equal in distribution among human beings, total individual worth will vary dramatically, though it can never fall below a very high threshold. Moreover, it is also plausible to suppose that, for both better and worse, human beings have it within their power to effect those variations. If that is true, it is possible not only for some human beings to make it *seem* like they can degrade others, it is possible for them actually to do so. More darkly, it is possible for them to pass off genuine degradation as a rather thorough eradication of worth: by degrading an individual in particularly salient respects, we can make her appear – to herself and others – to be worth*less*. It is a depressingly useful and common bait and switch.

So the claim that each human being has basic worth is consistent with the claim that we can degrade one another, sometimes in life-altering and tragic respects. That said, if each human being has basic worth, then there is a very high limit to how low we can go: although we can engineer circumstances so that a human being seems to be only a beast of burden, and though in so doing we can reduce her overall worth, we cannot make it the case that she lacks great worth.

3   Ambivalence about basic human worth?

Well, if each human being were to have basic worth, that would be a very fine thing. But do we? I suspect that most of us think that we do – something in the neighborhood, at least.[14] It is a platitude that 'all men are created equal,' or if not 'created' equal, then at least equal. Not equally *worthless*, of course: the claim is not that we are equal in the respect that none of us have intrinsic worth. That kind of equality would hardly be anything to write home about. Rather, we are equal in having great worth. You will not be re-invited to many dinner parties if you spout off against that.

I am doubtful, however, that we are as firmly committed to basic human worth as it might initially seem. We have a powerful penchant for carving humanity up into 'in-groups' and 'out-groups' and then assigning some lesser normative status to outsiders. That inclination to group egoism has been with us for a very long time and it is not going away anytime soon.

So, for example, however platitudinous the claim that each human being has basic worth seems to us, most of the human beings who have graced our planet would have denied it, had it crossed their minds in the first place. On this point, it is worth citing Claude Levi-Strauss in full:

> The concept of an all inclusive humanity, which makes no distinction between races or cultures, appeared very late in the history of mankind and did not spread very widely across the face of the globe. …For the majority of the human species, and for tens of thousands of years, the idea that humanity includes every human being on the face of the earth does not exist at all. The designation stops at the border of each tribe, or linguistic group, sometimes even at the edge of a village. So common is the practice that many of the peoples we call primitive call themselves by a name which means 'men' (or sometimes 'the good ones,' the 'excellent ones,' the 'fully complete one,'), thus implying that the other tribes, groups and villages do not partake in human virtue or even human nature, but are, for the most part, 'bad people,' 'nasty people,' 'land monkeys,' or 'lice eggs.' They often go so far as to deprive the stranger of any connection to the real world at all by making him a 'ghost' or an 'apparition.' Thus curious situations arise in which each interlocutor rejects the other as cruelly as he is rejected.[15]

Of course, it is not the case that only primitive societies have been unimpressed by the excellence of some of their species-mates. In fact, the platitude that each human being has basic worth has been denied by morally sensitive and rationally proficient persons who seem to have an adequate grasp of its meaning. So, for example, Aristotle claims that many human beings lack the full complement of rational capacities, are thereby incapable of governing themselves in a fully competent manner, thereby require direction by those who do have the full complement, and so are natural slaves, whom we are free to hunt if it suits us.[16] This rather bracing rejection of basic human worth was to have a long and sordid history of rationalizing the enslavement of countless numbers of Africans and Native Americans.[17]

Now this kind of frontal rejection of basic human worth is entirely beyond the pale: we do not fix on racial, gender or cultural features as a basis for dividing humanity up into those who have basic worth and those who do not. We are far too individualistic to conceive of our species-mates in so gross and static a manner. But there are other ways to deny basic worth. Rather than marking off portions of humanity on the basis of fixed characteristics like race or gender, we rely on performance-related criteria: it is by virtue of what they do, and so become, that some human beings lack basic worth.

Nowhere does this regrettable tendency manifest itself more clearly than in warfare: war powerfully threatens a soldier's already tenuous grasp of the worth of human beings with the consequence that it is only too common for soldiers to deny that the members of 'enemy out-groups' have great worth.[18] Consider in this regard Arthur 'Bomber' Harris's response to Winston Churchill's moral qualms over the obliteration of Dresden:

> I... assume that [Churchill's qualms amount to] something like this: no doubt in the past we were justified in attacking German cities. But to do so was always repugnant and now that the Germans are beaten anyway we can properly abstain from proceeding with those attacks. This is a doctrine to which I could never subscribe. Attacks on cities like any other act of war are intolerable unless they are strategically justified. But they are strategically justified insofar as they tend to shorten the war and so preserve the lives of Allied soldiers. To my mind we have absolutely no right to give them up unless it is certain they will not have this effect. I do not personally regard the whole of the remaining cities of Germany as worth the bones of one British Grenadier.[19]

Here we have as candid a justification of (what I take to be) the morally tragic area bombing campaign as we are likely to have and it seems squarely grounded on the claim that some human beings, Germans most particularly, lack much by way of worth. (If the area bombing campaign inflicted morally ghastly suffering and death on some 800,000 civilians,[20] and some large proportion occurred in German cities, and avoiding that large quantity of deaths does not warrant the death of even one British soldier, well, then even if Harris was speaking rather loosely, he seems to have believed that British worth far exceeds German.) Although Harris would no doubt not avail himself of the Aristotelian move that the Germans were not fully rational, he doubtlessly believed that the Germans were responsible for causing vast amounts of unjustifiable suffering and might have taken that as some justification for the denial that German citizens were worth every bit as much as British soldiers.[21] In so doing he would have articulated a common line of thought, one expressed most repugnantly in Theodore Kaufman's 1940 *Germany Must Perish!*, which began:

> Today's war is not a war against Adolf Hitler. Nor is it a war against the Nazis. It is a war of peoples against peoples, of civilized peoples envisioning Light against uncivilized barbarians who cherish darkness.... [Hitler, the Kaiser, Bismark are] merely mirrors reflecting centuries-old inbred lust of the German nation for conquest and mass murder.... This time Germany has forced TOTAL WAR upon the world. As a result, she must be prepared to pay a TOTAL PENALTY. And there is one, only one, such Total penalty: Germany must perish forever! In fact, not fancy![22]

As if smitten with the same malign virus, Russian soldiers raped and pillaged their way through Germany armed with Ilya Ehrenburg's comparably repulsive rationalization:

> Kill! There is nothing that is innocent in the German. Neither in the living nor in the unborn. Follow the directive of Comrade Stalin and trample into the ground forever the Fascist beast in his cave. Break by force the racial haughtiness of German women. Take them as your lawful prey. Kill, you brave advancing Red soldiers.[23]

It is in the context of a generalized dehumanization of the German people that one can best understand the Red Army General who was surprised to find that the German children searching for their parents in a blazing town 'were crying in exactly the same way as our children cry.'[24] And that dehumanization of the German people was itself a response to a long-term project of dehumanization and brutalization the Germans directed at their enemies, as the following Nazi propaganda leaflet exemplifies:

> Anyone who has ever looked into the face of a red commissar knows what the Bolsheviks are like. Here there is no need for theoretical expressions. We should insult the animals if we described these mostly Jewish men as beasts. They are an embodiment of the Satanic and insane hatred against the whole of noble humanity. The shape of these commissars reveals to us the rebellion of the *Untermenschen* against noble blood. The masses, whom they have sent to their deaths by making use of all means at their disposal such as ice-cold terror and insane incitement, would have brought and end to all meaningful life, had this eruption not been dammed at the last moment.[25]

Harris, Kaufman and Ehrenburg express a theme that recurs far too often in violent intra-communal conflict and which it would be utopian to believe will end anytime in the near future (much less that we have already gotten past it!): by virtue of their embracing a morally repugnant project our enemies makes it the case, not only that they forfeit certain rights, but that they no longer have the dignity, sacredness or worth on which those rights are grounded. Of course, this 'theme' has its contemporary manifestations. So, for example, when enemies butcher, mutilate or torture their brothers-in-arms, soldiers must resist the all too human tendency to carve humanity up into insiders and outsiders and then to deny worth to the latter. Very regrettably, some have not.[26]

So I suspect that we are ambivalent about basic human worth. Many (most?) of us are confident that each human being has basic worth. In so doing, we take for granted a claim that most human beings have simply assumed to be false and that runs contrary to our persisting tribal predilections. And when we are differently circumstanced our tribal tendencies erupt: when those we love are brutalized and degraded by our fellow human beings, *they* seem to have less than no worth and we have a strong disposition to treat them accordingly. Civilization is a very thin veneer.[27]

4 Secular grounds for basic human worth

That we are only tenuously committed to the claim that each human being has basic worth implies nothing at all about whether each human being has basic worth. If anything, it provides some reason for us to do what we can to articulate some clear and compelling argument for that claim. A crucial part of that argument will include some account of what 'grounds' basic worth. That is, if we make the very plausible assumption that basic worth is not just an inexplicable, surd fact about human beings,[28] then we will have to identify what it is about each human being by virtue of which each has basic worth. Moreover, given that we want as many of us to affirm basic worth as we can, it would be highly desirable for us to articulate some *secular* account of basic worth – to identify, without recourse to theological exotica, that feature of humanity that grounds basic worth. And that might seem rather easy to do, for human beings have easily identifiable and excellent features that render them markedly superior to rocks, trees, lions and quasars.

Nevertheless, identifying the desired substrate is no easy task. There are, of course, many features that might ground equality, or greatness, or permanence of worth, but it is hard to specify some feature that provides for all three for each human being.[29] So, to begin with a clearly unpromising example, each human being has a certain distinctively human genetic code. And if having that genetic code was a really terrific thing, then we would be able to put a quick end to our inquiry: since each human being has a distinctively human genetic code, since having that code generates great worth and since no human being can do anything to alter it (for the time being, at least), well, then we would have powerful reason to believe that each human has great, equal, indelible and so basic worth. But it is doubtful that each human being's having *any* kind of genetic code grounds much worth, much less great worth. To be sure, having a certain kind of genetic code plays a causal role in producing other things that ground great worth. But then it is not the case that having a certain kind of genetic code gives human beings basic worth. I take this to be obvious.

There are other candidates, of course, for there is no doubt that many human beings have various excellent properties – moral and intellectual virtues of various sorts. Gandhi was a great man, Mother Theresa a morally admirable woman, and their distinctive mix of excellences surely made it the case that each rates rather high in the scale of moral worth – far higher than Jeffrey Dahmer or Our Dear Leader. But that is the point: the moral virtues are very spottily distributed. Some human beings exhibit great virtue, and some do not. Hence, possession of moral virtues does not ground basic worth.[30]

Pretty clearly, we want to identify some property that is both universally distributed among human beings, that plausibly generates great worth, and that is in some sense a fixed possession of a living human being. What could fill that bill of particulars?

The most promising candidate is a terrific *capacity* – some ability that each human being possesses, even if only incipiently. So, for example, we might think that to be a human being just comes with having the capacity for rational agency – the capacity to act on the basis of reasons. And we might regard that capacity as an excellent one indeed: our capacity to shape our own lives in light of ends we find worthwhile is surely one of the features we most esteem about our species-mates (and ourselves, no doubt). Unfortunately, some human beings lack the capacity for rational agency. My grandmother, for example, spent the remaining years of her life quite unable to shape her life in light of ends she found worthwhile. Hence, actual possession of the capacity for rational agency cannot be what provides each human being with basic worth.[31]

It seems, however, that this gap in coverage is easily remedied. So we might think that basic worth is grounded on the fact that each human being is a member of a species the properly functioning members of which have the potential to develop a capacity for rational agency. This property my grandmother surely possessed and did so until her death. No doubt each and every human being indelibly has that property. Does it provide for basic worth? Although this proposal scores well with respect to equality and permanence, it seems to do rather poorly with respect to degree of worth: it is doubtful that being a member of a species other members of which have some terrific property is particularly wonderful and so seems incapable of grounding *great* worth.

Now this response might seem inadequate and critics might very well want to dig in their heels.

> Look, I've identified a feature that I take each human being to have, that I take to ground great worth, and that is a permanent possession of any living human being, viz., that each human being is a member of a species the properly functioning members of which have a capacity for rational agency. And your response is, what, simply to deny that that property grounds great worth? This is not argument; it's arbitrary dictum.

Here it will be helpful to reflect on the epistemic limitations any account of basic worth faces. As I have construed it, the concept of basic worth includes some notion of degrees of worth that reach a certain threshold. But in the best of circumstances claims about excellence are difficult to justify to the skeptical and that difficulty applies in spades to the judgment that some feature does or does not reach the (admittedly unspecified and unspecifiable) threshold required for basic worth. Given the cognitive capacities with which we are endowed, we cannot expect to demonstrate those kinds of evaluative judgments. They are grounded more on hunches and difficult to defend intuitions than anything that can pass for rigorous argument. Consequently, we can demonstrate neither that our favored account of basic worth is correct nor that its competitors are defective. What we can do is to articulate valuational judgments as clearly as we can, motivate them by example and counter-example, and articulate the meager arguments in the area. At the end of the day, we will likely disagree. Such is life.

With that in mind, let just say that I do not see how my being a member of a species the other members of which have excellent traits that I lack redounds in my favor. That kind of excellence by association does not fly in other cases: I acquire not a jot of moral virtue, musical talent or intellectual agility by virtue of the fact that my family members are so gifted. If I am none of those things, then my being related by family, communal or species membership to those who are helps me not a whit. They excel in those respects, and I do not, end of story.

There are no doubt many other candidates and I will not survey them all. For even this brief survey suggests a general objection. Secular accounts are unlikely to specify a feature that grounds basic worth because, as it happens, the more widely a given feature is distributed among human beings, the more plausible that it grounds equal worth but the less plausible that it grounds great worth, whereas the greater the worth that a given feature grounds, the less plausible that it also generates equal worth. In human beings, equality and greatness of value do not seem married together in any tight way. To be sure, this is no necessary truth: it is a generalization regarding the features that human beings actually possess, and those features could have been different than they are. But it does not need to be a necessary truth. We want to determine which feature each human being actually possesses that provides for basic worth and the problem is that, when we look straight at human beings, as they actually are, and take into account the kinds of features we actually share with each of our species-mates, we find that what we share does not count for much.

This is, however, as much a suggestion as an argument. So I will try to motivate my skepticism a bit further by explaining why I take the most plausible secular account of basic worth to be inadequate. As I noted, that secular account appeals to some capacity: human beings have basic worth by virtue of the fact that each human being possesses a capacity for self-consciousness, for rational agency, for moral agency, or the like. I will focus throughout on the sheer capacity for moral agency – on the ability human beings possess to act on the basis of moral reasons abstracted from the manner in which that capacity has been developed well or poorly by one or another human being. Simply put, I doubt that the sheer, undeveloped capacity for moral agency grounds much, if any, worth.[32] How can that be? If a given human being has the capacity intentionally to sacrifice her well-being in order to save the life of a stranger, and has the more general capacity to act out of respect for the moral law, then how can it not be the case that she has some most excellent feature? If *each* of us has that capacity, then how can it fail to be the case that each of us has some most excellent feature?

Well, it seems to me that the worth of a given capacity is itself a function of what that capacity enables its possessor to do. For those who appreciate the sport, the capacity to dunk a basketball is valuable because it enables its possessor to perform an act of admirable athleticism; more mundanely, we value the capacity to dunk because we value dunking. That seems pretty straightforward. And it seems general: we prize the capacity for moral agency because it enables us to act in ways that have great merit – with great charity and admirable self-sacrifice. We honor our capacity for rational agency because it enables us to pursue ends we regard as worthwhile – where the pursuit of our self-set ends is an intrinsic good, not only our achieving those ends.[33]

The problem is that, as human beings happen to be put together, the very capacities that enable us to achieve great goods also enable us to produce great evils. The very capacity that enables us to execute an efficient plan to protect the Chesapeake from environmental plunderers also enables us to calculate how we can get away with polluting it. The capacity that enables us to reach the heights of moral virtue also enables us to plunge with Dmitry Karamazov 'heels up' into sin and degradation.[34] And so on. The implication seems to be that the capacities which human beings enjoy are systemically ambiguous in what they enable us to do and therefore decidedly equivocal with respect to the worth they ground: if our capacity for moral agency generates great worth by virtue of its enabling us to perform acts of great moral worth, develop the moral virtues, and pursue the good, why does not that very capacity generate disexcellence precisely by virtue of its enabling us to degrade ourselves, to spurn the good, and to embrace evil? It is the very same capacity, after all, that enables us to pursue both projects. But if our capacities for rational reflection, free moral agency and such are equivocal with respect to the worth they ground, they seem unable to account for basic human worth.

Now this objection depends on the claim that the worth generated by a given capacity depends on what it enables its possessor to produce. But is that claim correct? Consider the following case.

Bart has it within his power either to decide or not to decide intentionally to perform a range of morally salient actions. Now the range of actions any human being can perform is limited in various respects and the same is the case for Bart: he can perform certain actions, but not others and he can do so for certain reasons but not others. But, as it happens, Bart's options are constrained in morally crucial respects: although it is genuinely up to him to act in various ways for various reasons, he is afflicted by a brain lesion that enables him freely to select from only morally corrupt actions. So, he can steal from the poor, or swindle the elderly, or molest the young, but he cannot feed the poor, or help the elderly across the street, or treat the young with due respect. Now so far as I can tell, Bart has a capacity for moral agency – he is sensitive to moral reasons and can freely, though not without constraint, choose between grades of evil. He is a free moral agent, for he has it within his power to act in a more or less corrupt manner. But of course, his capacity for moral action is of a decidedly crimped sort. And precisely because of what it enables, and does not enable, him to do, it seems that his capacity for moral agency generates no worth whatsoever.

Of course, we can think of a sunnier alternative, one in which Lisa too has it within her power intentionally to perform a limited range of actions for a range of salient reasons. But in her case, the range of actions and reasons for actions available to Lisa are morally quite admirable. I will not fill in the details, but you can be sure that they would have her choosing to bring apples to teachers, or to help old ladies across the street and for only the best of reasons. Now it seems to me that this capacity would ground great worth: precisely because of its unambiguously virtuous products, Lisa's capacity for moral action is quite excellent indeed.

Bart's capacity is disexcellent, Lisa's is excellent, precisely by virtue of how they enable their possessors to act. This seems to indicate that the excellence generated by capacities depends on what those capacities enable. And now what about us? Fortunately for us, although we could have been outfitted as Bart is, we have not. If we had, our capacity for moral agency would not ground great worth: better not to have a capacity for moral agency than to have that with which Bart is afflicted. So it seems to me. For better or worse, our sheer capacity for moral agency is systemically ambiguous, enabling us to achieve both great virtue and vice. Hence, our sheer capacity for moral agency does not ground great worth.[35]

Of course, matters are very different with respect to our *developed* capacity for moral agency. Some trade their inheritance for a mess of pottage: they embrace evil, degrade themselves, and with respect to them, it seems to me, their developed capacity for moral agency grounds less than no worth. Others are not so corrupt: for those who shape their character and moral identity so as to respect the moral law and embrace the good, their capacity for moral agency turns out to be excellent indeed. But, pretty clearly, the variable worth of our developed capacities for moral agency is not going to ground equal and so basic worth.

If this line of argument is correct, then what I take to be the most plausible secular account of basic worth fails: the claim that basic worth is grounded on our sheer capacity for moral agency seems a non-starter. It seems that, absent theism, Jeff McMahan correctly senses that 'our egalitarian commitments rest on distressingly thin foundations.'[36]

5   Religious grounds for basic human worth

As I said, when we look straight at human beings and take into account the kinds of features we share with each of our species-mates, we find that what we share does not count for very much. Few of our discrete properties count for much and none that count for much are shared by all. It seems that we have to look elsewhere – to our relational properties – to discern what makes for basic worth. Here I will just assert that no property that relates human beings to one another will account for basic worth – our relations are too contingent and variable for that possibility to pan out. It is at this point that theists tend to go … theistic: human beings have basic worth by virtue of some relationship they bear toward God. What sort of relation? There are various candidates, some of which are more promising than others.[37]

Consider one of the less promising candidates: each human being is dependent on God in the sense that each has been created and is always sustained in existence by God. That property is indeed one that each human being possesses, if familiar sorts of theism are correct, and it seems to be a property that no human being can do anything about. But it is a property that imparts little, if any, value. After all, if the familiar theistic story is correct, then everything that exists has been created by and depends for its existence on God, from quarks and leptons to koalas and quasars. But it is doubtful that each passing quark has great worth. Hence, being dependent on God does not suffice for basic worth. (Here again is one of those judgments about 'degrees of worth' that seems very plausible to me but that is exceedingly difficult to demonstrate to the determinedly skeptical: if it seems just obvious to you that dependence on God provides for great worth, and you are willing to countenance that claim that each created thing has equal worth, well, there is little to be said by way of persuasion.)

Consider another candidate: basic human worth is a function of the vast disparity in excellence between human beings and God. If none of the variations in worth that characterize distinct human beings are significant when each of us is compared to God, then human beings have powerful reason to think of ourselves as equal in worth. So in his book on justice, equality and the retarded, Robert Veatch argues as follows:

> Religious thinkers, at least in the major religious traditions of the modern West, all share a belief in an infinite God who transcends finite human beings. In comparison to the infinite, all finites are equal in their finitude as well as in their relationship to a Creator. ... The religious thinker can solve the problem of why [a severely retarded person] should be treated equally with other human beings by saying, in effect, all are equal in the eyes of God.[38]

Now perhaps this line of argument provides some pragmatic reason for me not to make, or even to think, much about the respects in which I surpass others. But it provides no reason, so far as I can tell, to believe that we have basic worth. For from the fact that none of us have much to crow about when we compare ourselves with God, it hardly follows that we have great worth. If anything, comparing ourselves with God elicits the suspicion that we lack anything at all by way of excellence. And the target claim is great and equal worth, not merely equal worth(lessness).

The most promising candidate for a relational property that grounds basic worth is, I suggest, that each human being is loved by God: human beings have basic worth by virtue of the fact that God loves each human being, none more than any other, but each a great deal.[39] How so?

We are all familiar with the phenomenon of *imparted worth*.[40] My son Nate has for years possessed a very ragged and homely stuffed creature, Elmo. Whatever the properties Elmo possessed when we first brought it home, Elmo now lacks much at all by way of worthy features: he is ugly, fragile and something of a health hazard. Nevertheless, Nate is deeply attached to Elmo and so cares very much what happens to Elmo. Because my son cares deeply about Elmo, *I* care about Elmo. I have perfectly good reason to be solicitous of Elmo's welfare, but not by virtue of Elmo's non-relational properties. The reasons I have to care about Elmo depend entirely on Nate's attachment to Elmo: Nate's attachment to Elmo imparts to his stuffed creature a worth that constitutes perfectly good reason for me to treat Elmo in the familiar ways – returning to pick it up at *great* inconvenience when he is been left behind, duly wash it rather than chuck it into the trash and so on. Just by virtue of my son's attachment, Elmo has a special moral standing that distinguishes that Elmo from all the otherwise more excellent Elmos for which I have no reason to treat with comparable solicitude.[41]

Now if it is true, as many (though not all) theists believe, that God is deeply invested in the life of each human being, if God loves each human being and so is attached to each far more closely than my son is to Elmo, then each human being thereby has great worth – great imparted worth. Moreover, if God loves each human being equally, as many (though not all[42]) theists believe, then each has great and equal worth. Finally, if God loves each human being resolutely, so that God persists in loving each person no matter how degraded or corrupt, then each human being has great, equal and indelible worth. Whatever our particular features, our particular selection of virtues and vices, whatever use to which we have put the sheer capacities that accompany properly functional humanity, each of us has basic worth by virtue of the fact that God loves every human being as God does.

So my commitment to basic human worth is, ultimately, a faith-move… and that in three senses. First, my account of basic human worth requires that certain facts about God obtain: that God exists, that God constantly and impartially loves each human being, and that God's love for human beings imparts great and equal worth to each human being. Second, I know of no way to demonstrate that any of those facts obtain. Third, there is powerful reason to deny the central claim at issue: personal experience and reflection on the human condition provide powerful evidence against the claim that each human being indelibly has great and equal worth. It certainly is not apparent that each of us has basic worth. Yet we do – so I believe.

6   A few objections to the theistic account of basic worth

It is not hard to imagine a number of objections to the theistic account of basic human worth I have sketched. I will briefly discuss several, from the less to the more weighty.

We might object to my theistic account because it seems to imply that, absent the theistic property I have identified, human beings lack worth. But it is obvious that human beings do have great worth, and so the theistic account must be wrong. But nothing I have said implies that human beings lack great worth absent some relation to God. Rather, the claim is that they lack basic worth: there is no guaranteed, but still very high, threshold of human worth absent relation to God. When God goes, on this way of thinking, we are left with widely varying levels of human worth with no floor to the variation, and so, I would suspect, many human beings who are of little moral account. Absent theism, indeed, theism of a somewhat particular sort, this seems to me to be an extremely plausible view.

It might seem that my theistic account of basic worth implies a defective understanding of the normative force of basic human worth. After all, it seems that I have reason to treat others as befits their great worth only if I happen to love God or care about those whom God loves. God's love for Our Dear Leader provides me with reason to treat that repulsive human being as having great worth only if I happen to love God – and I might not. But that seems wrongheaded: the normative force of basic worth should no more depend on my happening to love God than it should depend on my happening to love my wife or country or, indeed, my species. If human beings have basic worth, then I have reason to treat them with due respect whether or not I happen to love God.

This objection too seems to me to miss the mark. If theism is true, and there really does exist a maximally excellent Person who is responsible for my existence and to love Whom is to flourish, then I have compelling reason to respect those whom God loves whether or not I happen to do so. For to violate those whom God loves is to reject friendship with God and thereby to reject an unsurpassably great good. God might not exist, of course, or God might exist but I lack adequate reason to believe that God does, but if God does exist and is as familiarly described, then I cannot but have compelling normative reason to treat those whom God loves in a manner that befits God's love for them.

A more serious objection to the theistic view parallels a common complaint against other kinds of theological voluntarism. The concern is that the appeal to God's love renders basic worth objectionably arbitrary. Consider in this regard the analogy between God's love for each human being and Nate's attachment for Elmo. Although Nate happens to have developed an attachment to Elmo, matters could have turned out otherwise: he could have developed an attachment to some other stuffed creature – an Ernie, perhaps. In that case, I would have no reason to care about Elmo and some reason to care about Ernie. Similarly, might God have had no love for us but great love for some other species – chimps or whales but not human beings? Might God care not a whit about any of God's creatures, just as Nate might have had no attachment to any stuffed creature? If so, then our moral status could have been altered in some considerable respect and for nothing that has anything to do with anything any human being has done or refrained from doing. This seems incredible: so important a normative status as our having basic worth cannot depend on divine whim. It seems even more incredible that some other species could have had basic worth – chimps or whales – but that we do not. Much less that rocks, trees or atoms could and we do not.

But this last set of possibilities suggests a solution: we have to identify some constraints on what God can love. God's love for us does not just float down and happen rest on us rather than the chimps, whales or trees. It might be the case that it is unintelligible for God to love (in the relevant sense) those who cannot honor God. And it is plausible to suppose that God can be honored only by those who have certain features: cognitive and moral capacities of the familiar sort. That is, there are certain conditions for the possibility of God's loving something, and those conditions include a certain set of capacities. Those capacities do not, by themselves, provide for great worth, since they also enable us to repudiate God's love and so commit grave wrongs. Rather, they enable us to have the kind of relationship with God that grounds basic worth. So it is the relationship, not the conditions that make the relationship possible, that grounds great worth. And if that is the case, then the theistic account does not imply that chimps, rather than human beings, could have had basic worth.

Unfortunately, this response seems vulnerable to a different charge of arbitrariness. Suppose that God creates another species similar to human beings in all normatively relevant respects, most particularly with respect to the various capacities necessary to God's sensibly loving that species, but that God happens not to love the members of that species, or does not love them impartially, or the like. In that case the members of that other species lack a moral status that has important moral implications and for what seems to be no reason at all. Somewhere in this neighborhood, there is a disturbing arbitrariness, though I find it hard to fashion this worry into an argument.

Well, as with other criticisms of theological voluntarism, there are roughly two competing responses. First, we might argue that God's nature or enduring characteristics eliminate the possibility of any objectionable arbitrariness. Since having the status of basic worth is a great good in the life of a human being, and since God is a perfectly benevolent being, and since God can (so it seems) love each human being without any apparent moral cost, then God will, given God's nature, love any species relevantly like our own. So if God has created another species just like ours, then God has compelling reason to love them as God loves us, and so the scenario that motivates the objection is not really possible. This idea seems a bit quirky, since the notion of one person's loving another seems to include the notion of not being compelled to do so, even if the compulsion is not external, but God's love for others is bound to differ from our own in some respects.

Second, we might just accept the implications of the sketched scenario. Although mysterious, nothing untoward follows from the fact that God does not love the members of a species otherwise indistinguishable from our own. After all, the putative implications of this kind of theological voluntarism are very different in kind from those often taken to discredit simple versions of the divine command theory. The latter is, I take it, supposed to be objectionably arbitrary because God's commanding could make it the case that certain kinds of actions – murdering, raping, lying – could be morally required should God command them. I do not see how to reach anything like that disturbing conclusion from the theistic account of basic worth.

There are, however, further problems with this general line of argument. I have floated the idea that there are certain conditions of the possibility of God's sensibly loving human beings. But if there are such conditions, then what is the moral status of the human beings who do not satisfy those conditions – my Grandmother during the later stages of her life? If they do not have the necessary capacities, then God does not love them, and then they lack the property I have identified as grounding basic worth. If God can still love them without their having the necessary capacities then we are right back where we started: God's love might settle down on just anything, or on us but not some other species just like us, and this is troublesome.

I am not sure what to say in response to this objection. Perhaps there is some sense in which God loves not only individual human beings, but humanity – though that is a conception I have difficulty grasping. Perhaps God loves the irremediably impaired 'eschatologically,' for they will one day be able to respond to God's love in a way they cannot now respond. Perhaps theists should just bite the bullet and deny that those who lack the necessary capacities lack basic worth.[43] Clearly, there is more work to be done.

7 A practical conclusion

Let me conclude with a kind of practical reflection. It matters a great deal whether each human being has basic worth and it matters whether we have an adequate account of what makes for basic worth. To be sure, it matters more for some than for others, and among those for whom it matters more I include many of the military professionals with whom I now work. Let me explain.

It goes without saying that war provides many opportunities for moral corruption.[44] Combat soldiers are required to perform acts for which they would at least be incarcerated in peacetime. Far from effective legal authority, they are sometimes able to commit morally egregious acts without the realistic prospect of punishment. Moreover, it is sometimes in a soldier's interest to commit morally egregious acts. (As Michael Walzer says, combat is *always* a supreme emergency for individual soldiers.) Operating under a different set of rules, with little chance of punishment, and with what seem to be powerful reasons of self and communal interest, soldiers will sometimes be powerfully tempted to commit acts that shock the conscience. This temptation is vastly amplified when to these mundane factors we add moral horror: a soldier whose comrades are betrayed, brutalized, tortured or mutilated is naturally disposed to retaliate. And a combat soldier has the means at his disposal to do so.[45]

Because they have a reasonable prospect of finding themselves ensconced in such trying circumstances, it seems to me very important that soldiers are firmly convinced that even those who egregiously degrade their comrades have a worth, sacredness or dignity that equals their own and that cannot be forfeited. But certain accounts of what makes for basic worth seem to me to be unable the bear that weight. I have in mind, most particularly, the main alternative to the theistic view I favor, viz., the claim that what makes for basic worth is each human being's capacity for rational or moral agency. If a human being enjoys basic worth by virtue of his having the capacity for rational agency, and if he employs that capacity in such a way as to embrace a moral horror – say, he crucifies, dismembers and then displays the remains of, a frail and harmless prisoner of war in a cold and calculated attempt to deter other prisoners from stealing the paltry morsels they need to survive[46] or he uses mentally handicapped children as a mechanism to deliver Improvised Explosive Devices because those children are unable to heed the warnings issued to them by the soldiers targeted – then it seems to me entirely natural to conclude that his otherwise valuable capacity no longer worth grounds much if anything by way of worth. Indeed, this conclusion seems not only natural, but reasonable.

Though it is not incoherent to insist otherwise, it seems to me that our capacities provide us at most with a kind of conditional worth – a greatness of worth which we very much have it within our power to forfeit.[47] This seems to be the view of a great many people: not only the Arthur Harrises and Ilya Eherenburgs but the 'ordinary men' who have endured military combat. The biographical literature on war is pervaded by the conviction that enemy combatants have dehumanized themselves, and so forfeited their worth, by virtue of the atrocities they willingly commit.[48] Who knows whether they had ever heard of the capacities view of human worth? But if they had, and if they accepted it, their construal of their fellow human beings seems to me to be sensible – not obviously correct, not obviously incorrect, but perhaps correct, and perhaps even more likely correct than not.[49]

So my sense is that the main alternative to the theistic view is too frail a reed on which to ground our basic moral status and so we have good practical reason to affirm some more sturdy ground. No doubt, no account of basic worth is immune from abuse or corruption. The shock of moral horror is surely powerful enough to eviscerate the conviction that each human being indelibly has great and equal worth, no matter the basis for that conviction. The theistic account is no panacea. But it seems better able to resist our deeply ingrained inclination to deny basic worth than its main competitor.

To be sure, most of us do not often run into those who commit such horrors. Perhaps that is why it is so easy for affirmations of basic human worth to slip off our tongues. We should be grateful that it is so easy. And hopeful that it remains so.[50]

Notes

1. Of course, theists might also sometimes be led by their belief in God not to fulfill their moral obligations. This too is a role that belief in God might play, though a malign role.

2. For suggestive remarks that bear on this claim, see Jeremy Waldron, 'What Can Christian Teaching Add to the Debate about Torture,' *Theology Today* 63 (2006): 330–343.
3. This is not in any way to affirm the Divine Command Theory, according to which a moral obligation just is a command issued to us by God.
4. Michael J. Perry, *Toward a Theory of Human Rights: Religion, Law, Courts* (Cambridge: Cambridge University Press, 2007).
5. Nicholas Wolterstorff, *Justice: Rights and Wrongs* (Princeton: Princeton University Press, 2007). My treatment of this issue has been aided in innumerable ways by conversations with Nick Wolterstorff and is, so far as I can tell, consistent with the view he develops in his forthcoming book.
6. Duncan Forrester, *On Human Worth: A Christian Vindication of Equality* (London: SCM Press, 2001).
7. Jeremy Waldron, *God, Locke and Equality* (Cambridge: Cambridge University Press, 2002).
8. By 'intrinsic worth,' I mean something that is excellent for its own sake, not something that is excellent independently of its relational properties (of which instrumental usefulness is just one kind).
9. Jean Hampton, *The Intrinsic Worth of Persons* (Cambridge: Cambridge University Press, 2007), p. 122.
10. Of course, if a human being ceases to exist, then she lacks basic worth. So we should understand this last condition as the claim that no human being can do anything to make it the case that she exists yet lacks great and equal worth.
11. For helpful thoughts on this claim, see David Velleman, 'A Right to Self-Termination?,' *Ethics* 109 (April 1999): 606–628.
12. Michael Otsuka makes a comparable point about the permissibility of self-defense against lethal attack: 'the simple explanation of why you may kill a lethal agent that happens to be a grizzly bear on the attack is that you are a human person, whereas it is merely a grizzly bear, and human persons are worth more than grizzly bears.' 'Killing the Innocent in Self-Defense,' *Philosophy and Public Affairs* 23 (1994): 92. Interestingly, Otsuka's understanding of what makes for human worth has direct implications for the permissibility of using lethal force to defend against certain innocent attackers. Because Otsuka accepts the claim that human worth is grounded on the possession of excellent capacities, he sensibly concludes that 'a normal person is worth more than a human being whom mental illness has permanently rendered incapable of moral agency,' and hence that killing the former is worse than the latter. Michael Otsuka, 'Killing the Innocent in Self-Defense,' p. 92.
13. Though perhaps unusable to us inapplicable as a consequence of our not having the cognitive equipment reliably to make judgments about total individual worth.
14. See Jeremy Waldron, *God, Locke and Equality*, p. 3f.
15. Quoted in Michael J. Perry, *Toward a Theory of Human Rights*, pp. 22–23.
16. 'Now if nature makes nothing incomplete, and nothing in vain, the inference must be that she has made all animals for the sake of man. And so, from one point of view, the art of war is a natural part of acquisition, for the art of acquisition includes hunting, an art which we ought to practice against wild beasts and against men who, though intended by nature to be governed, will not submit; for war of such a kind is naturally just.' *The Politics* and *The Constitution of Athens*, edited by Stephen Everson (Cambridge: Cambridge University Press,

1996), p. 21. See, more generally, Peter Garnsey, *Ideas of Slavery from Aristotle to Augustine* (Cambridge: Cambridge University Press, 1996).

17. See Francesco de Vitoria, 'On the American Indians,' in *Political Writings*, Anthony Pagden and Jeremy Lawrence, eds (Cambridge: Cambridge University Press, 1991), pp. 239–251; Richard Tuck, *The Rights of War and Peace* (Oxford: Oxford University Press, 1991), pp. 44, 66–67; David Brion Davis, *Inhuman Bondage: The Rise and Fall of Slavery in the New World* (Oxford: Oxford University Press, 2006), p. 54f.

18. By 'enemy outgroups,' I mean both enemy combatants and the populations from which those enemy combatants emerge. This is a familiar theme in much of the literature on war. For two recent discussions of dehumanization in (even) 'good wars,' see Harry Stout, *On the Altar of the Nation* and A. C. Grayling, *Among the Dead Cities*. Jonathan Shay attributes this tendency to dehumanize enemy combatants to biblical religion, but it seems to me to be a 'human universal.' See *Achilles in Vietnam: Combat Trauma and the Undoing of Character* (New York, NY: Simon and Shuster, 1995). After all, and as Shay acknowledges, the Japanese conception of American soldiers during World War II was no less dehumanizing than the reverse – American soldiers were regularly construed as bestial demons who raped, collected body parts, and tortured innocents. See John Dower, *War Without Mercy*, pp. 234–261.

19. Quoted in Marshall De Bruhl, *Firestorm: Allied Airpower and the Destruction of Dresden* (New York, NY: Random House, 2006), p. 269. Of all people, the pugnacious Air Marshall knew that a good offense was a good defense, and so threw down the gauntlet: although the war against Germany was as good as won, Japan remained, and were the Allies willing to sacrifice the lives of American soldiers on the altar of an invasion of the Japanese homeland without 'softening up' the homeland prior to invasion?

20. See A. C. Grayling, *Among the Dead Cities* (New York, NY: Walker and Co., 2006), p. 5.

21. The idea was 'in the air,' so to speak. Consider the following BBC broadcast from 1942:

> We are even sorry for the women and children who may have suffered for the stupidity of their menfolk in putting Hitler in power and their cowardice in keeping him there. We are sorry for them, but when we remember Warsaw, Rotterdam, Coventry, and Belgrade, and wonder how many of the women and even the children of Cologne exulted at the activities of the Luftwaffe, then we harden our hearts. For the German women, and even the German children, ought to be capable of recognizing evil and rejecting it.

Quoted in Vera Brittain, *One Voice: Pacifist Writings from the Second World War* (New York, NY: Continuum, 2005), p. 104. This is the view adopted by another architect of area bombing, Curtis LeMay, after the firebombing of Tokyo: 'There are no innocent civilians...The entire population got into the act and worked to make those aeroplanes or munitions...men, women, and children.' Quoted in A. C. Grayling, *Among the Dead Cities*, p. 142.

22. Quoted in A. C. Grayling, *Among the Dead Cities*, p. 163.

23. Quoted in Robert Holmes, *Acts of War: The Behavior of Men in Battle* (New York, NY: Free Press, 1985), p. 390.

24. Anthony Beevor, *The Fall of Berlin 1945* (New York, NY: Penguin Books, 2002), p. 199.

25. Quoted in Omer Bartov, *Hitler's Army: Soldiers, Nazis and War in the Third Reich* (Oxford: Oxford University Press, 1992), p. 126.
26. Neither have some civilians. In one trenchant and grim variation on our theme, Jonathan Schonsheck has argued that suicide terrorists lack a moral right not to be tortured. If he is correct, the only moral impediment to our torturing a suicide terrorist (or, presumably, experimenting on a suicide terrorist for some worthy medical aim) is 'our need to be attentive to our own moral integrity.' ('Thwarting Suicide Terrorists: The Locus of Moral Constraints and the (Ir)Relevance of "Human Rights,"' *Universal Human Rights*, David A. Reidy, ed. (Lanham, MD: Rowman and Littlefield, 2005), p. 222. This extremely dubious normative claim is predicated on a prior assumption about moral status: because 'to be a bearer of moral rights is to be a respecter of moral rights..., the moral community does not automatically include as members the entirety of humanity,' most particularly those who demonstrate by thought and action their utter and perfidious repudiation of the worth of their fellow species-mates. ('Thwarting Suicide Terrorists,' p. 221.) Here we have, I take it, a candid denial of basic human worth that avoids outré appeals to race, gender and ethnicity. For a competing view, see Jeremy Waldron, 'What Can Christian Teaching Add to the Torture Debate about Torture,' *Theology Today* 63 (2006): 330–343.
27. No evidence for this claim is more powerful than the effects of combat on ordinary, human beings. I know of no better description of this process than in Eugene Sledge's *With the Old Breed at Peleliu and Okinawa* (Oxford: Oxford University Press, 1990). So, for example, after describing the gruesome scene of an American Marine's indifferently cutting teeth with gold fillings out of a living Japanese soldier, Sledge reflects:

> Such was the incredible cruelty that decent men could commit when reduced to a brutish existence in their fight for survival amid the violent death, terror, tension, fatigue, and filth that was the infantryman's war. Our code of conduct toward the enemy differed drastically from that prevailing back at the division C[ommand] P[ost]. ...To the noncombatants and those on the periphery of action, the war meant only boredom or occasional excitement; but to those who entered the meat grinder itself, the war was a nether world of horror from which escape seemed less and less likely as the casualties mounted and the fighting dragged on and on. Time had no meaning; life had no meaning. The fierce struggle for survival in the abyss of Peleliu eroded the veneer of civilization and made savages of us all. We existed in an environment totally incomprehensible to men behind the lines – service troops and civilians.
>
> (*With the Old Breed*, pp. 120–121)

> For several recent discussions of dehumanization in (even) 'good wars,' see John Dower, *War Without Mercy: Race and Power in the Pacific War* (New York, NY: Pantheon Books, 1986), particularly pp. 32–73; Harry Stout, *On the Altar of the Nation: A Moral History of the Civil War* (New York: Viking Books, 2006); and A. C. Grayling, *Among the Dead Cities: The History and Moral Legacy of the WWII Bombing of Civilians in Germany and Japan* (New York: Walker and Company, 2006). See also Jonathan Shay, *Achilles in Vietnam*, pp. 103ff.

28. See Jeremy Waldron, *God, Locke and Equality*, p. 69.

29. I do not assume that there must be just one feature that each human being possesses by virtue of which each has great, equal and indelible worth. In principle, basic human worth might be grounded on several distinct properties.
30. See Jean Hampton, *The Intrinsic Worth of Persons*, p. 116ff.
31. Of course, we might deny that irreparably damaged human beings like my grandmother lack basic worth. See, for example, Michael Otsuka, 'Killing the Innocent in Self-Defense,' pp. 91–92.
32. I confess that I am not sure how to construe the worth provided to a human being by her capacity for moral agency. For reasons I soon articulate, I am inclined to deny that the capacity for moral agency engenders anything by way of intrinsic excellence – that capacity is a necessary causal condition of our achieving great goods, but is not itself a great good. But as I later suggest, perhaps the worth provided by our capacity for moral agency is of a conditional sort – the sheer, undeveloped capacity for moral agency engenders great and equal worth... until developed well or poorly. If the first is correct, then the capacity move does not provide an adequate account of basic worth because capacities cannot ground intrinsic worth. If the second, the capacity move fails because capacities cannot ground indelible worth.
33. Moreover, two instances of the same kind of capacity have differential worth insofar as they enable their possessor to achieve differentially excellent ends. If A's capacity for rational reflection enables her to count the blades of grass on her front lawn but not reflect on the mysteries of the universe, and if B's capacity for rational reflection enables her both to count the blades of grass on her front lawn and to reflect on the mysteries of the universe, then, so far forth, A's capacity for rational reflection has less worth than B's. We can make sense of these comparative judgments regarding the excellence of different instances of the same general capacity only if we recognize that the excellence of a given capacity is a function of the goods that a given capacity enables its possessor to achieve.
34. Fyodor Dostoevsky, *The Brothers Karamazov*, Richard Pevear and Larissa Volokhonsky, trans. (New York, NY: Vintage Books, 1991), p. 115.
35. Note that nothing I have argued implies that we lack powerful reason to prize our capacities for moral agency and rational reflection. For those capacities enable us to achieve great goods – they are a necessary causal condition of our achieving those great goods. But, of course, a necessary causal condition of a great good need not be a great good – from the fact that my having a body that obeys the laws of physics is a necessary causal condition of my achieving the great good of admirably sacrificing my life for my child it does not follow that my having a body that obeys the laws of physics is a great good. I'll return to this point in due course.
36. Jeff McMahan, 'Challenges to Human Dignity,' *Journal of Ethics*, forthcoming.
37. Of course, there could be Martians out there who bear to each human being the kind of relation I take God to bear to each human being. If so, then perhaps there is an adequate secular account of basic human worth. Since I have never seen this view articulated, I will await an advocate before I address it.
38. Robert Veatch, *The Foundations of Justice: Why the Retarded and the Rest of Us Have Claims to Equality* (Oxford: Oxford University Press, 1986), p. 13.
39. What about the property of being created in God's image? That depends on what being created in God's image means. If the respect in which human beings 'image' God is that both God and human beings have some excellent capacity (for moral agency or rationality, or creativity), then the appeal to the *imago Dei* doesn't really

advance matters beyond the impasse that blocked secular accounts of basic worth. I take it that many theologians have understood the *imago Dei* in just that way. Not all, though – Karl Barth comes to mind as an exception. On this topic, which I do not really have the expertise to address adequately, see Nicholas Wolterstorff, *Justice*, forthcoming.

40. The term in Nick Wolterstorff's.

41. I am assuming that Nate's love for Elmo is a 'worthy' love in that his attachment to Elmo violates no-one's rights, isn't psychologically damaging, and the like. This assumption in no way militates against the claim that Nate's attachment to Elmo imparts worth to Elmo. What is crucial, of course, is that the relational propriety of Nate's being attached to Elmo need not presuppose that *Elmo* has some prior excellence (though Elmo might). My thanks to Thaddeus Metz for flagging this issue.

42. 'Muslim superiority was a deeply rooted dogma. When the Byzantine emperor asked for an exchange of prisoners, al-Mu'tasim replied: 'We, Arabs, can not admit the possibility of comparing Muslims with Romans [Byzantines], because God values the former more highly than the latter.' B'at Yeor, *The Decline of Eastern Christianity Under Islam* (Madison, NJ: Fairleigh Dickenson University Press, 1996), p. 82.

43. In that case, theists would still be free to argue that the most plausible secular account of basic worth – that grounds basic worth on capacities alone – is inferior to the best theistic account of basic worth – which presupposes that each human being loved by God has certain capacities, but does not claim that those capacities suffice by themselves for basic worth.

44. Surely, Vera Brittain is on to something when she notes that 'it can hardly be over-emphasized that the endurance of pain, however bitter and unprovoked, never rots our more fibre with one tenth of the speed that follows its affliction.' *One Voice*, p. 70.

45. See, for example, William Langewiesche, 'Rules of Engagement,' *Vanity Fair*, November 2006. It can be accessed at: http://www.vanityfair.com/politics/features/2006/11/haditha200611.

46. See Yuki Tanaka, *Hidden Horrors: Japanese War Crimes in World War II* (Boulder, CO: Westview Press, 1996), pp. 63f.

47. For reasons I earlier indicated, I believe that our sheer capacities provide us with negligible worth. But if we deny that, and claim that our sheer capacities ground great worth in spite of the fact that those capacities just are (in part) capacities to do great evil, then it still seems plausible to suppose that the worth that our sheer capacities provide is conditional: we can augment or diminish our worth by the manner in which we develop those capacities.

48. See John Dower, *War Without Mercy*, pp. 33–73. For example, '*Time*, in a good example of Old Testament fervor, informed its readers on March 15, 1943, that 'low-flying fighters turned lifeboats towed by motor barges, and packed with Jap survivors, into bloody sieves. Loosed on the Japs was the same ferocity which they had often displayed. This time, few, if any, Japs in battle green reached shore.' When, two weeks later, *Time* published a single letter to the editor questioning the morality of such 'cold-blooded slaughter,' this triggered a spate of subsequent letters ridiculing the notion that 'brotherly love' had any place in the current conflict. One respondent began with a list of Japanese atrocities, and then asked if the original letter writer would be 'remorseful about killing a helpless rattlesnake after he had spent his strike.' Dower, *War Without Mercy*, p. 67.

49. Some reflection on forfeiture seems relevant here. There is a widespread sense that, although each human being has certain (natural, human) rights, each human being has it within her power to forfeit those rights: although I have a natural human right to life, if I culpably use lethal force against you, I have thereby forfeited my right to life. A human being who forfeits her right to life does not necessarily forfeit her worth, not even if her right to life is grounded on her worth (a plausible view, I think). Nevertheless, it seems possible for a human being to forfeit her worth, although that possibility depends on what makes for her worth. If God's love for a human being imparts to her basic human worth, and if God's love is constant, then there's nothing a human being can do to forfeit her worth. (Though she can still forfeit worth-grounded rights.) But if we accept the capacities view, I think it's plausible to suppose that a human being can forfeit her worth, and perhaps some implicit commitment to the capacities view explains not only the sense that atrocities committed in war dehumanize those who commit them, but also the idea expressed by some philosophers that human beings can degrade themselves and so acquire the moral status of a beast. See, for example, Michael J. Perry's reference to the teaching of the Catholic Church (and Aquinas in particular) in *Towards a Theory of Human Rights*, p. 40, (though I think that Perry's discussion does not distinguish between forfeiture of particular rights and forfeiture of what he calls dignity. See also Jeremy Waldron's discussion of Locke on the bestialization of offenders, *God, Locke and Equality*, p. 146f.
50. Many thanks to Terence Cuneo, Tim Jackson, Thaddeus Metz, Michael Perry, Steven Smith, Nick Wolterstorff and George Wright for their help in guiding me through this thicket.

11
Imperfection as Sufficient for a Meaningful Life: How Much is Enough?

Thaddeus Metz

1 Introduction

In this chapter, I address the debate between naturalists and supernaturalists with regard to meaning in life. The concept of a meaningful (or significant or important) life is, roughly, the idea of a person's existence that is intrinsically desirable for having achieved worthwhile ends other than being happy, or for exhibiting qualities worthy of great pride or admiration.[1] The supernaturalist believes that any such final value in our lives is constituted by a certain relationship with a transcendent or religious realm. In the Western version of supernaturalism that I explore here, this view implies that if neither God nor a soul exists, or if they exist but we fail to relate to them in the appropriate way, then our lives utterly lack meaning. Or, if some meaning is possible under these conditions for the supernaturalist, it is not a meaning with a depth or relevance that could enable anyone's life to count as 'meaningful' on balance. In contrast, the naturalist maintains that a life that is meaningful on the whole is possible in a purely immanent or this-worldly realm as known by science.

The desire for perfection drives supernaturalism about life's meaning. Implicitly or explicitly, the thesis that meaning logically depends on a maximally great condition often motivates the view that God or a soul is what makes our lives significant. It also probably *best* motivates this view, for no other thesis would make as much sense of the implication that Charles Darwin's, Mother Teresa's and Amadeus Mozart's lives (at least in their stereotypical characterizations) would be insignificant in the absence of supernatural entities. Consider briefly how the following recent arguments for supernaturalism appeal to the thesis that perfection of some sort is necessary for meaning.

With respect to God, supernaturalists commonly hold that only a perfectly good being could ground invariant moral norms, where our lives would be meaningless if no such norms existed (Craig, 1994; Cottingham, 2003;

Cottingham, 2005). Others maintain that only a being with the superlative final goods of atemporality, independence and omniscience could give each of us a specially tailored purpose the fulfilment of which confers meaning on our lives (Affolter, 2007). Still others hold that only a certain relationship with a personal creator of the universe, where creativity is constitutive of perfection, could ground meaning (Quinn, n.d.; cf. Morris, 1991). And, finally, others argue that a God-based account of meaning is best justified by the view that meaning turns on positively orienting one's life towards a being whose nature exhibits the greatest perfections to the greatest compossible degree (Metz, 2000; Ward, 2000).

With regard to a soul, the relationship between perfection and meaning is not as readily apparent, but is, logically speaking, just as tight. One, Thomist rationale is that one must have a soul in order to obtain the meaning that alone comes from loving or communing with God, a perfect being (Morris, 1992). And other rationales for the view that meaning requires a soul ultimately rely on claims about perfection (the following, compressed analysis is systematically defended in Metz, 2003). For example, some argue, with Leo Tolstoy (1882), that nothing is worth doing unless one will live forever (Craig, 1994). If we ask why nothing is worth doing unless one will live forever, the answer that provides some pull is that meaning comes from honouring an infinite or maximally great condition, which would require an eternity in a supernatural realm. In addition, there are those who maintain that life would be meaningless if there were no afterlife in which the injustices of this world were rectified (Davis, 1987). If we ask why an *eternal* afterlife would be required to obtain distributive, retributive or reparative justice, the best explanation seems to be that meaning comes from being ideally virtuous and receiving a proportionate reward. And a proportionate reward would plausibly involve satisfying a person's strongest desires, one of which would be for perfect flourishing, possible only in a supernatural realm (Heaven).

So, supernaturalism appears plausible insofar it is plausible to think that a meaningful life can come only from a world in which there is a perfect value of some kind. Call the view that meaningfulness depends on perfection the 'perfection thesis'. There are different ways to try to support the perfection thesis, but I do not explore them here. And although I believe neither supernaturalism nor the perfection thesis that drives it, I do not in this chapter seek to convince the reader that either is false. Instead, my aim is merely to develop the contrasting 'imperfection thesis', the claim that a life that is significant on balance does not require any perfect value.

Although it is logically possible for a naturalist to hold the perfection thesis, most naturalists would reject it in favour of the claim that meaningfulness does not require perfection of any sort. More specifically, since most naturalists would claim that meaning depends merely on a less than ideal value, the question arises as to how much value is sufficient for a life to be on balance meaningful. Where do we draw the line between a life including or being oriented towards an iota of value, at one extreme, and a life including or being oriented towards a perfect value, at the other? In the absence of any principled specification of what degree of less than perfect value is sufficient for a meaningful life, the naturalist view is poorly developed. Furthermore, the supernaturalist can at least claim the virtue of simplicity, for infinity or a maximally finite state (however you might conceive of perfection) is a simpler ground of meaning than some degree of value in between it and zero (Swinburne, 1991). It would be useful for the naturalist to specify in a principled way the less than ideal degree of value that determines when a life counts as 'meaningful', that is, to present the most attractive version of the imperfection thesis. That is what I aim to achieve here.

I argue that principles that naturalists have offered (or at least suggested) in the literature are all implausible. None fits the considered judgments that naturalists themselves would, upon reflection, have about which degree of value is sufficient for a person's existence to be significant. Working within a naturalist mindset, I demonstrate that a new theory needs to be developed, and I also develop one that I believe should be weighed up against the perfection thesis in future work.

I begin by criticizing naturalist claims that the amount of value needed for one's life to be meaningful on balance is determined in an individualistic way (2). According to this view, the standards for judging the meaningfulness of lives vary from individual to individual. Then, I examine and reject existing social conceptions of the value needed for meaning (3). This kind of view is that whether an individual's life is significant logically depends on facts about a certain group she belongs to, whether it be a society, species or something else. I propose a new version of the social view, setting out the basic instance of the imperfection thesis that a naturalist ought to put forth as a counter to the perfection thesis. I also indicate some ways that naturalists could reasonably question and refine it (4). Throughout the chapter I proceed dialectically, that is, by presenting a principle, offering objections to it, presenting another principle that avoids the objections, offering new objections and so on. The principle that remains at the end both avoids and explains all previous criticisms, and hence is the strongest available. I conclude by indicating the next stage of enquiry that would make sense to pursue in order to advance the debate between naturalists and supernaturalists (5).

2 Individual conceptions

In the literature one finds several accounts of which amount of less than perfect value is sufficient for meaning in life. It is useful to divide them into two different kinds of theories. On the one hand, there are social views that say that whether a person's life is meaningful on balance logically depends on how she fares in comparison to some group of which she is a member. On the other, there are individual views according to which a person's life can be properly judged to be meaningful on the whole regardless of the group she belongs to and solely in virtue of certain facts about her. In this section, I consider and ultimately reject versions of the latter view.

2.1 Subjectivism: Objects of a person's pro-attitudes

In the last few years, Brooke Alan Trisel (2002, 2004) has explicitly done the most to argue against the view that perfection is required for meaning in life. His principal target are those who believe that life is futile, meaningless or not worthwhile since we cannot satisfy our strongest desires or realize states of affairs that we judge to be most important, among them being in a certain immortal state, having an infinite effect on future generations, and playing a role in God's plan. Trisel suggests that there is a simple way to avoid making one's life undesirable: change one's desires or other relevant subjective dispositions.

> Since no purpose has been imposed on humankind from without, we are free, to a large extent, to choose our own purposes in life, as many existentialists have emphasized. Not only are we free to choose *which* purposes we will and will not pursue, we are *free to choose how high* to set our expectations.
>
> (Trisel, 2002, p. 79)

This remark and other facets of Trisel's discussion bring to mind[2] the following account of when and in virtue of what a person's life counts as meaningful:

(1) A human's life is meaningful on balance just insofar as she has brought about many objects of her strongest pro-attitudes, with the most meaningful life being one in which a person's strongest pro-attitudes are directed toward objects that were brought about with ease.

On this view, there are no ends that a person ought to pursue other than those that she sets for herself and are attainable. The standards for evaluating an individual's life are relative to the individual's contingent mental states and hence vary from person to person. If a person seeks out gross imperfection that is easily attained, then perfection (and hence a supernatural realm) is not necessary for her life to be meaningful.

Although I am sympathetic to the claim that life can be meaningful without perfection, I find unattractive this subjectivist explanation of why. This view implies that a meaningful life is awfully easy to come by, as easy as making the inhalation of oxygen, the ingestion of food and the discharge of waste one's highest ends. To avoid these counterexamples, one might revise the view as follows:

> (2) A human's life is meaningful on balance just insofar as she has brought about many objects of her strongest pro-attitudes, with the most meaningful life being one in which a person's strongest pro-attitudes are directed toward objects that she brought about with difficulty.

Trisel points out that we often fail to have a sense of accomplishment when we obtain easily obtainable goals (2002, p. 79), which he deems to be enough reason to think that only challenging goals are relevant to meaning in life.

Now, I presume that having a sense of accomplishment should be relevant for a subjectivist simply because and only if it is typically one of our highest-order goals. After all, subjectivism cannot entail that we ought to have any particular goal or rank it in any particular way, except relative to some other goals that we happen to have. And, so, if having a sense of accomplishment were not a person's highest-order goal, then the counterexamples regarding breathing, eating and excreting would resurface. In addition, it is not obvious that challenging projects are necessary to feel a sense of accomplishment – imagine taking a 'pride pill' or electrically stimulating a certain part of the brain to produce the sensation.

We could, however, read (2) as being an impure subjective theory, one that simply conjoins a non-subjective criterion regarding degree of effort with the subjective one about object of variable mental states. William James (1900), for one, has maintained that a person's life is meaningful just insofar as she achieves her contingent goals that require effort to achieve.

However, there are important counterexamples even to this quasi-subjective theory. For instance, if a life were meaningful in virtue of obtaining one's highly ranked ends that were difficult to achieve, then a life could be meaningful for maintaining 3732 hairs on one's head throughout one's life (Taylor, 1992, p. 36). Although this project would be simple in a way, it would require a lot of concentration and stamina and at least for these reasons would be challenging.

While there are manoeuvres open to the subjectivist to try to avoid such counterexamples, they merely buy some time. Ultimately, the subjectivist must bite the bullet in respect of her theory being permissive as to what counts as a meaningful life, and, in my judgment, the theory is too permissive. It would be interesting if there were an objective theory that avoided the counterexamples to subjectivism, while indicating that meaningfulness is determined by facts about individuals. I explore such a theory next.[3]

2.2   Maximum objective good available to a person

Some who have explicitly maintained that perfection is too high a standard for evaluating the significance of a human being's existence have asserted individualism but rejected subjectivism. That is, they have contended that whether a life is meaningful on balance is a function solely of facts about the individual considered apart from her membership in any group, but they have maintained that what is valuable is not simply a matter of what agents happen to value. In a way, this is an odd combination of views, for the natural explanation of why meaningfulness is relative to individuals would be that it is relative to their mental states. However, it is coherent to hold that there are objectively good conditions and that the only ones pertaining to whether a person's life is meaningful are those that are in some sense 'available to her'.

There are two instances of this view in the literature, the most common one being the claim that if a state of affairs is beyond the control of an individual, it neither adds nor detracts from the meaning in her life. The intuitive idea here is that meaning is a normative category that we should consider when deciding how to live. If something is utterly beyond our reach, then, by virtue of ought implies can, it should not figure into our deliberations about what to do. Kurt Baier expresses this sort of judgment in the following:

> (T)he standard by which a thing's ability to satisfy certain criteria of excellence is rightly judged depends on the ability . . . . to meet a given criterion . . . . (W)hen I was young, the life of an eagle seemed to me vastly superior to my own life and that of other people. But, as I mentioned, this question has not greatly exercised many people, and that for good reason, since we have no choice in the matter.
>
> (1997, pp. 63, 63–4)

Baier's attitude seems to be not to cry over spilled milk and more generally not to worry about things that are beyond one's control. If something cannot be prevented, changed or brought about, then it should make a difference neither to what one chooses to do nor to the way one appraises one's life (see also Trisel 2002, pp. 73–6, 79–80; Trisel 2004, pp. 377–8, 385–6). And if perfection of the relevant sort did not exist in our world, its absence would not affect the significance of our existence.

Note that the principle Baier provides is merely a necessary condition for the meaningfulness of a life; a condition must be within a person's control for it to influence whether her life matters or not. I am more interested, however, in sufficient conditions for meaningfulness that a naturalist or other critic of the perfection thesis might be tempted to hold. Furthermore, I am concerned in this section to evaluate sufficient conditions for meaningfulness that vary from person to person but not merely in virtue of their differing mental states. E. M. Adams (2002) provides a principle that meets these criteria.

According to Adams, there are conditions that are objectively good in that they are worthwhile not simply because they are the object of an individual's pro-attitudes. Addressing the nature of these objective goods is not pertinent here; they could be achievements, experiences or whatever else is plausibly the bearer of final value. The point is that there are some things that are good not merely because of our orientation to them, and there is also a fact of the matter about how much of these conditions a given individual can realize. People vary biologically, psychologically and socially, with some being able to do more objective good than others. Those who are healthy are prima facie more able to promote value than those who are sick; those who have self-esteem on the face of it have a greater capacity to do good than those who are depressed; and those who live in societies with minimal repression and substantial resources are in some respects in a better position to achieve worthy ends than otherwise. However, the proper way to judge a person's life is not by judging how much value she brought about in comparison with others or with an ideal condition. Instead, according to Adams:

> The most important question for us is not the length of one's life but how well one used one's time in developing one's powers, defining one's identity and life plan, and working for an order of goodness....One's life is meaningful to the extent that it is the life reality requires of one, given one's abilities and circumstances. There are normative requirements impinging on one from within one's own constitution and from within one's time and place.
>
> (2002, p. 80)

A straightforward reading of Adams grounds the following principle:

> (3) A human's life is meaningful on balance just insofar as she has achieved a high proportion of the maximum amount of final value (relevant to meaning)[4] that she could have brought about.

Adams's view entails that if one did, say, 90 per cent of what one could have done to promote the 'order of goodness', then one's life would be meaningful on balance, whereas if one did only 35 per cent, it would not be. It follows that perfection is not necessary for meaning in life, supposing it is not within our reach. Instead, meaning is simply a function of how well one does at promoting imperfect value in light of what is within one's control, or, more accurately, within one's particular and limited capacities.[5]

There are several counterexamples to this theory to consider. First, think about a case in which your child and spouse get hit by a bus and die (Metz, 2005, pp. 221–2). Even though you could not control when (or that) they died, their deaths would surely have some effect on the meaning of your life. Adams's principle entails that if the prevention of their deaths were not within your power, then they would be just as irrelevant to the meaning in your life as is (for her) the fact that you cannot prevent your own death. However, it is counterintuitive to think that meaningfulness is not lessened by the loss of loving relationships when others die.

In addition to the claim that a state of affairs must be *achievable* for an individual for it to count with regard to the meaning in her life, Adams claims that meaning is a function solely of the *degree* to which the good states of affairs that are achievable have in fact been achieved. Here are two counterexamples to the latter claim. First, consider an innocent person who has been kidnapped and held in a cage, with absolutely no means of escape. If Adams were correct that meaningfulness is a function of the percentage of one's capabilities that one has used, then whether the person's life is meaningful on balance and how much would not be negatively affected by the kidnap. Once the person's opportunities were unavoidably reduced, according to Adams's view, meaningfulness would be a function of the extent to which those opportunities that remain would be used. Indeed, her view entails that great meaning would be possible in this scenario, more than in the course of a normal life, if the kidnapped person's opportunities were few in number and easily 'maxed out'. However, this seems absurd.

It is tempting to want to refer to the opportunities that would be available 'to a normal life', but that would be to drop an individualist account of meaningfulness in favour of a social one; for what determines a 'normal life' would be a function of a group to which the person belongs, not the nature of the person herself. The only way consistent with individualism to avoid the counterexample, it seems, would be to modify (3) to speak of a high percentage of the goodness available to an individual 'supposing she were not the victim of injustice'. Here, Adams could appeal to the opportunities available to the individual in a counterfactual world in which people did not impose unjustified limitations on her.

However, this manoeuvre seems ad hoc, and it ultimately fails to resolve the problem. Consider the suggestion that people who are *severely* retarded, handicapped and impoverished (as a result of the natural lottery, not the social one) on balance do not have meaningful lives. Adams's view entails that they could have terrifically meaningful lives, if they fully realized whatever few opportunities to promote 'the order of goodness' were available to them. However, my intuition suggests that the number and kind of opportunities available to a person affects whether her life can count as 'meaningful', not merely, as per Adams, the degree to which a person has realized whatever (perhaps very limited) opportunities have come her way.

Some readers might balk at this judgment for sounding harsh. In particular, some have the intuition that any plausible account of meaning must entail that everyone is at least capable of living a meaningful life (e.g. Cottingham, 2003, pp. 69–70). I, however, believe that the present cases are more powerful than this intuition; they show that it is more plausible to think that meaning can be undercut by dramatic losses at the natural and social lottery than that meaning can always survive any such losses. Note that judging some people's lives to have little meaning in them, viz., not enough to count as 'meaningful' on the whole, is consistent with believing that everyone's life is equal from a moral point of view. Inequality of meaningfulness does not imply inequality of moral status. Indeed, the fact that someone has little meaning in her life could ground the moral judgment that she is entitled to more help and resources than those with more meaning. Furthermore, readers should reflect on why they presumably do not want more ignorance, worse health and less wealth. Why would you prefer not to become an Alzheimer's patient? Part of the best explanation, I submit, is that one senses that a life with much fewer capabilities would lack meaning, or at least the meaning available to a life with more capabilities.[6] If it is true that being (born) very dumb, sick and poor can affect the degree of meaning in one's life, then Adams's thesis that meaning is a function merely of how much one has exercised whatever capabilities one has is false.

Before turning to a different sort of theory, I address the reason that I suspect is mistakenly leading many to incline towards Adams's (and Baier's) view. Recall the suggestion that meaning is a practical matter. Most of those writing on life's meaning believe that the meaning in an individual's life can come in degrees, and they are interested in the ways an individual could have more meaning in her life. Relatively little of the field is concerned with any meaning the universe or the human species as such may have. This action-guiding interest might suggest that the relevant sort of meaning judgments are fundamentally 'normative' in the sense of being governed by the dictum that 'ought implies can', such that to judge a condition able to confer meaning on a person's life implies that she can realize it.

However, the inference to the relevance of ought implies can is weak. Although it is true that meaning comes in degrees, that it varies within a life and also between lives, and that we ought to seek more of it rather than less, all these claims are consistent with the view that meaning is at bottom evaluative rather than normative. That is, even supposing meaning is basically a good rather than a should, we can be interested in it for the difference it can make it to our lives to no less a degree than we are in the good of happiness. When we ask how to make lives meaningful on balance, we need not suppose that the only coherent answer is that meaningfulness is a function of whether a person *realized a certain proportion of the value available to her*, Baier's and Adams's view. Instead, the answer could be that a life is meaningful on balance insofar as a person *realized value available to her that is a certain proportion of some group-based standard*.

The examples above suggest that a social standard for assessing meaningfulness is correct. When we judge that being severely handicapped or permanently kidnapped reduces the available meaning in a life, we are comparing such lives with others that do not suffer from these afflictions. When we are inclined to judge these lives to be meaningless or close to it, such a judgment requires appealing to conditions beyond what the given individual is capable of achieving. In sum, the best explanation of why certain lives are not meaningful on balance is that they fail to measure up to some supra-individual standard, for instance, they fail to achieve what the normal human achieves. I therefore turn to social conceptions of the amount of meaning constitutive of a life that counts as 'meaningful'.

3 Social conceptions

The accounts of meaningfulness in the previous section imply that whether a person's life is meaningful or not is a function solely of facts about that person, considered apart from membership in any group. The extent to which one satisfies one's desires or the degree to which one has realized the objective goodness of which one is capable involve no essential reference to group membership. In contrast, the accounts of meaningfulness considered in this section imply that one cannot ascertain whether someone's life is meaningful in isolation from society or humanity. I critically explore three types of social conceptions of meaningfulness to be found in the recent literature.

3.1 Communal criteria

In a recent article, Berit Brogaard and Barry Smith (2005) put forth a social conception of meaning in life, according to which one's life is meaningful to the degree that one has engaged in projects in a way that rank highly on public criteria for success. A life counts as meaningful on balance when one's activities have largely measured up to the community's standards.

More specifically, Brogaard and Smith proffer three necessary and sufficient conditions for a life to have engaged in non-trivial projects and hence obtained meaning.[7] First, for an activity to confer meaning on life, one's community must have a way to judge it as better or worse, or as successful or not. To use Brogaard's and Smith's example, daydreaming is not a meaningful activity since there are no public criteria for judging it as done well or poorly. Second, one's community must be aware of the activity, or at least have criteria that 'can be easily applied in the public light of day' (Brogaard and Smith, 2005, p. 446) to the activity. This is the reason Brogaard and Smith suggest for thinking that mass murder is not meaningful, for it needs 'to some extent to be practiced in the dark' (2005, p. 447). Third, the activity must in fact be successful in the light of the community's criteria. These three elements of non-trivial projects suggest the following view, which obviously does not require perfection for meaning:

> (4) A human's life is meaningful on balance just insofar as she has engaged in many activities that measure up highly to standards that one's community is in a position to apply.

One question to ask with regard to this view is which community matters, and one problem to raise for this view is that every answer to this question has counterintuitive implications. Suppose, for instance, the relevant community is whatever one most identifies with. In that event, one might identify most with the Nazi Party or the Flat Earth Society and do well by their standards at, say, purifying the race or spreading the word, respectively. However, surely little or no meaning would come from these activities.

To avoid the problem of being too permissive as to what counts as meaningful, then, one might go to the opposite extreme and suggest that the relevant community is the human race as a whole, or humanity at a given time. However, this view seems too restrictive, implying that majorities are necessarily correct when it comes to what counts as a non-trivial pursuit and that the individual cannot do something meaningful until his fellows agree that it is. Consider, here, the first scientists in the modern era. The dominant institutions of the time, as well as the general populace, failed to appreciate the grand project of empirically testing hypotheses, positing physical unobservables as the best explanation of observables, appealing to Ockham's Razor and so on. Furthermore, at the time, many scientists had to practice their work 'in the dark', that is, could not share their findings without risking ostracism, punishment or even death. Of course, humanity eventually developed criteria by which to judge such activities, which now do not have to be practiced behind closed doors; but the point is that these activities were meaningful before then, that is, at the time they were done.

I submit that any community or public one posits as relevant to determining whether an activity is meaningful will suffer from being too permissive for enabling an individual to get meaning from virtually anything, on the one hand, or too restrictive for entailing that minorities are always wrong about what confers meaning, on the other. It is plausible to think that whether a life counts as 'meaningful' is a function of a group to which one belongs, but implausible, I suggest, to hold that the group constitutes meaningfulness simply by virtue of the pro-attitudes of (a majority of) its members. In short, intersubjectivism suffers the same weakness that I above ascribed to subjectivism.

3.2   The human norm of objective good

Baier posits a social but objective standard for specifying the amount of final value one must engage with in order to have a life that counts as 'meaningful'. Over a span of 40 years, Baier (1957, 1997) has maintained that one appropriate way to judge the meaning or, more generally, worth of a human's life is in comparison with the typical lives of other humans. When comparing human lives, the absence of immortality or some other perfect condition does not matter. As Baier remarks, '(O)ur question would be more difficult if some human beings were immortal or at least survived the death of their body. That all must die appears to make the finality of death irrelevant to assessing the comparative worth of human lives' (1997, p. 66). This comparative standard is vague as it stands, and I now criticize three, more specific versions of it.

In one text, Baier develops a concrete way to judge lives by drawing analogies with the proper way to judge other things such as tallness and students:

> Ordinarily, the standard we employ is the average of the kind. We call a man and a tree tall if they are well above the average of their kind.... The same principles must apply to judging lives.... A good and worthwhile life is one that is well above average. A bad one is one well below.... The Christian evaluation of earthly lives is misguided because it adopts a quite unjustifiably high standard.... Even if it were true that there is available to us an after-life which is flawless and perfect, it would still not be legitimate to judge earthly lives by this standard. We do not fail every candidate who is not an Einstein.
>
> (1957, p. 127)

These remarks suggest the following standard for when a human's existence is on the whole significant:

(5) A human's life is meaningful on balance just insofar as it has more final value (relevant to meaning) than the average human's life.

One obvious problem with this principle is that it entails that meaning is 'zero-sum', that is, that it is *impossible* for everyone's life to be meaningful (Belliotti, 2001, p. 73). Of course, it is implausible to think that everyone's life is in fact meaningful, but that point is not relevant. So long as there is a possible world in which everyone's life is meaningful, Baier's suggestion about which lives count as 'meaningful' is incorrect since it entails that those people with less than the average amount of meaning (or the final value constitutive of it) have meaningless lives. And if we can conceive of a world in which everyone develops herself through close relationships, intricate skills and sophisticated projects, then there is a possible world in which the lives of all are significant.

There is another way to read Baier so that this counterexample is avoided. Instead of deeming a human being's life to be meaningful on balance just insofar as it has more objective goodness than the average human's, one might deem it to be one that has at least as much as the typical human.

(6) A human's life is meaningful on balance just insofar as it has at least as much final value (relevant to meaning) as most human beings.

So, instead of better than average as per (5), according to (6) one must be (at least) equal to most, for one's life to count as 'meaningful'. This latter principle would have us ascertain the range of objective goodness that a large majority of human beings realize and then see whether a given individual falls within that range. This principle leaves open the possibility that everyone falls within the same range, and hence does not entail that some must have meaningless lives if some have meaningful ones. And the principle still serves the function of denying that an immortal soul in a certain state or any other condition of perfection is required to have a meaningful life.

However, (6) still has the counterintuitive implication that it would be *impossible* for a person whose life has somewhat less final value than most to have enough for her life to be meaningful on balance.[8] We can imagine a world in which the lives of most human beings have quite a lot of final value in them and that those who have somewhat less still have enough to give them significant lives on the whole. To see the point, return to Baier's student analogy. We can readily think of a group of students who are generally excellent, with a minority not performing as well but nonetheless well enough to count as 'satisfactory'.

Furthermore, (6), along with (5), entails that a promising way to make one's life meaningful would be to kill off most human beings and then subject the few remaining ones to torture (Belliotti, 2001, p. 73). That way, one's own life would be not only better than average, but also at least equal to most.

Where has Baier gone wrong? Perhaps he is led astray by the analogies he draws, which are upon reflection not as strong as he believes. Tallness is different from meaningfulness, on the face of it. Tallness seems inherently comparative in the sense that something small must exist in order for there to be something tall. However, meaningfulness is not obviously comparative in this way; we can imagine a world in which human lives are all meaningful or all meaningless. In addition, while being a good student is not comparative in the way that tallness is, it seems plausible to think that whether a student is good is not merely a function of whether she is better than average or equal to most. For, again, the middling and the typical might be terribly bad. So, tallness is perhaps a function of an average but is disanalogous to meaningfulness, whereas being a good student seems more analogous to meaningfulness but is not merely a function of usual performance.

Let me suggest a way to flesh out Baier's hunch that a human norm fixes when a life counts as 'meaningful' that differs from the better than average or equal to most principles and avoids the problems I have raised for them. Consider this way to ground meaning in normality[9]:

> (7) A human's life is meaningful on balance just insofar as it has at least as much final value (relevant to meaning) as is characteristic for human life.

What is characteristic of human life is, I think, well understood as a dispositional feature of it, rather than an actual one. Whereas the criteria of better than average and equal to most peg the final value sufficient for meaning-fulness to an amount that human beings have in fact exhibited, the present criterion does not. It instead invokes an amount that human beings are bio-logically, psychologically and socially disposed to realize. It could be that the amount of final value that human beings have in fact realized is greater or smaller than what is characteristic for them to realize, just as most human beings in fact have fewer teeth than the 32 that are characteristic for them (as Elizabeth Anscombe famously noted).

So construed, (7) avoids the counterexamples that plague Baier's (5) and (6). It entails that everyone's life could be meaningful, since everyone could realize the amount of final value that is characteristic of human life, avoiding the problem with (5). It entails that a person's life can be meaningful even if she has realized less final value than most have, so long as she has realized what is characteristic of human life, thereby evading the objection to (6). And it entails that a life that is better than the lives of all others who are tortured is not necessarily meaningful, for that life could still fail to realize the amount of final value that is characteristic of human life, hence by-passing the objection that applies to both (5) and (6).

So far, so good. But (7) faces the criticism that it oddly entails that it is *impossible* for everyone's life to be meaningless, a criticism that also applies to (5) and (6). Someone is always going to be better than average,[10] someone is always going to fit into the category of most, and someone is always going to meet what is characteristic of the species. However, it seems possible for there to be a world in which human lives are universally meaningless; simply imagine we were all thrown into hell.

In reply, the friend of (7) might suggest that it in fact entails that it is pos-sible for all lives to be meaningless. Even if we were all thrown into hell, that condition might not be characteristic of human life; we could be disposed for something better, even if a contingent force 'luckily' ended up damning everyone. However, I am not sure what it would mean to speak of what is 'characteristic' of human life, or what such a life is 'disposed' to be like, if in fact all human beings were in hell. It seems that a necessary condition of something's being characteristic of a species is that a certain percentage of the members of that species meet this norm.

Another problem with (7) is that we seem able to appraise what is charac-teristic of human life from a more absolute scale. To see the point, consider an analogy. Childbirth is characteristically extraordinarily painful for human females, and so if the appeal to what is characteristic of human life exhausted our evaluation of its value, we would lack the resources to claim that a typical childbirth is 'bad'; the only bad labour would be one that is worse than what is characteristic, which is counterintuitive. Just as we should not restrict our evaluation of childbirth to what is characteristic of it, so we should not restrict our evaluation of human life to what is characteristic of it. The amount of final value that grounds meaning in a characteristic human life could intuitively be low.[11] The same is true of the amount of final value that is average or typical, meaning that the present objection also applies to (5) and (6).

I admit that the objections to (7) are not as damning as some of the objections to earlier principles. (7) is worth more exploration, I readily grant. However, if there were another principle that captured what is attractive about (7) while also avoiding its prima facie problems, it should be considered. In the rest of this chapter I suppose that judging whether a life is meaningful on the whole requires a standard independent of the human norm. Since the average, typical or even characteristic human life could have an intuitively low amount of meaning, and since appeal to a human norm entails that it is impossible for all human lives to be meaningless, I seek a more absolute scale, albeit one still fixed by reference to facts about the human species. Baier, in fact, has proposed such a scale.

3.3   Maximum objective good available to humanity

In his last work to address meaning in life, Baier notes that a comparative standard is not the only one we sensibly use to appraise the worth or meaning of a life. While being better than the norm would make one life more meaningful than another, Baier acknowledges that it would not be enough to make it count as 'meaningful' on the whole.

> How much more valuable, significant, and rewarding than the average life must a life be to be a good one? Must it be vastly, perhaps infinitely more so than the best possible earthly lives, as those would seem to imply who claim that if human existence ends in death, our earthly lives cannot be meaningful, significant, or good ones? Is not this an exorbitantly high standard?.... Might not the appropriate standard be one that relates to the best possible lives here on earth?
>
> (Baier, 1997, p. 66)

Although this passage suggests that a life could be meaningful only if it were better than average to a certain extent, I ignore that claim since it invites the kinds of counterexamples considered above. What I find more promising in Baier's remarks is this principle:

> (8) A human's life is meaningful on balance just insofar as it is not very far below the maximum amount of final value (relevant to meaning) that a human could have on earth.

By virtue of being more absolute, this account of how much less than perfect value is constitutive of a meaningful life avoids the counterexamples raised to the social accounts considered so far. Unlike the communal criteria view, it does not imply that meaning is a function of the variable pro-attitudes of the majority of a community. Unlike the better than average, equal to most and characteristic views, it leaves open the possibilities that all human beings could live meaningless lives (if they all were quite far below the maximum) and that what is normal for human life is too low. In sum, (8) is independent of convention and norm and is for that reason compelling, in my view.

However, as attractive as (8) is, I find it arbitrary and poorly motivated. It seems unprincipled to suggest that whether a human being's life counts as 'meaningful' should be a function of any *location* such as the earth.[12] Why choose the earth? Why not the earth plus the moon and an orbiting space station? Or why not something less than the earth, say, its habitable continents? Any suggestion about where to draw the line in terms of location will be capricious, I submit. After all, suppose human beings will colonize Mars and age on that planet much more slowly than us. Imagine they will live twice as long and without mental or physical impairment. When judging whether the amount of final value in a human's life is sufficient to make it meaningful on the whole, such a possibility seems relevant and should not be automatically excluded.

Another problem with (8), as it stands, is that it is vague. Speaking of the value that a human 'could have' leaves open the sort of possibility involved. It strikes me as not only in line with Baier's intentions, but also plausible from a naturalist viewpoint to suggest that the relevant sort of possibility is nomological, as opposed to, say, logical or metaphysical. Most naturalists believe that meaning in life is a function of certain conditions of a world as known by science, with remotely possible worlds being irrelevant.

Let us therefore revise (8), as follows:

> (9) A human's life is meaningful on balance just insofar as it is not very far below the maximum amount of final value (relevant to meaning) that a human can achieve, given the laws of nature.

I am not aware of anyone in the literature who has explicitly advocated (9), though it is not far from (8) and might be what Baier had in mind. I think (9) is close to the sort of imperfection thesis that a naturalist ought to find attractive. If one believes that perfection is not necessary for a meaningful life and that such a life is available in a world as known by science, then, by virtue of the dialectical progression in this chapter, one should find (9) compelling. (9) not only avoids all the objections to previous principles, but also provides a plausible explanation of them: (1), (2) and (3) are incorrect because they are individualist (as opposed to social); (4) is incorrect because it is intersubjectivist (as opposed to objectivist); (5), (6) and (7) are incorrect because they focus on a human norm (as opposed to a human maximum); and (8) is incorrect because it is arbitrary (as opposed to principled).

4   Refining the favoured conception

In this section, I present objections to (9). I find the objections to be more speculative and less forceful than ones made to previous principles. I raise them tentatively as issues on which naturalists and other friends of the imperfection thesis could (more) reasonably disagree.

One apparent problem with (9) is that it might counterintuitively make meaning too far out of our reach. Although our lives are not as meaningful as 'freaks' such as artistic and intellectual geniuses who have put their talents to effective use, our lives are perhaps 'not very far' below theirs and so are still able to count as 'meaningful'. Suppose, however, that a 'superfreak' were realized, a once in ten billion occurrence of a human being whose powers are so great that our lives turn out to be 'very far' from his and hence all meaningless. I doubt that a superfreak is nomologically possible, and if it is not, then no revision to (9) is necessary. However, if a superfreak were possible in the light of the laws of nature, then to avoid the counterexample, we could adopt this principle:

> (10) A human's life is meaningful on balance just insofar as it is not very far below the maximum amount of final value (relevant to meaning) that a human is likely to achieve, given the laws of nature.

When I speak of the 'maximum that a human is likely to achieve', the reader should think of the range of the most meaningful lives that humans could lead, and then ascertain which in this range is the least improbable to occur. That life is the relevant maximum to use when judging the meaningfulness of everyone's life.

I am not sure whether (10) resolves the problem, for it might still entail that our lives, or at least the lives of our ancestors, have been meaningless. What humanity has produced so far could turn out to be quite far removed from the kinds of superlative lives that are most probable. However, if that were true, we might be prepared to bite the bullet. After all, we now judge our ancestors' lives to have been nasty, brutish and short; we live to about 80 with anesthesia, whereas they made it to 30 or so without it. Perhaps one day we will discover so much about what humanity is capable of with regard to meaning in life that it will seem plausible to judge what we have done up to now not to be worthy of the title of 'meaningful' on balance, even if we have had some meaning.

Another, more fantastic counterexample to both (9) and (10) is the case of an 'inhuman superfreak', something like Nietzsche's *Übermensch*. Imagine, for instance, that knowledge of the human genome enabled scientists to manipulate the genes of a human being so that he would become a great individual but no longer human. Suppose that such genetic manipulation resulted in much longer life, greater intelligence and better health. Suppose that after the process the person's DNA were no longer human and that he could not mate with humans. And suppose that the choice of whether to undergo the process were widely available. It might be that, under these conditions, the relevant maximum to consider when appraising human lives would not be based on facts about our species.

Note that the thought experiment should not be dismissed out of hand, at least if one finds the Mars counterexample to (8) compelling. The Mars case had us imagine that human beings could substantially enhance the powers they have – and hence the meaning available to them – simply by being in a location other than the earth. If the reader is inclined to think that changing circumstances could in principle affect the relevant maximum available to invoke when appraising meaningfulness, then, analogously, she should think that an altered constitution could do the same.

However, some might try to drive a wedge between the external and the internal, that is, try to argue that biological species or at least objective kind is alone relevant to meaningfulness, marking a difference between the Mars case and the case of the inhuman superfreak. For instance, Martha Nussbaum has argued that it is inappropriate to judge the value of human lives with reference to any non-human lives. She says of an eternal life that

> its constitutive conditions would be so entirely different from ours that we cannot really imagine what they would be. Nor, if we could, would they be of any immediate importance for us.... We are not attempting to show that an immortal existence could not have value, beauty, and meaning internal to itself.... What we are attempting to show is the extent to which *our* values would be absent in that life; and that is the thing most relevant to a therapeutic treatment of our always impossible wish to have that life in place of our own. It is, as well, the only perspective on value from which we can coherently proceed, in asking a question for *ourselves*: for in asking about ourselves there is not much point in asking whether a certain life seems good from the point of view of creatures that we have no chance of ever being, or rather creatures becoming identical to which we would no longer be ourselves.
>
> (Nussbaum, 1989, p. 340; see also Lenman, 1995; Tabensky, 2003)

Nussbaum here offers three reasons for thinking that the case of the inhuman superfreak should not lead us to revise (9) or (10). One is that we could never become an inhuman superfreak, but the thought experiment of course invites us to suppose that we could and then to see whether we would be inclined to judge the quality of our lives in the light of the possibility. Another is that we cannot know enough about the life of any non-human creature to know whether it would be desirable, but that seems false. I surely know that it is better to be a normal, adult human being than a fruit fly.

Just because we invariably know ourselves best does not mean we cannot justifiably claim to know what it would be like to have a quite different sort of life.[13]

Nussbaum's third and most interesting suggestion is that even if we could become another being and could know what it would be like, the possibility would not be relevant to appraising our lives. This point is more asserted than defended in the quote above, but the most straightforward motivation for it is the idea that a meaningful life cannot involve suicide. Put that way, the point sounds irrefutable.

Upon reflection, however, it does not obviously tell against the idea that our lives should be judged relative to the inhuman superfreak, for two reasons. First, one can grant the point that for a condition to confer meaning on one's life, the condition must not alter what one essentially is, but deny that being human is what one essentially is. If one is essentially, say, a non-branching stream of consciousness intimately connected causally and intentionally over time, then one could remain who one essentially is even if one were to change species and become an inhuman superfreak.

Second, extending the work of Derek Parfit (1986) from issues of prudence and morality to meaning, one could reasonably reject the principle that one must remain essentially who one is in order to obtain meaning from a state of affairs. After all, it is typical to think that one's life can obtain meaning by virtue of sacrificing it in order to help others. Suppose one dies as a result of donating a kidney to a family member or that one jumps on a grenade to protect one's fellow soldiers and promote a just cause. Meaning arguably accrues to one's life upon its end. If killing oneself for the sake of others quite distinct from oneself can confer meaning on one's life, then killing oneself for the sake of an inhuman superfreak who is closely related to oneself can probably do the same.

If one holds the judgment that whether our lives are meaningful could be a function of the extent to which we approximate the meaning available to the inhuman superfreak, then one should find the following appealing:

> (11) A human's life is meaningful on balance just insofar as it is not very far below the maximum amount of final value (relevant to meaning) that a being that was born human is likely to achieve, given the laws of nature.

One might wonder, now, whether (11)'s requirement of initially being human is truly necessary. Imagine that an inhuman superfreak like Superman lived among us, but that we had no opportunity to become one of his species. Should merely being in the presence of another, greater species be considered relevant to judging whether our lives count as 'meaningful' or not, if one is a naturalist friend of the imperfection thesis?

My answer is a firm 'no'. After all, some naturalists are theists. That is, some who believe that a meaningful life is possible in a world lacking a perfect, supernatural realm believe that such a realm does exist, for example, that we are in God's presence. Awareness of being in God's presence is not enough for a naturalist to hold the perfection thesis or supernaturalism, that is, not sufficient to think that perfection possible only in a transcendent realm is the relevant standard to use when appraising the meaningfulness of human lives. And so, even if a naturalist were acquainted with beings lesser than God but greater than us, she should not think that these beings set the relevant standard for whether our lives are meaningful, if the amount of meaning they can acquire were in no way available to us. Hence, if one is inclined to depart from (9), one should probably not go beyond (10) or (11).

5 Conclusion

In this chapter, I have sought to develop a principled alternative to the perfection thesis. My aim has been to indicate with some precision how much less than perfect value is constitutive of a meaningful life, from the perspective of naturalists who deny that perfection is necessary for it. I have argued against existing imperfection theses in the literature that significance is a function of whether an individual has realized: much of what she values; a high proportion of the final value available to her; much of what her society values; more final value than the human average; at least as much final value as most humans have; and at least as much final value as is characteristic of human life. Instead, I have argued that the relevant standard by which to judge a human being's life as meaningful or not refers to the maximum amount of final value available to human beings. More specifically, one's life is meaningful insofar as one has realized a degree of final value (of the sort that constitutes meaning) that is not very far below the most that could (likely) be achieved by human beings in the physical world. This instance of the imperfection thesis avoids and well explains the counterexamples facing the others, and it provides a concrete and intuitively appealing contrast to the perfection thesis. Having specified and defended this version of the imperfection thesis should help to improve our understanding of naturalism as well as to advance debate between it and supernaturalism. If I am correct that supernaturalism is motivated by the perfection thesis and naturalism by the opposite, then we should gain traction in the debate between them by evaluating their underlying rationales. The field can now do so with what appears to be the naturalist's favoured rendition of the imperfection thesis. The next question to be asked, then, is whether it or the perfection thesis better accounts for relatively uncontroversial judgments about meaning in life.[14]

Notes

1. I largely rely on the reader's intuitive sense of 'meaning in life'. For a systematic analysis of the phrase, see Metz (2001).
2. I do not claim that this is Trisel's view (which he explicitly disavows in correspondence with me), but rather that it is inspired by many of his remarks. His views are actually closer to something like (2) below. More clear instances of (1) were commonly held in the late 1960s and early 1970s, for example, Barnes (1967); Edwards (1967); Taylor (1970).
3. In rejecting subjective factors as sufficient for a meaningful life, I want to leave open the possibility that they are necessary or contributory. For instance, even if believing one's life to be meaningful were not enough to make it so, one might reasonably hold that one's life would be meaningless if one believed it were or that one's life would be more meaningful if one believed it to be. In the rest of my discussion, I set aside these kinds of roles that subjective factors might play in constituting a meaningful life. I thank Christopher Eberle for noting the need to clarify this point.
4. Although I speak of an 'amount' of final value, I do not mean to imply that the only value relevant to meaning in life is aggregative, that is, that the meaning of a life is merely the sum of its valuable parts. The final value relevant to meaning could also be a function of the pattern of the life as a whole, viz., the order of its parts. I take it that if the pattern of a life as a whole confers meaning on it, that will also be a matter of degree (some patterns will confer more meaning than others) and hence that holistic factors could figure into the overall 'amount' of final value relevant to meaning.
5. Note that the concept of being able to realize a condition is not the same idea as a condition being within one's control. I cannot always control whether others love me, but, if they do, then it is something within my reach. I also cannot control the remote consequences of my actions (or at least not nearly as much as the action itself or its proximate consequences), but if my action brings about a certain state of affairs in the long run and far away, then I was indeed able to achieve it.
6. One might reply that living with fewer capabilities would be a less happy life, as opposed to a less meaningful one. But there need not be less happiness, at least if a life in the experience machine were available. And if there would be less happiness, it would result in part from the individual's own judgment that she is not able to obtain as much meaning as she would like.
7. At least when these projects were intended by the agent, have been challenging for the agent, and meet some additional 'internal' criteria.
8. I thank Yujin Nagasawa for this criticism.
9. I am indebted to Frans Svensson for this powerful and interesting suggestion.
10. Except, of course, in the rare case in which everyone has exactly the same amount of value – in which case no one's life would be meaningful since no one would be above average!
11. Compare Thomas Nagel on the way death is characteristic of human life:

> Normality seems to have nothing to do with it, for the fact that we will all inevitably die in a few score years cannot by itself imply that it would not be good to live longer. Suppose that we were all inevitably going to die in

> *agony* – physical agony lasting six months. Would inevitability make *that* prospect any less unpleasant?
>
> (1979, p. 10)

12. Yujin Nagasawa has suggested to me that the charitable way to read Baier would be to construe 'earth' not in terms of a planet but instead as shorthand for 'an earthly or this-wordly existence', viz., as what I label '(9)' below.
13. See the various responses to Thomas Nagel's claim that we cannot know what it is like to be a bat.
14. For comments on an earlier draft of this essay, I am grateful to Christopher Eberle, Yujin Nagasawa, Frans Svensson, Brooke Alan Trisel and participants in a research seminar at the University of the Witwatersrand Philosophy Department.

References

Adams, E. M. (2002) 'The Meaning of Life', *International Journal for Philosophy of Religion* 51: 71–81.

Affolter, Jacob (2007) 'Human Nature as God's Purpose', *Religious Studies* 43: 443–455.

Baier, Kurt (1957) 'The Meaning of Life', Inaugural Lecture at Canberra University College, repr. in Klemke 2000, pp. 101–132.

Baier, Kurt (1997) *Problems of Life and Death: A Humanist Perspective.* Amherst, NY: Prometheus Books.

Barnes, Hazel (1967) *An Existentialist Ethic.* New York: Alfred A. Knopf, selections repr. in Klemke 2000, pp. 160–166.

Belliotti, Raymond (2001) *What is the Meaning of Human Life?* Amsterdam: Rodopi.

Brogaard, Berit and Smith, Barry (2005) 'On Luck, Responsibility and the Meaning of Life', *Philosophical Papers* 34: 443–458.

Cottingham, John (2003) *On the Meaning of Life.* London: Routledge.

Cottingham, John (2005) *The Spiritual Dimension.* Cambridge: Cambridge University Press.

Craig, William (1994) *Reasonable Faith, Revised Edition.* Wheaton, IL: Crossway Books, selections repr. in Klemke 2000, pp. 40–56.

Davis, William (1987) 'The Meaning of Life', *Metaphilosophy* 18: 288–305.

Edwards, Paul (1967) 'The Meaning and Value of Life', in Paul Edwards, ed., *The Encyclopedia of Philosophy, Vol. 4.* Upper Saddle River, NJ: Prentice-Hall, Inc., repr. in Klemke 2000, pp. 133–152.

James, William (1900) 'What Makes a Life Significant?', in *On Some of Life's Ideals.* New York: Henry Holt and Company, pp. 49–94.

Klemke, E. D., ed. (2000) *The Meaning of Life, 2nd Edition.* New York: Oxford University Press.

Lenman, James (1995) 'Immortality: A Letter', *Cogito* 9: 164–169.

Metz, Thaddeus (2000) 'Could God's Purpose Be the Source of Life's Meaning?', *Religious Studies* 36: 293–313.

Metz, Thaddeus (2001) 'The Concept of a Meaningful Life', *American Philosophical Quarterly* 38: 137–153.

Metz, Thaddeus (2003) 'The Immortality Requirement for Life's Meaning', *Ratio* 16: 161–177.

Metz, Thaddeus (2005) 'Critical Notice: Baier and Cottingham on the Meaning of Life', *Disputatio* 19: 215–228.

Morris, Thomas (1991) 'Metaphysical Dependence, Independence, and Perfection', in Scott MacDonald, ed., *Being and Goodness*. Ithaca: Cornell University Press, pp. 278–297.

Morris, Thomas (1992) *Making Sense of It All: Pascal and the Meaning of Life*. Grand Rapids: Willliam B. Eerdmans Publishing Company.

Nagel, Thomas (1979) 'Death', repr. in *Mortal Questions*. New York: Cambridge, pp. 1–10.

Nussbaum, Martha (1989) 'Mortal Immortals: Lucretius on Death and the Voice of Nature', *Philosophy and Phenomenological Research* 50: 303–351.

Parfit, Derek (1986) *Reasons and Persons*. Oxford: Clarendon Press.

Quinn, Philip (n.d.) Personal correspondence.

Swinburne, Richard (1991) *The Existence of God, Revised Edition*. Oxford: Oxford University Press.

Tabensky, Pedro (2003) *Happiness: Personhood, Community, Purpose*. Ashgate: Aldershot.

Taylor, Charles (1992) *The Ethics of Authenticity*. Cambridge: Harvard University Press.

Taylor, Richard (1970) *Good and Evil*. New York: Macmillan Publishing Co., selections repr. in Klemke 2000, pp. 167–175.

Tolstoy, Leo (1882) *My Confession* <http://www.ccel.org>.

Trisel, Brooke Alan (2002) 'Futility and the Meaning of Life Debate', *Sorites* 14: 70–84.

Trisel, Brooke Alan (2004) 'Human Extinction and the Value of Our Efforts', *The Philosophical Forum* 35: 371–391.

Ward, Keith (2000) 'Religion and the Question of Meaning', in Joseph Runzo and Nancy Martin, eds, *The Meaning of Life in the World Religions*. Oxford: Oneworld Publications, pp. 11–30.

Index